# THE SOUTH

**Jerry E. Jennings**
**Marion H. Smith**

Jerry E. Jennings is a writer and editor of textbooks for young people. A graduate of Michigan State University, Mr. Jennings has continued his education at Columbia University. Through extensive travel, he has gained firsthand knowledge of the South. Marion H. Smith is a writer and editor of children's textbooks. She is a graduate of Michigan State University, and has also studied at the University of Michigan. Together, Mr. Jennings and Mrs. Smith have written about the South in a direct and vivid style that students can easily understand.

COPYRIGHT 1977, THE FIDELER COMPANY

All rights reserved in the U.S.A. and foreign countries. This book or parts thereof must not be reproduced in any form without permission. Printed in the U.S.A. by offset lithography.

Earlier Edition Copyright The Fideler Company 1973.
LIBRARY OF CONGRESS CATALOG CARD NUMBER: 76-729
ISBN: 0-88296-063-6

## BOOKS IN THIS SERIES

| | | |
|---|---|---|
| FAMILIES* | UNITED STATES* | CANADA AND LATIN AMERICA |
| FAMILIES AROUND THE WORLD* | THE NORTHEAST | CANADA  SOUTH AMERICA |
| OUR NEEDS * | THE SOUTH | MEXICO  CARIBBEAN LANDS |
| OUR EARTH * | MIDWEST AND GREAT PLAINS | AMERICAN NEIGHBORS |
| GREAT IDEAS THAT BUILT OUR NATION * | THE WEST | |

WORLD CULTURES*

| | | (Dual editions) |
|---|---|---|
| BRITISH ISLES | GERMANY | EUROPE—BRITISH ISLES AND GERMANY |
| FRANCE | SOVIET UNION | EUROPE—FRANCE AND SOVIET UNION |
| INDIA | SOUTHEAST ASIA | ASIA—INDIA AND SOUTHEAST ASIA |
| AFRICA | SOUTH AMERICA | AFRICA AND SOUTH AMERICA |

*Teacher's Guide is available

Cover Illustrations
1. See pages 80-81
2. See pages 18-19
3. See pages 198-199
4. See pages 6-7
5. See pages 96-97
6. See pages 108-109

**THE FIDELER COMPANY** Grand Rapids, Michigan / Toronto, Canada

# THE SOUTH

## CONTRIBUTORS

John F. Lounsbury
Chairman of Department
of Geography
Arizona State University
Tempe, Arizona

| | |
|---|---|
| Lee Abbott | Joyce Kortes |
| Silence M. Andrews | Wayne M. McDowell |
| Robert H. Bauer | Beverly M. Miller |
| Betty-Jo Buell | Mary Mitus |
| Robert Bunda | Timothy C. Mulder |
| Rita Colvin | Connie Negaran |
| Michael C. Cuti | Carol S. Prescott |
| Raymond E. Fideler | Bev Roche |
| Ruth E. Fideler | Dorothy M. Rogers |
| Sharon Heiden | Alice Vail |

Audrey Witham

**In the Blue Ridge section** of North Carolina are some of the highest peaks in the South. This picture shows rhododendrons blooming on a mountainside in the Blue Ridge.

# CONTENTS

PART 1 Land and Climate
   1 A Global View . . . . . . . . . . . . . . . . 8
   2 Land . . . . . . . . . . . . . . . . . . . . . . 18
   3 Climate . . . . . . . . . . . . . . . . . . . . 34

PART 2 History
   4 Settlers Come to the South . . . . . . . . 54
   5 The Revolution and the New Nation . . . 68
   6 The Union Endures . . . . . . . . . . . . . 76
   7 The Growth of the New South . . . . . . 86

PART 3 People
   8 People and Cities . . . . . . . . . . . . . . 92
   9 Citizenship in a Democracy . . . . . . . . 118
  10 The Arts . . . . . . . . . . . . . . . . . . . . 152

PART 4 Earning a Living
  11 Farming . . . . . . . . . . . . . . . . . . . . 162
  12 Natural Resources . . . . . . . . . . . . . . 176
  13 Industry . . . . . . . . . . . . . . . . . . . . 196

PART 5 Great Ideas That Built Our Nation
  14 Ten Great Ideas . . . . . . . . . . . . . . . 212

PART 6 States of the South
    Alabama . . . . . . . . . . . . . . . . . . . 244
    Arkansas . . . . . . . . . . . . . . . . . . . 245
    Florida . . . . . . . . . . . . . . . . . . . . 246
    Georgia . . . . . . . . . . . . . . . . . . . . 247
    Kentucky . . . . . . . . . . . . . . . . . . . 248
    Louisiana . . . . . . . . . . . . . . . . . . . 249
    Mississippi . . . . . . . . . . . . . . . . . . 250
    North Carolina . . . . . . . . . . . . . . . 251
    South Carolina . . . . . . . . . . . . . . . 252
    Tennessee . . . . . . . . . . . . . . . . . . 253
    Virginia . . . . . . . . . . . . . . . . . . . . 254
    Facts About Our States . . . . . . . . . . 255
    Thinking and Solving Problems . . . . . 256
    Learning Social Studies Skills . . . . . . 259
    Learning Map Skills . . . . . . . . . . . . 266
    Glossary . . . . . . . . . . . . . . . . . . . 272
    Index . . . . . . . . . . . . . . . . . . . . . 283
    Maps, Charts, and Special Features . . . 287
    Acknowledgments . . . . . . . . . . . . . 288

# Part 1
# Land and Climate

One group of states in our country is known as the South. Do you know exactly where the South is located? What do you know about the land and climate of the states in the South? Do you know the answers to the following questions?

- What is the conterminous United States?
- What are the main groups of states into which the conterminous United States may be divided?
- How many states are in the South? Which ones are they?
- The South includes parts of four of our country's main land regions. What are these regions?
- Although the climate is much the same in most parts of the South, there are some differences from place to place. Why is this so?

As you read the chapters in Part 1 of this book, you will discover answers to these and many other questions. The pictures and maps in these chapters provide additional information that will be helpful to you in doing research about the South.

**A sandy beach on Jekyll Island, Georgia.** This is one of the Sea Islands, a chain of islands that lie along the Atlantic coast of South Carolina, Georgia, and the northern part of Florida.

# 1 A Global View

**The stars in the night sky are part of the Milky Way.** When you look at the sky on a clear night, you see hundreds of stars glittering against the deep blackness of space. These stars are part of an enormous star system, or galaxy, called the Milky Way. The Milky Way is one of billions of separate galaxies scattered through the vast, nearly empty space of the universe. Each of these galaxies is made up of billions of stars and other heavenly bodies.

**The Milky Way is a spiral galaxy.** As the painting below shows, the Milky Way has a spiral shape like that of a pinwheel. In one arm of the pinwheel is our own special star, the sun, together with the earth and the other heavenly bodies that make up our solar system.

Much of our knowledge about stars and other heavenly bodies has been gained by astronomers using huge telescopes such as the one shown in the picture at left. The painting above shows how our galaxy, the Milky Way, might appear to an observer in another galaxy. The "+" sign marks the place in the Milky Way where scientists believe that our solar system may be located.

**Our sun is the center of the solar system.** Our sun, like the other stars in the universe, is a huge, whirling ball of burning gases. The other parts of our solar system are balls of fairly solid material that revolve around the sun. These include nine main planets. (See chart below.) Some of the main planets, such as our earth, have one or more moons. The solar system also includes thousands of small planets, called asteroids, that circle the sun between the orbits of Mars and Jupiter.

The nine main planets differ greatly in size and in distance from the sun. They also differ in the time it takes them to revolve around the sun. Our earth makes this revolution once each year. Our moon circles the earth about once each month.

**Our solar system includes nine main planets.** Some of these main planets, such as our earth, have one or more moons. The solar system also includes thousands of small planets, called asteroids, that circle the sun between Mars and Jupiter.

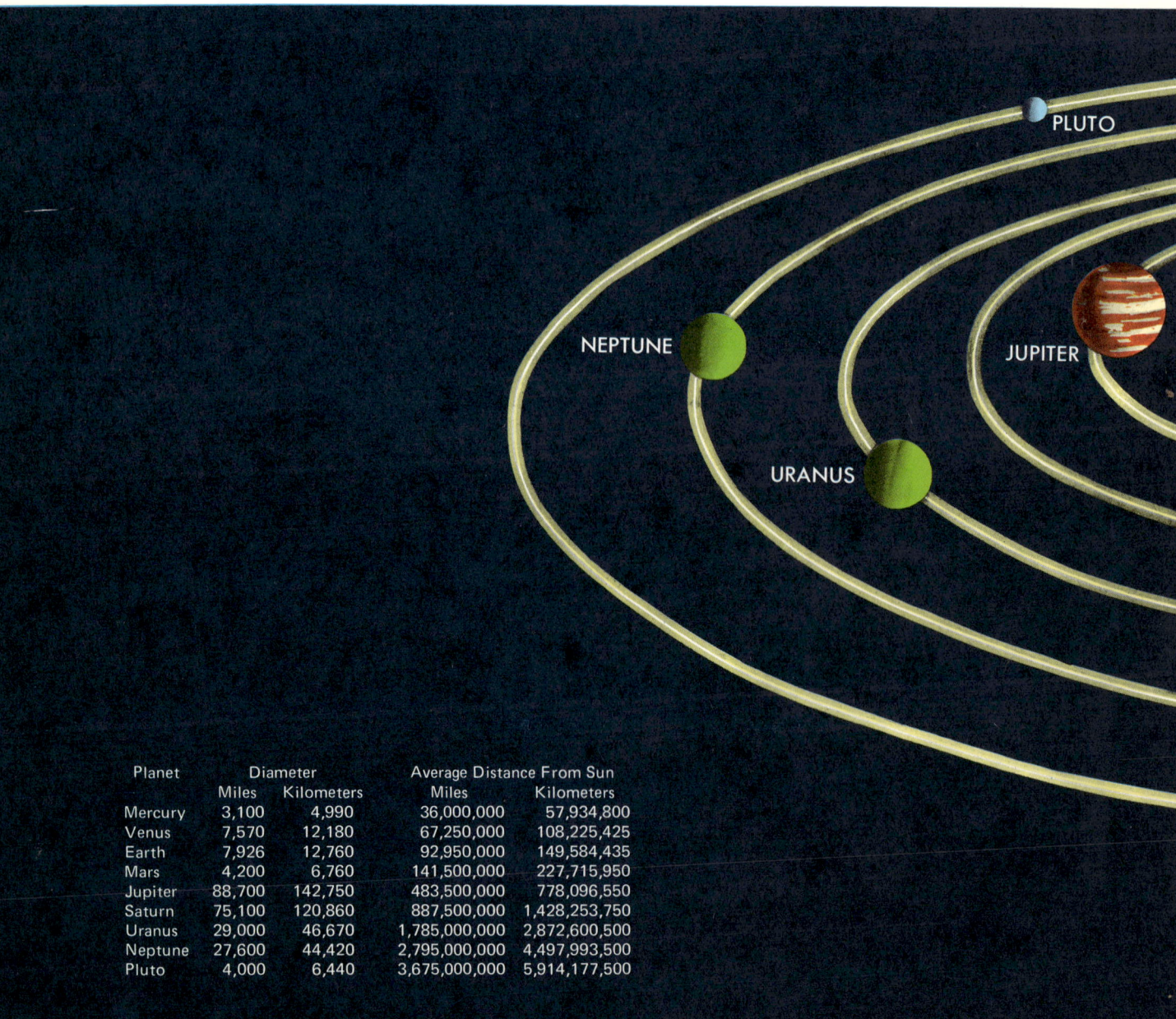

| Planet | Diameter | | Average Distance From Sun | |
|---|---|---|---|---|
| | Miles | Kilometers | Miles | Kilometers |
| Mercury | 3,100 | 4,990 | 36,000,000 | 57,934,800 |
| Venus | 7,570 | 12,180 | 67,250,000 | 108,225,425 |
| Earth | 7,926 | 12,760 | 92,950,000 | 149,584,435 |
| Mars | 4,200 | 6,760 | 141,500,000 | 227,715,950 |
| Jupiter | 88,700 | 142,750 | 483,500,000 | 778,096,550 |
| Saturn | 75,100 | 120,860 | 887,500,000 | 1,428,253,750 |
| Uranus | 29,000 | 46,670 | 1,785,000,000 | 2,872,600,500 |
| Neptune | 27,600 | 44,420 | 2,795,000,000 | 4,497,993,500 |
| Pluto | 4,000 | 6,440 | 3,675,000,000 | 5,914,177,500 |

**Learning about the solar system.** During recent years, we have begun to explore some of our neighbors in the solar system. A number of American astronauts have landed on the moon. The photographs and rock samples brought back by these astronauts have provided much information about the moon. Various instruments have been left on the moon to transmit additional information back to the earth. The Soviet Union has sent a number of unmanned spacecraft to the moon, but Soviet astronauts have not yet landed on its surface.

Both the United States and the Soviet Union have sent unmanned spacecraft to investigate other planets. An American spacecraft, Mariner 9, orbited Mars in 1971 and 1972 and sent back television pictures of its surface. About the same time, a Soviet spacecraft landed an instrument capsule on Mars. The Soviet Union has also sent several space probes to Venus. Two American spacecraft, Pioneer 10 and Pioneer 11, have sent back much new information about the planet Jupiter. In 1974, the American spacecraft Mariner 10 became the first space probe to explore two planets. It flew past Venus and then curved around to fly very close to the planet Mercury. Mariner 10 provided scientists with the first close-up photographs of Mercury's surface.

**Looking at the earth from space.** In addition to learning about some of our neighbors in the solar system, we have also gained new knowledge about our own planet through observations made from space. For example, satellites and space probes have provided useful data about weather on the earth. Astronauts have taken many photographs of the earth from spacecraft orbiting the earth or the moon.

**An envelope of air surrounds our planet.** Photographs of the sunlit earth taken from the blackness of outer space show that the curving surface of our planet is partly hidden by a layer of fluffy white clouds. These are part of

The surface of our earth is covered partly with land and partly with water. The largest masses of land are continents, and the largest bodies of water are oceans. The picture of a globe at left shows the Eastern Hemisphere. On this side of the earth are the continents of Africa, Eurasia, and Australia. The picture below shows the Western Hemisphere, with the continents of North and South America. Antarctica, a continent around the South Pole, is not shown.

| Continents and Oceans | Area in Square Miles | Area in Square Kilometers |
|---|---|---|
| **CONTINENTS** | | |
| Africa | 11,707,000 | 30,321,000 |
| Antarctica | 5,100,000 | 13,200,000 |
| Australia | 2,968,000 | 7,687,000 |
| Eurasia | | |
|   Europe | 4,063,000 | 10,523,000 |
|   Asia | 16,966,000 | 43,942,000 |
| North America | 9,417,000 | 24,390,000 |
| South America | 6,884,000 | 17,829,000 |
| **OCEANS** | | |
| Arctic | 5,440,000 | 14,090,000 |
| Atlantic | 31,530,000 | 81,662,000 |
| Indian | 28,356,000 | 73,442,000 |
| Pacific | 63,800,000 | 165,200,000 |

the atmosphere, which is the precious envelope of air that completely surrounds our planet. Without this envelope of air, people could not live on the earth. The atmosphere provides the oxygen* we breathe. It protects us by night from the bleak cold of outer space, and by day from the burning rays of the sun. If there were no atmosphere to hold moisture, there would be no rain on the earth. Plants could not live, and without vegetation there could be no animal life. Plants provide food for human beings and other ani-

*See Glossary

mals and also replenish the oxygen we use up from the air. Thus, the atmosphere is our planet's greatest treasure.

**The earth's surface is made up of oceans and continents.** Photographs of the earth from outer space also show the sparkling blue waters of the earth's great oceans and seas. These waters cover about three fourths of the earth's surface. The largest landmasses on the earth are called continents. The earth's six continents, together with its many islands, make up about one fourth of the surface of our planet.

**Most of the United States is located on the continent of North America.** If we were to fly over the continents, we would not see any boundary lines. We could not tell where one country ends and another begins. On maps, boundary lines are drawn to show where different countries are located. Sometimes, a boundary may follow a physical feature such as a river or a mountain range. Boundaries are established by agreements, or treaties, among the different nations. As new agreements are made, boundaries change. Sometimes the changes are very great, but often they are slight.

The continent of North America is where most of our country, the United States, is located. The map on this page shows us the boundary lines between the different countries of North America. We can see that our closest neighbors are Canada and Mexico.

**The South is part of the conterminous United States.** There are fifty states in the United States. Two of these, Alaska and Hawaii, are separated from all the others. Alaska, like most of our country, is located on the continent of North America. Hawaii, however, is an island

*Continued on page 16*

### The United States

This map shows the location of the fifty states that make up our country. Two of these, Alaska and Hawaii, are separated from the others. Alaska is located in the far northern part of North America, and Hawaii is an island state located in the Pacific Ocean. The remaining forty-eight states form the part of our country known as the conterminous United States. In addition, our country controls the island of Puerto Rico and the Virgin Islands of the United States, as well as various other territories.

state located in the Pacific Ocean. (Compare map on page 13 with map on pages 14 and 15.) The part of our country that is made up of the other forty-eight states is called the conterminous United States.

The states in the conterminous United States may be divided into groups. One of these is the South, which is made up of eleven states in the southeastern part of our country. These states are Alabama, Arkansas, Florida, Georgia, Kentucky, Louisiana, Mississippi, North Carolina, South Carolina, Tennessee, and Virginia. The South is bordered on the east by the Atlantic Ocean, and on the south by the Gulf of Mexico.

**Great changes are taking place in the South.** At the beginning of the present century, the South was not as prosperous as most other parts of the United States. More than half of the people earned their living by farming. There were few factories. Most manufactured articles were obtained from northern states, where there was more industry. Nearly all of the South's main crop, cotton, was shipped to other parts of the country to be made into cloth.

Today, better farming methods and new manufacturing industries have

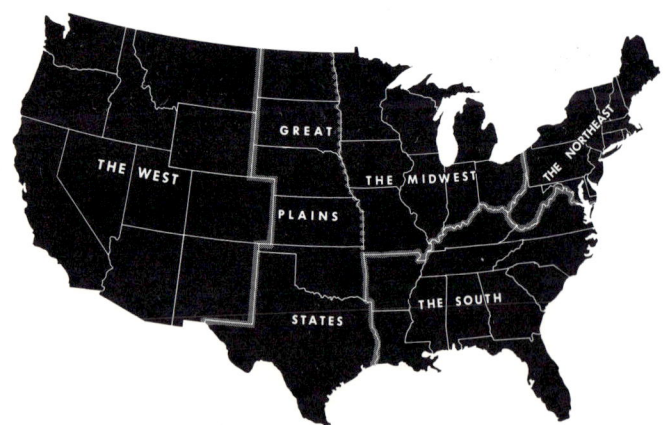

The states in the conterminous United States may be divided into five main groups. These are the Northeast, the South, the Midwest, the Great Plains states, and the West. Sometimes the Midwest and the Great Plains states are combined into one group, known as the Midwest and Great Plains. Compare the map at left with the large map on pages 14 and 15. Then list the states in each of the five main groups.

A view of the Florida peninsula, taken from an orbiting spacecraft. The South is made up of eleven states in the southeastern part of our country. The Atlantic Ocean borders this region on the east, and the Gulf of Mexico borders it on the south.

brought the South a higher standard of living. Many different products come from its farms and factories. Crops such as soybeans and peanuts are grown, as well as cotton and tobacco. Furniture, paper, textiles, and many other items are manufactured in the South and sold throughout the country. In exchange, the South buys things other states have to sell. In the chapters that follow, you will learn more about the South. You will also learn many things about the people who make their homes in this important part of our country.

**Using Natural Resources**

See pages 226-229

Nature has given the South many valuable resources. Among these are sunshine, fertile soil, and abundant rainfall.
1. How did colonists in the South use these resources during the early days of our country?
2. What are some of the ways in which the people of the South use these resources today?

Chapters 3 and 11, as well as this chapter, will help you discover answers to these questions.

# 2  Land

If you were to fly over the South in an airplane, you would see that all parts of it are not alike. You would notice that some areas are low and almost level. In other parts of the South, you would see rolling plateaus, wooded mountains, or deep valleys. These different features affect the ways in which people in the various parts of the South live and work.

## The Coastal Plain

More than half of the South lies in a vast region of the United States called the Coastal Plain. The map on page 21 shows us that this region extends along most of the Atlantic coast of our country. In the north, the Coastal Plain is narrow. Farther south, it becomes wider, and spreads out westward in a broad, irregular band along the Gulf of Mexico. The map also shows us that part or all of every state in the South lies in the Coastal Plain region.

Near the sea, the Coastal Plain is low and flat. Sandy beaches stretch for miles along parts of the coast. Many very low areas are covered with shallow

The picture above shows farmers harvesting rice on the Coastal Plain in Arkansas. More than half of the South lies in the vast Coastal Plain region, which borders the Atlantic Ocean and the Gulf of Mexico. (See map at right.) Much of the Coastal Plain is low and level. In other parts of the South, there are rolling plateaus, wooded mountains, and deep valleys.

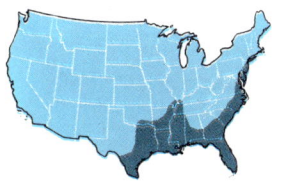

water much of the time. Some of these areas are freshwater swamps or marshes. Others are covered with salt water. Where the land is not so wet, there are huge forests of pine trees. In some places, there are fields of vegetables, rice, sugarcane, or other crops.

Farther inland, the Coastal Plain gradually rises higher above sea level and becomes gently rolling. The light, sandy soil of this area is good for growing such crops as corn, tobacco, and peanuts.

Many broad, muddy rivers wind across the Coastal Plain on their way to the Atlantic Ocean or the Gulf of Mexico. They carry soil that rainwater has washed away from the land farther upstream. Time after time, these rivers have overflowed their banks and left some of this soil on the flooded land. For this reason, much of the land along the rivers is covered with a deep layer of rich, dark soil. Cotton and other crops grow well on these fertile alluvial* lowlands.

Some of the largest cities in the South have grown up near the mouths of rivers or along bays on the seacoast. Here there are fine harbors where ships can come to load and unload their cargoes.

*See Glossary

**Jacksonville, Florida,** is situated on the St. Johns River, in the Coastal Plain region of the South. Many broad, winding rivers flow across the Coastal Plain and empty into the Atlantic Ocean or the Gulf of Mexico. Most of the South's large port cities are located in this region.

## The Appalachian Highlands

The Appalachian Highlands region of our country extends from central Georgia and Alabama northeastward to Canada. (Compare maps on pages 15 and 21.) In this region are mountains, plateaus, and valleys. The land here is higher and more rugged than the land in the Coastal Plain region. In the South, the Appalachian Highlands region is divided into four sections. These are the Piedmont Plateau, the Blue Ridge, the Appalachian Ridges and Valleys, and the Appalachian Plateau.

**The Piedmont Plateau.** Most of the Piedmont Plateau section of the Appalachian Highlands lies in the South. The name of this broad, rolling plateau means "foot of the mountain." The Piedmont slopes gently upward from east to west. In some places, the Piedmont is more than 125 miles wide. (See map on page 21.)

The Piedmont Plateau is one of the South's most productive farming areas. Fields of cotton, tobacco, and other crops cover much of the land. In order to get good yields, however, Piedmont farmers must use up-to-date farming methods. They must plow their hilly fields carefully to prevent erosion. They must also add fertilizer to the soil, and rotate their crops. (See pages

Our country's Appalachian Highlands region extends from central Alabama and Georgia northeastward to Canada. Which states of the South lie partly in this highland region?

This picture shows hikers in the Appalachian Highlands. In the South, the Appalachian Highlands region is divided into four sections. These are the Piedmont Plateau, the Blue Ridge, the Appalachian Ridges and Valleys, and the Appalachian Plateau. The South's highest mountains are in the Blue Ridge. Some of the peaks rise more than six thousand feet above sea level.

166-168.) In earlier times, many farmers in the South did not know about such methods of keeping the land fertile. In some parts of the Piedmont, the topsoil has been worn out or washed away. Where this has happened, the land can no longer be used for growing crops such as cotton and tobacco. Forests, orchards, and pastures now cover many of these areas.

**The Fall Line.** Many swift rivers cross the Piedmont as they flow toward the Atlantic Ocean or the Gulf of Mexico. Rapids and low waterfalls are formed as these rivers drop from the plateau onto the Coastal Plain. For this reason, the border between the Piedmont Plateau and Coastal Plain is called the Fall Line. The map on page 29 shows the location of this line. By comparing this map with the maps on pages 15 and 21, you can see that the Fall Line extends along the border between the Coastal Plain and the Piedmont all the way from northeastern New Jersey to central Alabama.

The drawing below shows that the land of the Coastal Plain slopes gently upward from the ocean to the Piedmont Plateau. In most places along the Fall Line, there is not much difference in elevation between the Piedmont and the Coastal Plain. Only in places where rivers flow from the plateau to the plain does the elevation drop sharply. The drawing also helps to explain how rapids and waterfalls were formed at these places. As you can see, the Piedmont is hard rock under the surface soil, but the Coastal Plain is made up of soft sand and clay. As a result, rivers flowing to the sea carry away much more soil from the plain than from the plateau. Through the centuries, these rivers have carved valleys in the plain, almost down to sea level. Near the ocean, where the land is low, the valleys are shallow. Farther inland, however, where the land slopes upward, the valleys are deeper. As the rivers drop from the rocky Piedmont into these valleys, they form rapids and waterfalls.

During the early days of our country, settlers traveling upstream from the coast by boat were stopped by the falls and rapids at the Fall Line. Here the settlers had to unload their goods. As a result, many of them settled nearby. Later, people in settlements along the Fall Line found that they could use the

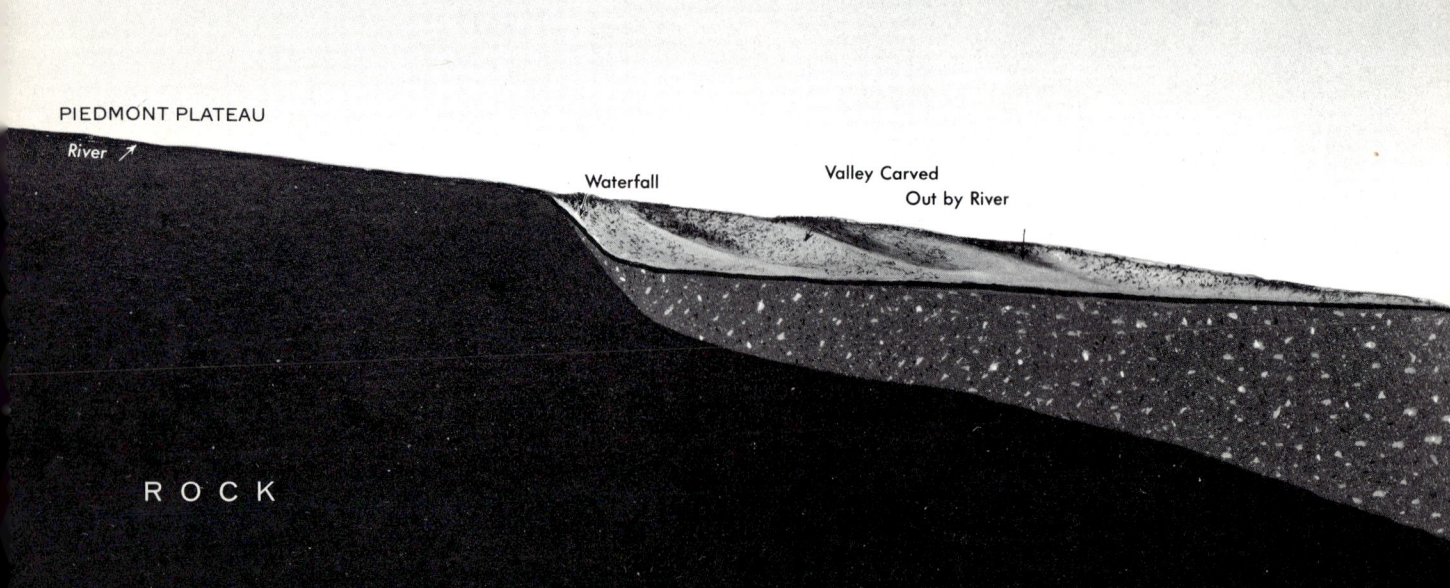

A cotton mill in Columbus, Georgia, on the border between the Piedmont Plateau and the Coastal Plain. The drawing below explains why this border is known as the Fall Line.

power of the falling water to run machines in mills and factories. Some of the early settlements that started on rivers along the Fall Line have grown into important cities. (See map on page 29.)

Today there are many hydroelectric power stations along the Fall Line and on the Piedmont Plateau. They produce electricity for homes and factories. More factories are located in this area than in any other part of the South.

Many rapids and waterfalls are formed as rivers flow from the Piedmont Plateau to the Coastal Plain. The border between the highlands and the lowlands is known as the Fall Line.

**The Blue Ridge.** From northern Georgia into southern Pennsylvania, ranges of forest-covered mountains overlook the Piedmont Plateau. Because its wooded slopes often appear blue from a distance, this chain of mountain ranges is called the Blue Ridge. These ranges are millions of years old. Through the years, wind and water have rounded the mountaintops and smoothed the slopes.

The map on page 21 shows that the southern part of the Blue Ridge section is wider than the northern part. Where it straddles the Tennessee-North Carolina border, the Blue Ridge is about seventy miles wide. Here are the Great Smoky Mountains, the Black Mountains, and several other mountain ranges. Mount Mitchell, in the Black Mountains, is the highest peak in the South. It rises to 6,684 feet above sea level.

Most mountain slopes in the Blue Ridge are too steep for farming. They are covered with dense forests of oak, walnut, and other hardwood trees. However, many small farms lie in the valleys between the mountains.

When our country was being settled, pioneers traveling westward into Kentucky and Tennessee found it difficult to cross the Blue Ridge. The Blue Ridge is still a barrier to transportation. It is difficult to build roads and railroads through this area.

**The Blue Ridge** is a chain of mountain ranges in the Appalachian Highlands. Ever since colonial days, the Blue Ridge has been a barrier to transportation. It is difficult to build roads and railroads through this rugged area.

**In the Great Valley,** which lies west of the Blue Ridge, much of the land is flat or gently rolling. Flowing through different parts of the Great Valley are several large rivers. Douglas Dam, shown in the photograph above, is on a branch of the Tennessee River.

**The Appalachian Ridges and Valleys.** West of the Blue Ridge is an area of alternating ridges and valleys. This section, called the Appalachian Ridges and Valleys, is shown on the map on page 21. The most important part of this section is a long chain of river valleys known as the Great Valley. In the South, most of the land in the Great Valley is flat or gently rolling, and the soil is fertile. A patchwork of farms, meadows, and orchards covers the countryside. Flowing through different parts of the Great Valley are several large rivers, including the Shenandoah, the Tennessee, and the Coosa.

Many cities and towns are located in the Great Valley. Among the largest are Chattanooga and Knoxville, both in Tennessee. Important highways and railroads run lengthwise along the valley floor. Hydroelectric power is produced by dams and power plants that have been built on rivers in the valley. Industrial plants in Chattanooga and other cities use much of this power in manufacturing chemicals, textiles, and many other products.

West of the Great Valley are long, parallel ridges. The steep sides of these ridges are blanketed with forests. Between the ridges are narrow valleys that are used for farming.

**The Appalachian Plateau.** A large highland area lies west of the Appalachian Ridges and Valleys. This is the Appalachian Plateau. (See map on page 21.) Most of this section of the South is usually called the Cumberland Plateau.

The Appalachian Plateau slopes gradually downward from east to west. If you were to look down at the plateau from an airplane flying high above it, the surface of the land would appear smooth. If you were to fly lower, however, you could see the thousands of valleys that have been cut into the plateau. Long ago, the surface of the plateau was unbroken. As time passed, however, rushing streams and rivers carved out narrow, steep-sided valleys.

In most of the Appalachian Plateau section of the South, the land is not suitable for farming. Forests of oak, hickory, and other hardwoods cover some of the more rugged areas. There are small fields of corn and tobacco in the narrow valleys. However, so much soil has been washed away by rain or worn out by careless farming that the land no longer produces good crops. For this reason, many farmers in this section of the South are very poor.

If you were to travel through the Appalachian Plateau section, you would not see many large towns. There is little industry. Although this area has rich coal deposits, most of the coal mined here is sent by rail to other parts of our country. There are few highways, for the deep valleys make it difficult to build good roads.

The **Appalachian Plateau** is a large highland area. Here rushing streams have carved thousands of narrow, steep-sided valleys.

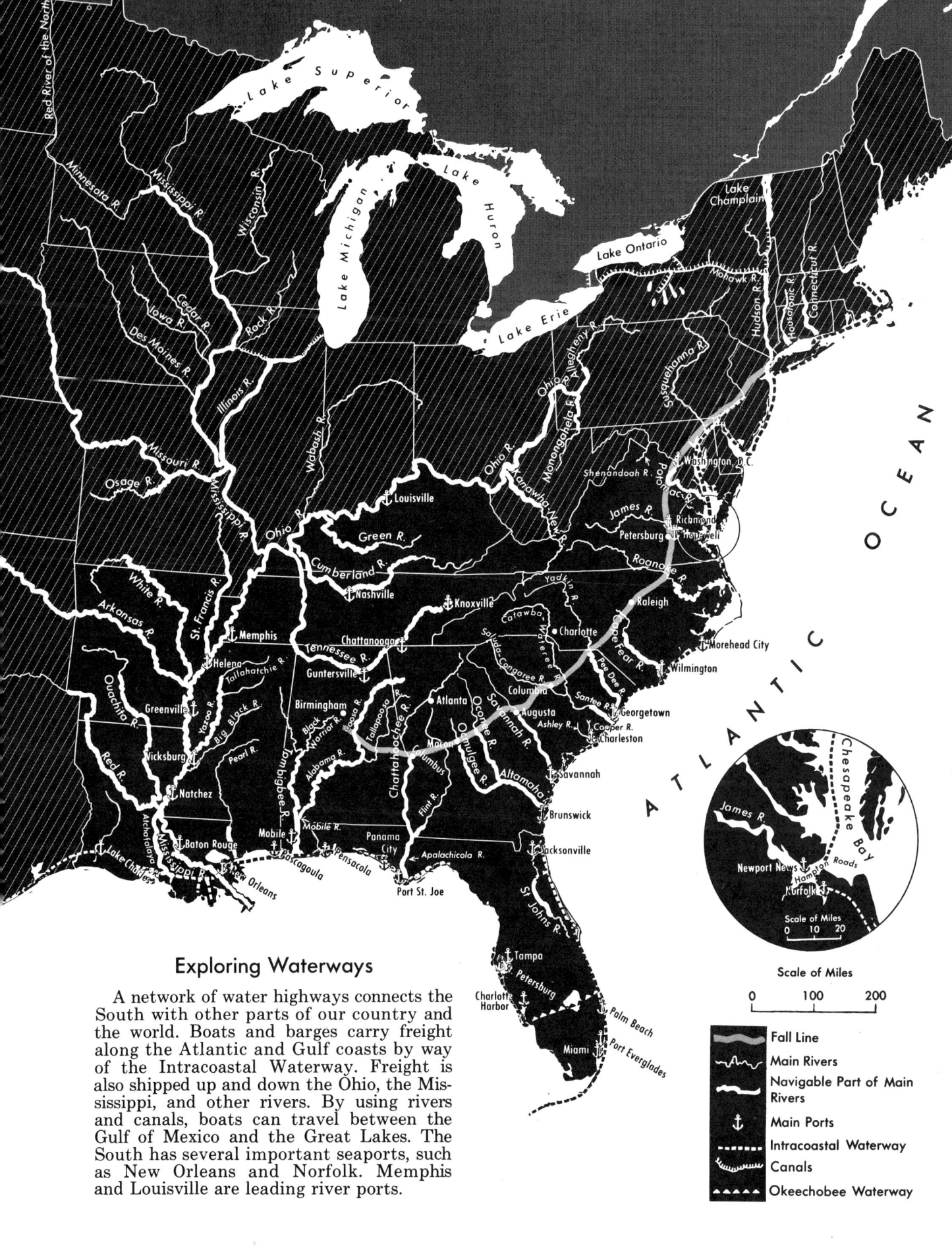

## Exploring Waterways

A network of water highways connects the South with other parts of our country and the world. Boats and barges carry freight along the Atlantic and Gulf coasts by way of the Intracoastal Waterway. Freight is also shipped up and down the Ohio, the Mississippi, and other rivers. By using rivers and canals, boats can travel between the Gulf of Mexico and the Great Lakes. The South has several important seaports, such as New Orleans and Norfolk. Memphis and Louisville are leading river ports.

Many horses and cattle graze on the rich pasturelands of Kentucky's Bluegrass. This area is a fertile, basin-shaped lowland in the Interior Plains region. The Nashville Basin of Tennessee is much like the Bluegrass, but other parts of the Interior Plains region in the South are hillier and less fertile. Why do you suppose the Bluegrass is called by that name?

# The Interior Plains

West of the Appalachian Plateau is an area of hilly land that extends southward across Kentucky and Tennessee and into northern Alabama. This area of the South is lower than the Appalachian Plateau, but it is not as low as the Coastal Plain. It is part of a huge region in the central part of our country known as the Interior Plains. (See map on page 21.)

Two important basin-shaped lowlands lie within the Interior Plains region of the South. These are the Bluegrass in northern Kentucky and the Nashville Basin in Tennessee. (See maps on pages 248 and 253.) In these areas, much of the land is flat or gently rolling, and the soil is very good for growing crops. In the summertime, green fields of tobacco cover much of the Bluegrass. There are also many large pastures where cattle and horses graze on the rich bluegrass* that gives this area its name. In the Nashville Basin are many dairy and tobacco farms.

The rest of the Interior Plains region in the South is hillier than the Bluegrass and the Nashville Basin. Also, the soil is less fertile. Much of the land is wooded, but there are fields of corn and tobacco in the valleys and on many steep hillsides. Just as on the Appalachian Plateau, rivers have carried away some of the soil and left deep gullies.

As the map at right shows, the vast Interior Plains region covers most of the central part of the United States. Which states of the South lie partly in the Interior Plains region?

**The Ozark Plateau** of Arkansas is part of the Interior Highlands region of the South. This plateau is mainly an area of rolling tablelands. Although there are rugged hills and mountains in some parts of the Interior Highlands, they are not as high as those of the Appalachian Highlands.

## The Interior Highlands

The northwestern part of Arkansas is in a region of our country called the Interior Highlands. This region extends from the Mississippi and Missouri rivers southwestward into eastern Oklahoma. The mountains and plateaus in this region are not as high as those in the Appalachian Highlands.

The northern part of the Interior Highlands region is known as the Ozark Plateau. (See map on page 245.) In Arkansas, farm fields and forests cover the broad, rolling hills of this area. There are also orchards of peach and apple trees. Along the southern edge of the Ozark Plateau are steep ridges separated by deep river valleys. These ridges are called the Boston Mountains.

The Interior Highlands region of our country includes the northwestern part of Arkansas.

In the southern part of the Interior Highlands region are the Ouachita Mountains. They extend from east to west across part of Arkansas and into Oklahoma. The highest peaks in the Ouachita range are only about 2,800 feet above sea level. Most of the mountain slopes are covered with dense forests of hardwood trees. Lumbering is an important industry in this area.

Between the Ozark Plateau and the Ouachita Mountains is a narrow lowland called the Arkansas Valley. Here the land is gently rolling, and the soil is fertile. In the Arkansas Valley are many fields of cotton, strawberries, and other crops.

In this chapter you have learned about the four main land regions in the South. You have discovered some of the ways in which the mountains, plains, and other land features of these regions affect the lives of people who live in this part of the United States.

**Solve a Problem**
The South has a wide variety of land features. How do these features affect the people who live in the South? The following questions suggest hypotheses you may need to make to solve this problem.
1. How do the land features of the South affect the way people earn a living?
2. How do the land features help to determine where people live?

The chapters in Part 4 of this book, as well as this chapter, will help you solve this problem.

See pages 256-258

**Develop Important Understandings**
To find the information needed to answer the following questions, you will need to do research about the land and water features of the South.
1. Along the Mississippi and other rivers that flow across the Coastal Plain of the South, much of the land is covered with a deep layer of fertile soil. Explain why.
2. No large cities have grown up in the Blue Ridge section of the South. What facts can you discover that help to explain this?
3. Describe some of the up-to-date farming methods used by farmers in the Piedmont Plateau. Explain why farmers must use each of these methods.

**Share New Understandings**
Imagine that you have a pen pal in a foreign country and that you want to tell your friend about the main land regions of the South. Do research in this book to discover the most important land and water features of each of the South's land regions. Then write your pen pal a letter describing what you might see if you were to travel in each of these regions. Be sure to use words that will create pictures in your friend's mind.

**A Challenging Topic To Explore**
During the last four hundred years, the land in the South has been changed in many ways. People have cut down forests and planted crops. They have built towns and cities. Coal and other minerals have been dug from the earth. Write a report describing some of the ways in which people have changed the land of the South. Include information about changes that have resulted from:
1. farming      3. lumbering
2. mining       4. work done by the TVA
   5. the growth of cities

In your report, consider both the beneficial and harmful effects of the changes you describe. The suggestions on pages 259-264 will be helpful in locating information and in writing an interesting report.

# 3  Climate

Imagine that we are visiting the city of Miami Beach, Florida, on the first day of February. As we leave our hotel for a walk, we notice that the air is warm and the sun is bright. The people we meet are dressed in light summer clothing. In a park nearby, we see hibiscus and other colorful flowers in bloom. Because there are palm trees growing in the park, we know that the weather here is never very cold.

We stop at a drugstore to buy a newspaper. On the front page, we read that a blizzard is sweeping across the northern part of the United States. Snow has been falling for three days. In some places, the temperature is below zero. We are glad to be here in Miami Beach, enjoying the warm sunshine.

**The South has mild winters and warm summers.** In order to learn more about the climate of the South, turn to the map on the left-hand side of page 44. This map shows average temperatures in North America during the month of January. Notice that in most of the northern part of the conterminous* United States, the average temperature in January is below thirty-two degrees. You will realize that winters are cold there when you remember that thirty-two degrees is the temperature at which water freezes. In nearly all of the South, however, the average temperature in January is above thirty-two degrees. The only places in the South that receive much snow are high in the mountains.

*See Glossary

The picture on these pages shows truckloads of ripe oranges in a Florida orchard. The frost-free period, or growing season, is longer in the South than it is in the northern part of our country. In some sections of Florida, oranges and other warm-weather crops can be grown. More than three fourths of all the citrus fruit grown in our country comes from this state.

**Develop Important Understandings**

Use the following questions to guide your research about the climate of the South.
1. What is the difference between "weather" and "climate"? (See the Glossary.)
2. What is the main reason why winters are mild in the South?
3. Why are winters milder along the coasts of the South than they are farther inland?
4. How does a long growing season help farmers in the South?
5. Which parts of the South have the longest growing season? (See top map on page 170.)
6. Why are summers cooler in the high mountains of the Blue Ridge than in other parts of the South?

The main reason why winters are mild in the South is that the southern part of our country is nearer the equator than the northern part. The special feature on pages 42 and 43 helps to explain how distance from the equator influences climate.

Winters in the South are somewhat milder along the coasts than they are farther inland. This is because large bodies of water lose their heat more slowly than the land. Warm winds from the Gulf of Mexico and the Atlantic Ocean help to delay the coming of frost to the coastal areas.

Except in the mountains, summers in the South are long and warm. The period of time during which crops can be grown without danger of frost is longer in the South than it is farther north. This frost-free period is called the growing season. As you can see by the map at the top of page 170, most of the South has a growing season of more than two hundred days. In southern Florida, crops can be grown outdoors all year round.

A long growing season helps farmers. In the South, crops can be planted and harvested earlier than they can in

**Sailing on Louisiana's Lake Pontchartrain,** near the Gulf of Mexico. Cool breezes bring pleasant summer weather to the parts of the South that lie near the sea.

Warm winds from the Gulf of Mexico bring most of the South's rainfall. These winds blow northward from the sea toward the land, especially in the summertime. They contain moisture that has evaporated* from the surface of the Gulf. As these winds blow over the land, they drop their moisture as rain. Along the Atlantic coast, some rain is brought by winds that blow in from the ocean.

**The climate in all parts of the South is not the same.** You have learned that the climate in most parts of the South is much the same. Winters are mild, summers are warm, and rain is plentiful. However, there are some differences of climate from place to place. For example, the climate of southern Florida is not like the climate in the Blue Ridge of Virginia. The rest of this chapter contains information about the climate in various parts of the South.

**Climate on the Coastal Plain.** If you could visit the Coastal Plain region of the South, you might discover for yourself many facts about the climate. Let's imagine that you are going to stay with friends in Montgomery, Alabama, for a whole year. (See map on page 15.) The climate in this city is typical of the climate in most parts of the Coastal Plain.

<u>Summer.</u> In summertime, the weather in Montgomery is warm and humid, just as it is nearly everywhere on the Coastal Plain. During your stay, the weather is sometimes hot. The temperature seldom rises as high as it

northern states. These crops can be sold in areas where winters are long and cold. Also, farmers in some parts of the South can grow such crops as cotton and oranges, which cannot be grown in the northern part of the United States.

**Rainfall is heavy in the South.** Although people sometimes talk about "the sunny South," the southern states receive more rainfall than any other main group of states in our country. The map on page 41 shows us that almost all parts of the South receive more than forty inches of rainfall each year.

does in some other parts of our country, such as the deserts and plains of the West. There, however, the air is dry. Here on the Coastal Plain the air is moist. You feel warmer and more uncomfortable than you would if the air were dry.

During the summer, the weather in the parts of the South near the Atlantic and Gulf coasts is usually a little cooler than it is farther inland. Large bodies of water like the Atlantic Ocean and the Gulf of Mexico become warm more slowly in summer than the land does. Cool sea breezes bring pleasant weather to coastal areas.

Thunderstorms. It is an afternoon in July. All day long, the weather in Montgomery has been so hot and damp that you have been uncomfortable. Now large, black clouds fill the sky. Thunder rolls, lightning flashes, and rain pours down in torrents. When the thunderstorm finally ends, the air seems cooler and fresher.

During the summer, Montgomery has many thunderstorms. The special feature on page 48 gives information about the causes of such storms. Some parts of the Coastal Plain of the South receive more than seventy thunderstorms each year.

**Physical Needs**

The picture at left shows a family camping at a state park in Louisiana, in the Coastal Plain region of the South. Do you think that the members of this family have the same physical needs that you do? (See pages 99 and 100.) Do they need food? Exercise? Fresh air? Protection from heat and cold? How does this picture suggest ways in which the members of the family meet their physical needs?

Hurricanes sometimes strike the Coastal Plain region of the South, uprooting trees and smashing buildings. Near the sea, high waves may also cause serious damage. Where do hurricanes form?

40

Thunderstorms bring heavy rains. Sometimes they bring as much as ten inches of rain within twenty-four hours. Although heavy summer rains are good for growing crops, they wash much soil into rivers and streams.

Hurricanes. During the summer and early fall, hurricanes sometimes strike the Coastal Plain. Hurricanes are violent storms that begin in the tropics, over large bodies of water. The hurricanes that strike the United States begin over the Atlantic Ocean or the Caribbean Sea. (See special feature on page 49.) During a hurricane, rainfall is heavy and winds blow at seventy-five miles an hour or more. Hurricanes can uproot trees and smash houses. The high waves that come with hurricanes often sink boats and cause great damage along low-lying coasts. Sometimes many people are killed.

Winter. During your year in Montgomery, the weather never becomes very cold. Winters are short and mild throughout the Coastal Plain region of the South. Snow seldom falls in this area. When it does, it usually melts quickly. Winters are mildest near the coasts.

In the southern half of the Florida peninsula, several years may pass without a heavy frost. Farmers here can grow oranges and other fruits that need a year-round

*Continued on page 44*

As this map shows, the average yearly rainfall varies from place to place in the United States. Throughout the South, rainfall is plentiful.

## Average Annual Rainfall

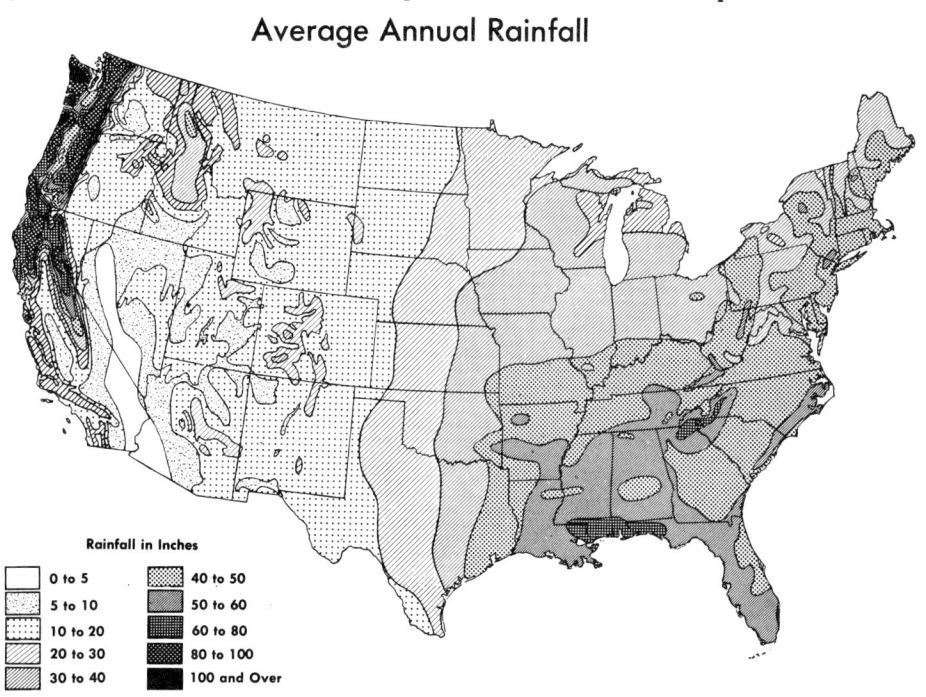

**SUMMER IN THE NORTHERN HEMISPHERE**

The chart above shows how the earth is lighted by the sun at noon on June 21, the first day of summer in the Northern Hemisphere.

# THE SEASONS

The year is divided into four natural periods, or seasons, which we call summer, autumn, winter, and spring. Each season is marked by changes in the length of day and night and by changes in temperature.

The seasons are caused by the tilt of the earth's axis and the revolution of the earth around the sun. It takes one year for the earth to revolve around the sun. On this trip, the earth remains tilted at the same angle to the path along which it travels. The chart below shows how this causes the Northern Hemisphere to be tilted toward the sun on June 21 and away from the sun on December 22. On March 21 and September 22, the Northern Hemisphere is tilted neither toward the sun nor away from it.

The chart on the left shows that on June 21 the sun shines directly on the Tropic of Cancer.* This is the northernmost point ever reached by the sun's direct rays. In the Northern Hemisphere, June 21 is the first day of summer and the longest day of the year.

The chart on the right shows that on December 22 the sun shines directly on the Tropic of Capricorn.* This is the southernmost point ever reached by the sun's direct

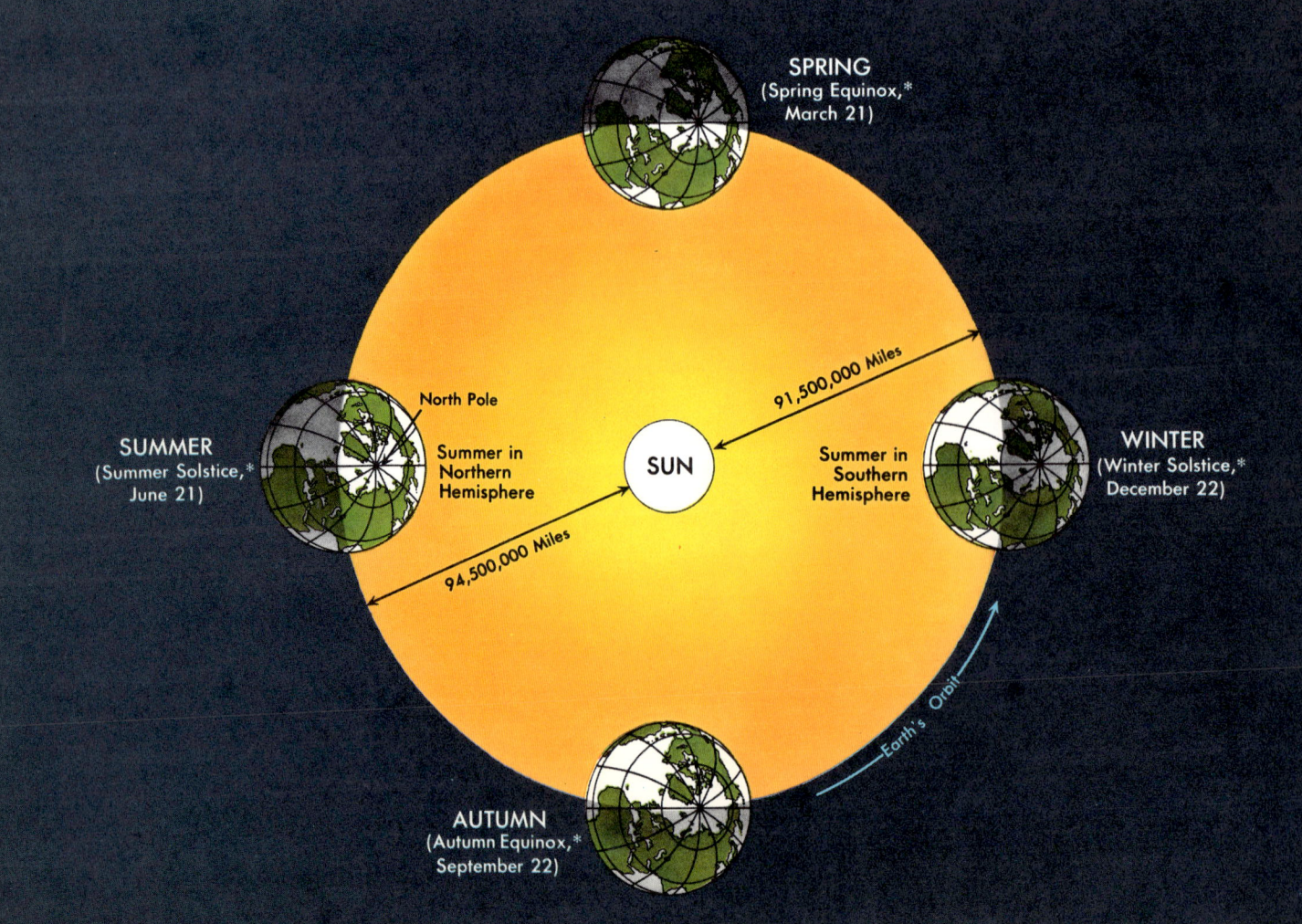

# OF THE YEAR

rays. In the Northern Hemisphere, December 22 is the first day of winter and the shortest day of the year.

When one hemisphere is tilted toward the sun, the other is tilted away from the sun. For this reason, the seasons in the Southern Hemisphere are just the opposite of those in the Northern Hemisphere. Summer in the Southern Hemisphere begins on December 22, and winter begins on June 21.

Temperatures are affected by the slant of the sun's rays as they strike the surface of the earth. Study the chart and the picture of Tallahassee, Florida, below to see why this is so.

Near the equator, the sun is almost directly overhead throughout the year. For this reason, the weather near the equator is always hot, except in the mountains. In areas farther away from the equator, the sun's rays are more slanted. Therefore, the weather is usually cooler.

The northern part of the United States is farther from the equator than the southern part of our country. This explains why the weather is generally cooler in the north than it is in the south.

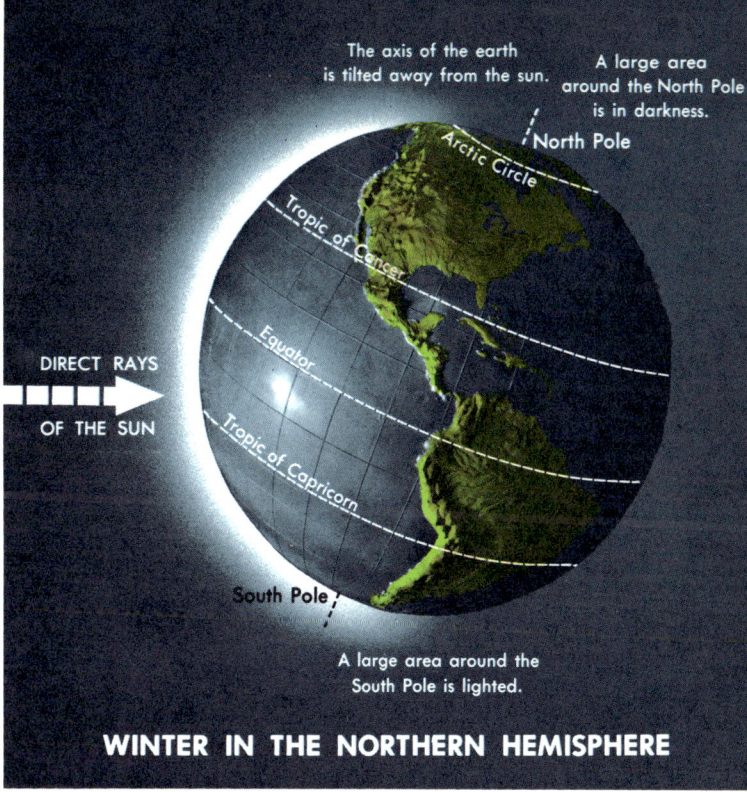

The chart above shows how the earth is lighted by the sun at noon on December 22, the first day of winter in the Northern Hemisphere.

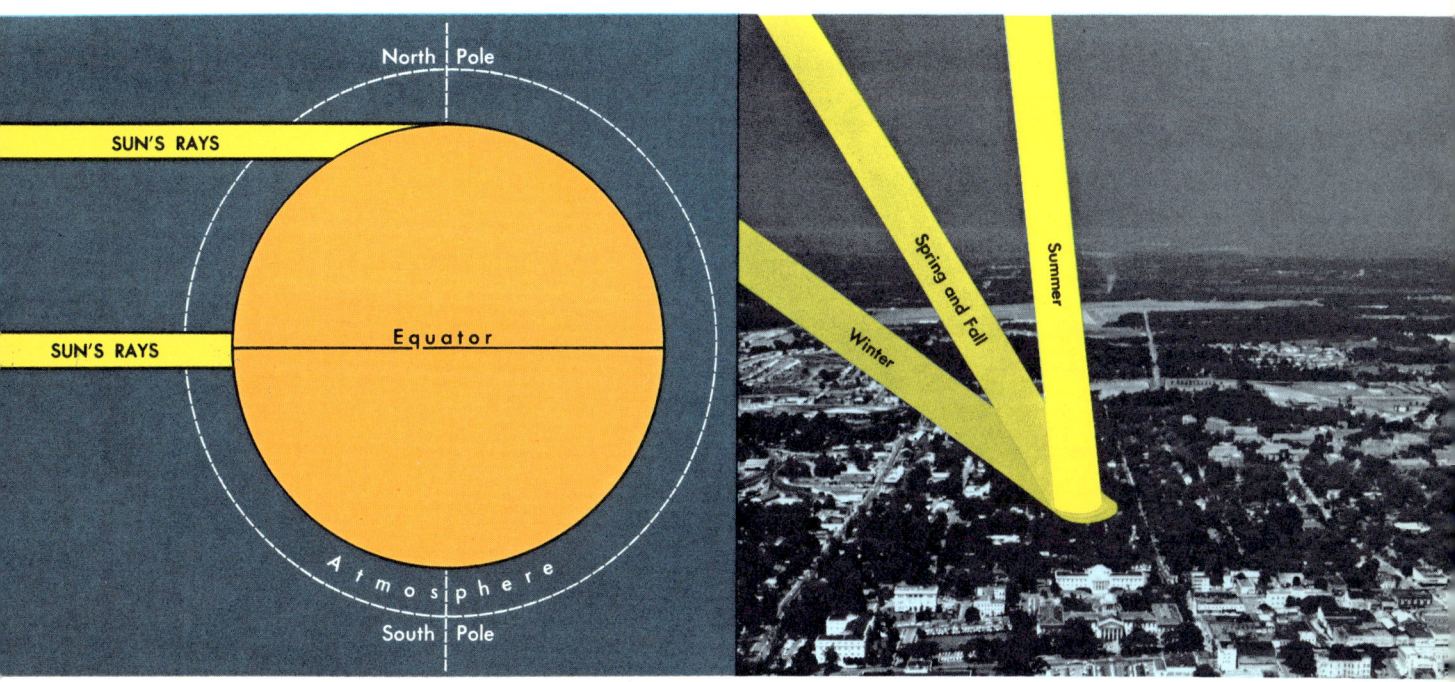

The chart above shows that when the sun's rays strike the earth at a slant, they must travel through more atmosphere than when they strike it directly. This affects temperatures because the atmosphere absorbs heat from the sun's rays. The more atmosphere the rays must pass through, the less heat they retain to warm the earth. This is one reason why temperatures are higher if the sun is directly overhead than they are if the sun is low in the sky.

This picture also helps to explain how changes in temperature are caused by the different angles at which the sun's rays strike the surface of the earth. During the summer, the noonday sun is high in the sky. The rays of the sun are concentrated into narrow areas. As a result, they produce much heat. During the winter, the noonday sun is low in the sky. The slanting rays of the sun are spread over much wider areas, so they produce less heat.

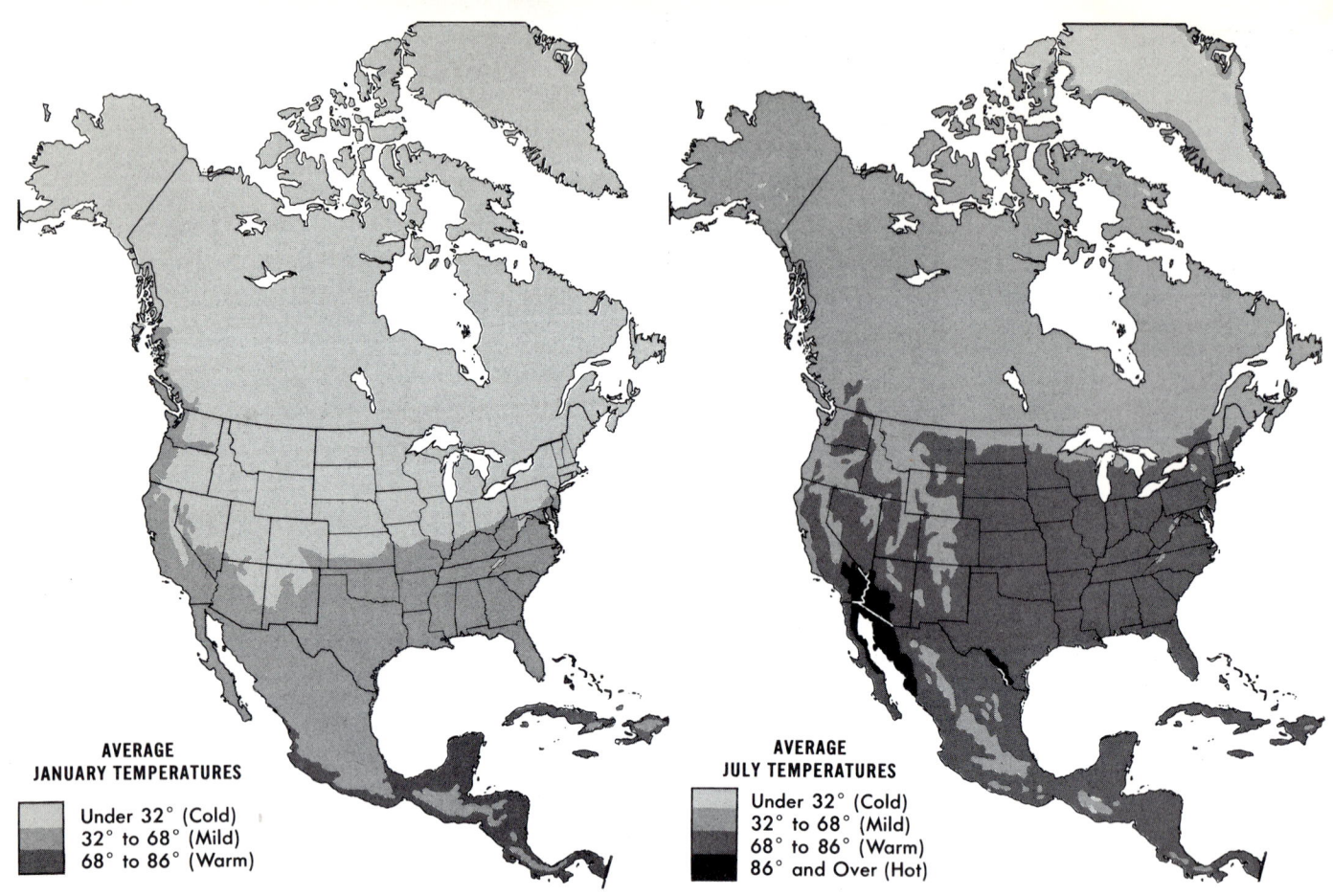

**Average temperatures** in North America during January and July. Winters are mild and summers are warm in all parts of the South except the high mountains of the Appalachian Highlands region.

growing season. They can also grow vegetables in the winter for sale to people who live in the northern part of our country. During the winter, millions of people come to Florida to enjoy the mild, sunny climate.

Even in Florida, however, the temperature may drop below freezing during the winter. Freezing temperatures are caused by cold air from the north, which sometimes brings a few days of cold weather. A heavy frost may cause great damage to crops.

**Climate in the Appalachian Highlands.** In the Appalachian Highlands region, climate varies with elevation. The higher you go above sea level, the cooler the air becomes. As you may have learned in your science class, the earth gives off heat that it has received from the sun. At low elevations, much of this heat is absorbed by the moisture and particles of dust in the air. At high elevations, however, the air is much cleaner and drier. Therefore, it cannot absorb as much heat. As a result, the temperature is usually cooler at high elevations than it is at lower elevations. Each three to four hundred feet of altitude makes a difference of one degree in temperature.

Summer. In the Piedmont Plateau section of the Appalachian Highlands, the climate is much like that of the Coastal Plain. Summers here are warm and humid. The growing season on the Piedmont varies from about 180 days in Virginia to 240 days in Georgia.

In the higher parts of the Appalachian Highlands, summers are cooler and more pleasant than they are on the Piedmont Plateau. The coolest summer weather in the Appalachian Highlands is found in the high mountains of the Blue Ridge. Many people spend their summer vacations in these mountains.

Winter. Winters are more severe in the high mountains than they are at lower elevations in the Appalachian Highlands. The first frost comes earlier in the fall. Often, a white blanket of snow covers the high peaks. In the spring, as soon as the danger of frost is over, crops such as corn and tobacco may be planted on the mountain slopes that are suitable for farming. The growing season in the mountains is only about 160 days long.

**Winter in the Appalachian Highlands of Virginia.** The high mountains are the only places in the South that receive much snow. Winters are generally less severe at lower elevations.

Rainfall. Most parts of the Appalachian Highlands region receive more than forty inches of rainfall each year. Rainfall is heaviest in the Blue Ridge. In this section, the mountain slopes are covered with dense, green forests. The heavy rainfall helps the trees to grow. Also, because it is cooler in the mountains, water does not evaporate quickly from the soil. Trees grow well where the ground holds plenty of water for their roots.

The Blue Ridge receives large amounts of moisture all year round. Warm, moist air blows inland from the Atlantic Ocean and the Gulf of Mexico. When the air reaches the mountains, it is forced to rise. The higher it rises, the cooler it becomes. Some of the moisture condenses and falls as rain or snow.

**Climate in other regions of the South.** Summers are warm in the Interior Plains region of the South. However, the growing season here is generally shorter than it is on the Coastal Plain. This is mainly because the Interior Plains region lies farther north than most parts of the Coastal Plain. Also, the warm sea winds that delay the coming of frost to the coasts do not reach this far inland.

Farmers in the Interior Plains grow crops such as tobacco and corn. Many horses, cattle, and other livestock are also raised here. Cotton, which needs a growing season of about two hundred days, is grown in Alabama and in small areas in Tennessee.

*Continued on page 51*

**Fontana Lake in North Carolina.** Many people spend their vacations in the high mountains of the Blue Ridge, where summers are cool and pleasant.

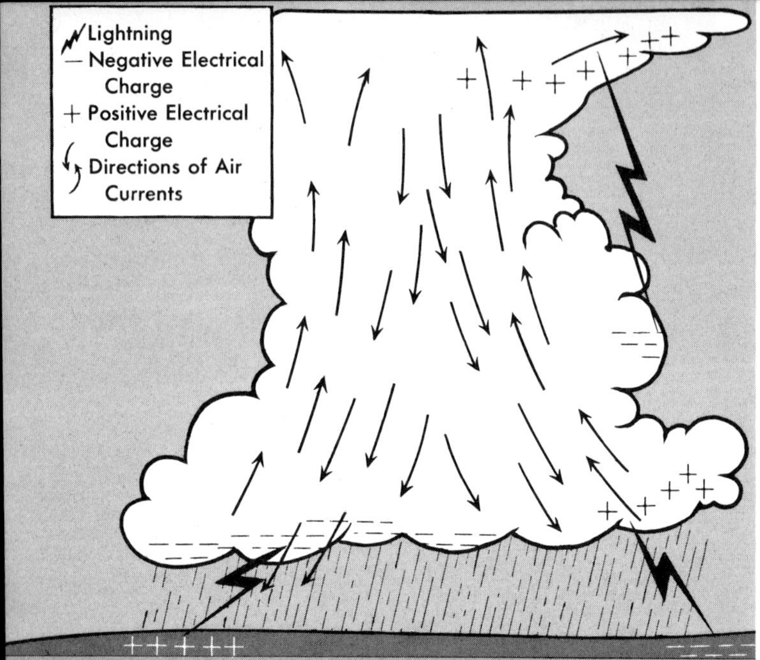

**Legend:**
- ⚡ Lightning
- − Negative Electrical Charge
- + Positive Electrical Charge
- ↻ Directions of Air Currents

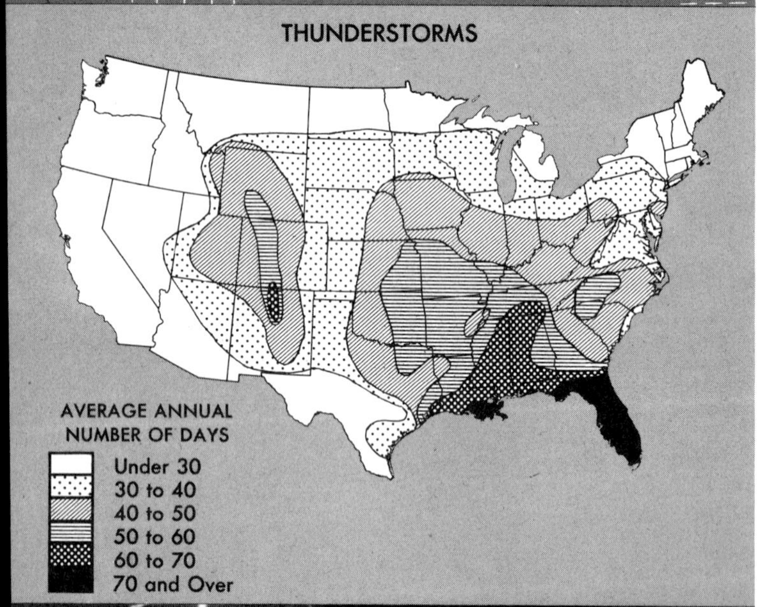

**THUNDERSTORMS**

AVERAGE ANNUAL NUMBER OF DAYS
- Under 30
- 30 to 40
- 40 to 50
- 50 to 60
- 60 to 70
- 70 and Over

# Thunderstorms

A thunderstorm is a heavy shower of rain accompanied by gusty winds, thunder, lightning, and sometimes hail. Thunderstorms are most frequent over areas of warm land in or near the tropics. Few such storms occur beyond 60° north or south latitude.

Practically all rain is formed by the rising and cooling of moist air. As the air cools, moisture condenses into tiny droplets of water. If there are enough droplets, a rain cloud forms. Then the droplets combine as raindrops, and a shower results. One raindrop may contain as many as 8 million cloud droplets.

A thunderstorm may occur when a warm land surface heats moist air very rapidly. This heating creates strong currents of rising air. When rain clouds form, the rising air currents sweep them upward, several miles above the earth's surface. Falling raindrops are broken up into fine particles by the rising air. These particles develop electrical charges, some negative (-) and some positive (+). Particles with the same charge collect in different parts of a cloud, or form new raindrops that fall to earth. When the difference in charge becomes great enough, electricity may be discharged between parts of one cloud, between two clouds, or between a cloud and the ground. This discharge, or flash of lightning, heats the air through which it passes. The heated air expands violently, creating the sound waves that we call thunder. Since it takes about five seconds for a sound wave to travel a mile, a person can tell how far away a storm is by counting the seconds between a flash of lightning and the thunder that follows.

# Hurricanes

A hurricane, or typhoon as it is called in some parts of the world, is the most destructive storm known. It is made up of violent winds that whirl around a calm center, called the eye. The eye is usually about fifteen miles in diameter, but the entire storm may be as much as five hundred miles across. Such a storm is not considered a true hurricane unless the whirling winds near the center blow at a speed of seventy-five miles an hour or more. The storm itself, however, travels rather slowly, at about fifteen or twenty miles an hour.

Hurricanes form in the tropics, over large bodies of warm water. They are most frequent in summer and fall. North of the equator, hurricanes travel in a northwestward direction until they reach about 25 or 30 degrees north latitude. Then they may change direction and move northeastward. South of the equator, hurricanes move first southwestward and then southeastward. The map below shows where hurricanes are most frequently formed, and the directions they generally follow.

Usually, several hurricanes form each year over the Atlantic Ocean. Some of these storms remain over the sea. Others, however, strike the islands of the West Indies or the coast of North America. The violent winds of a hurricane often cause great destruction of property. Sometimes many people are killed. The enormous tidal waves and heavy rains that come with hurricanes may also cause damage. Fortunately, hurricanes seldom reach far inland. This is because their winds are slowed down by friction when they blow over the land.

**ROTATION OF WINDS IN A HURRICANE**

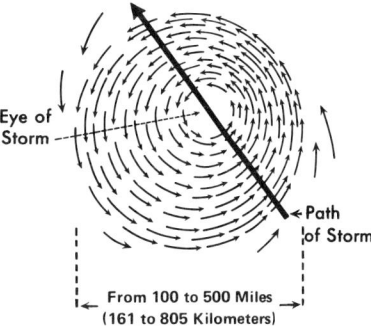

From 100 to 500 Miles
(161 to 805 Kilometers)

A hurricane is made up of violent winds that whirl around a calm center called the eye. (See illustration above.) In the Northern Hemisphere, the whirling winds of hurricanes and other circular storms blow in a counter-clockwise direction. (See chart at left.) In the Southern Hemisphere, they blow in a clockwise direction.

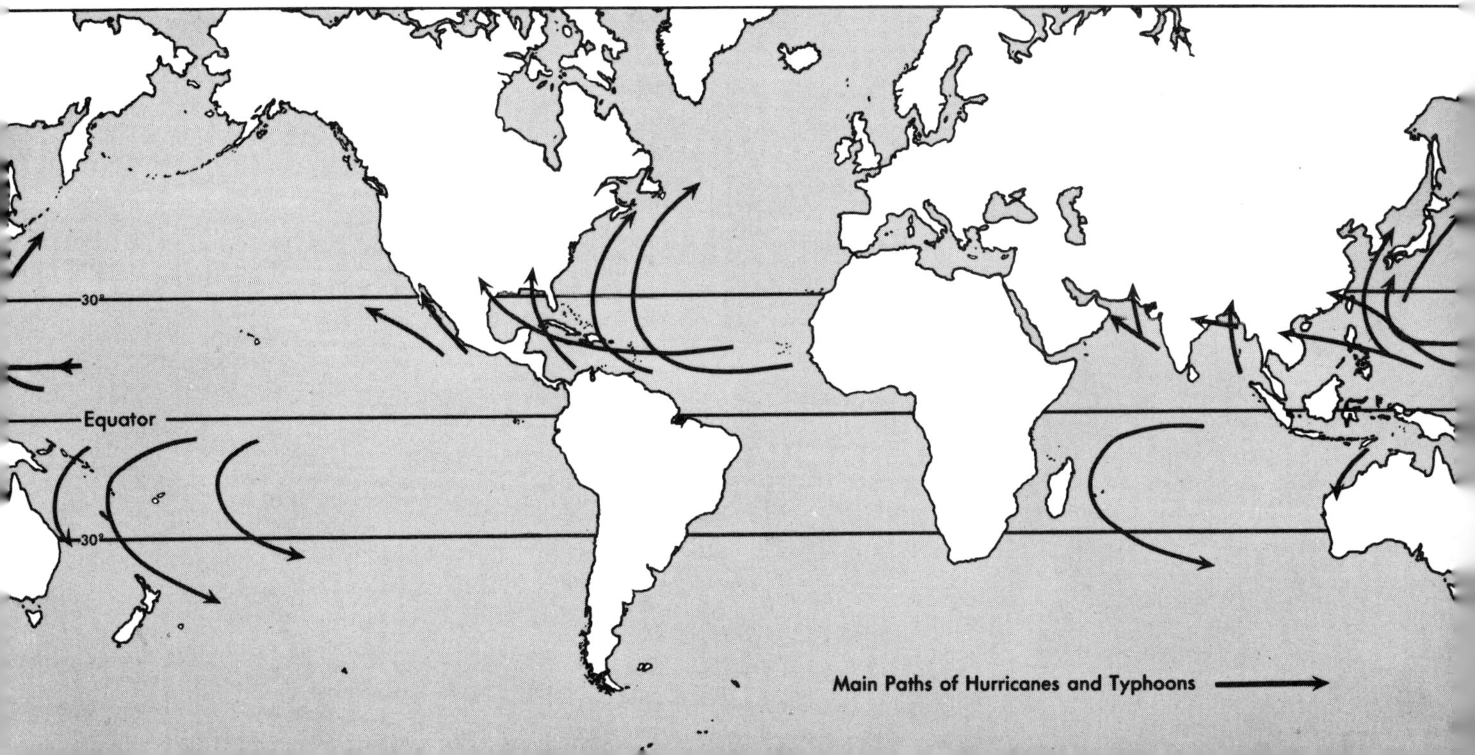

Main Paths of Hurricanes and Typhoons ⟶

Mainly because of its more northern location, the Interior Plains region has longer and somewhat cooler winters than the Coastal Plain. During the winter months, the parts of Kentucky and Tennessee that lie in the Interior Plains usually receive about ten inches of snow.

The Interior Highlands region of the South is not high enough above sea level for altitude to have much effect on temperature. However, the weather here is usually a little cooler and less humid than it is on the Coastal Plain nearby. Summer days are hot, but nights are cool. Winters are short and mild, with very little snow. The snow that does fall seldom remains on the ground very long.

**Problems To Solve**

1. Some parts of the Coastal Plain of the South receive more than seventy thunderstorms each year. <u>Why do so many of these storms occur here?</u> The following questions suggest hypotheses you will need to consider.
    a. How do the high temperatures in these parts of the Coastal Plain affect the formation of thunderstorms?
    b. How does warm, moist air from the Gulf of Mexico and the Atlantic Ocean affect the formation of thunderstorms?
2. <u>How does climate affect farming in the South?</u> In forming hypotheses, you will want to consider how farming is affected by rainfall and length of growing season.
See pages 256-258

**Fishermen on the White River,** in the Interior Highlands of Arkansas. The weather in the Interior Highlands region is usually a little cooler and less humid than it is on the Coastal Plain.

51

**A reconstruction of the fort built at Jamestown, Virginia, in 1607.** This was the first permanent English settlement in America. In the years that followed the founding of Jamestown, many more settlers came to the South from England and other parts of the British Isles.

# Part 2
# History

Your study of the South's history will be an exciting adventure if you think and read the way historians do. Historians know they can never learn about everything that has happened in our world. Of the millions of events that have taken place since ancient times, only a small number have been recorded. Still, there are more historical records than any person could study in a lifetime, even about a single subject such as the Civil War.

Historians must first select the events they wish to emphasize. Then they must gather data that will help explain these events. To make the investigation in an orderly way, the historian uses the problem-solving method, which is described in "Thinking and Solving Problems" on pages 256-258. Perhaps you would like to use this method to solve the following problem about the history of the South.

> Why did the South recover from the effects of the Civil War much more slowly than the North?

The following questions suggest some hypotheses that will be helpful in solving this problem.

- Where did most of the battles of the war take place?
- What happened to the state governments in the South after the war?
- How did the ending of slavery affect the South's system of agriculture?

# 4 Settlers Come to the South

## The First Americans

Thousands of years ago, people were already living in the part of our country that we now call the South. Most of these people had straight black hair, copper-colored skin, and dark eyes. Today they are known as Indians, or Native Americans.

**The first Americans came from Asia.** Scientists believe that the ancestors of the Native Americans came to this continent from Asia—the eastern part of the continent of Eurasia. This migration may have begun as long as 100,000 years ago. In the far north, Asia is separated from North America only by a narrow strait. (See the small picture of a globe below.) At various times in the past, the oceans and seas of the world were much lower than they are now. During those times a bridge of land may have connected Asia and North America. People could have traveled from one continent to the other across this land bridge.

The picture of a globe at left shows that Asia and North America are very close together in the far north. Scientists believe that the first people to live in North America came here from Asia. How do scientists think people traveled from one continent to the other?

The Indians, or Native Americans, in the South used many kinds of tools to help them meet their needs. In the picture above, a man is making a dugout canoe by burning out the center of a log. He is holding some wet clay, which he smears on the wood where he does not want the fire to burn. Later he will smooth the inside and outside of the log with scrapers made of stone and shell. Do research to discover some other kinds of tools used by the Native Americans.

Using Tools

See pages 230-235

A few of the people who came from Asia stayed in the far north to hunt seal and other game. Most of them, however, traveled southward to places where it was warmer. As the years went by, they settled throughout North and South America.

**Several Indian tribes made their homes in the South.** The area we now call the South attracted many Indians. Here, food was plentiful. In the forests were deer, bear, and small game such as squirrel and rabbit. There were many fish in the lakes and streams, and in the shallow bays along the Atlantic and Gulf coasts. The warm, rainy climate and fertile soil made it easy for the Indians to grow crops. Here, too, materials for clothing, shelter, and tools were readily available.

At the time European colonists first began to settle in America, there were about 150,000 Indians living in the South. These Indians belonged to several different groups, or tribes. Each tribe spoke a different language and had its own way of life. Among the largest Indian tribes in the South were the Chickasaw, the Choctaw, the Creek, and the Cherokee.

**Most southern Indians were peaceful farmers.** Most of the Indians in the South were good farmers. Their main crops were corn, beans, squash, melons, and tobacco. The Indians also grew sunflowers for the seeds, which were eaten. They cultivated their crops with hoes that had blades of shell or bone.

The Indians also obtained food by hunting and fishing. For these activities they used such implements as bows and arrows, knives, spears, and blowguns.* The southern Indians made their tools and weapons out of materials such as wood, stone, reed, bone, and shell. Their boats were dugouts made by burning out large logs.

The Indians of the South lived in villages of well-constructed houses. Many tribes built houses that were oblong in shape. They were open at each end and had curved, thatched roofs. Other tribes built round houses with cone-shaped roofs. The Indians also constructed buildings such as council houses and temples. Some of the southern tribes built their temples on top of earthen mounds.

The mild climate of the South made it unnecessary for the Indians to wear much clothing. However, they knew how to make moccasins, shirts, robes, and other articles of clothing out of deerskin and other animal hides and furs. They also made robes out of turkey feathers, and wove cloth from plant fibers and animal hairs.

Many other useful and ornamental articles were made by the southern Indians. They wove mats and baskets out of reeds and cornhusks. Their dishes and other utensils were made of wood or pottery. Wood carvings were made for use in temples and in religious ceremonies. The Indians also fashioned beautiful jewelry out of shells and pearls. This jewelry also served as money.

The Indians of the South were generally peaceful. Since each tribe had enough land and enough food, the Indians were seldom at war with one another. Most of the time, they hunted, fished, tended their crops, or traded with their neighbors for things they wanted.

*See Glossary

# Early Explorers

**Columbus sails to America.** Five hundred years ago, Europeans who wanted to visit Asia had to travel eastward. The trip was long and hard, and much of it had to be made by land. Even so, many people journeyed from Europe to Asia in order to obtain spices, silks, and other precious goods.

An explorer named Christopher Columbus was determined to find a better route to Asia. Like many educated Europeans at that time, Columbus believed the earth was round. He felt sure he could reach Asia by sailing westward across the unknown waters of the Atlantic Ocean. In 1492 Columbus and a small band of sailors set out from Spain in three frail ships.

Many weeks later, Columbus and his men landed on the shore of a small island far to the west. Columbus thought that he was somewhere near the coast of Asia. Although he later made three more trips to America, Columbus never realized that he had reached a new part of the world.

**Columbus and his men landed on the shore of a small island.** They thought they were near Asia. However, Columbus had really reached a new part of the world. Other explorers later found there were two great continents in the New World. These were North and South America.

Before long, other European explorers were sailing westward to learn more about the lands that Columbus had found. They soon discovered that Columbus had been mistaken about reaching Asia. To the west of the Atlantic Ocean lay two huge, unknown continents. These became known as North America and South America.

**Ponce de León claims Florida for Spain.** The first European explorer to reach the area that we now call the South was a Spaniard named Juan Ponce de León. He had helped to establish a Spanish settlement on the island of Puerto Rico. (See map on page 13.) In 1510 he was appointed governor of the island.

Ponce de León had heard tales of a magic spring whose waters were supposed to make old people young again. In 1513 he set out from Puerto Rico to find this magic spring, or "Fountain of Youth." On Easter, which the Spanish call *pascua florida*, Ponce de León saw what he believed was a huge island. He

**Freedom**

See pages 212-213

The picture at left shows the Spanish explorer Hernando de Soto and his soldiers crossing the Mississippi River in 1541. De Soto's expedition traveled for hundreds of miles through the wilderness in search of gold. During this journey, the Spaniards captured Indians to serve as guides and slaves.

1. Do you think the Indians who lived in the South enjoyed very much freedom before the Europeans came? What makes you think this?
2. Why do you suppose the Spaniards felt that they could take away the freedom of other human beings?
3. How do you suppose the captured Indians felt about their loss of freedom?
4. Do you think all human beings share a deep desire for freedom? Explain.

named this land Florida, and claimed it for Spain.

In 1521 Ponce de León made a second expedition to Florida, where he hoped to start a colony. Soon after reaching Florida, he was wounded in a battle with Indians. Later, he died. Although Ponce de León never found a Fountain of Youth, he opened the way for other people to explore the South.

**De Soto finds the Mississippi River.** In 1538 a wealthy Spanish nobleman named Hernando de Soto sailed to the New World. De Soto had heard tales that Florida was a "land of gold." He was willing to spend his fortune to conquer this land.

De Soto was named governor of Cuba and Florida by the King of Spain. After a year's stay in Cuba, he sailed to the west coast of Florida. With him was a large group of soldiers and noblemen, wearing colorful uniforms. These men began a march that was to take them through much of the South looking for gold.

Hernando de Soto and his men set sail for the New World in 1538. Although their search for gold ended in failure, they explored much of the region that we now call the South. De Soto died in the spring of 1542, and his men buried him in the Mississippi River.

On the journey, De Soto and his men captured Indians to serve as guides and slaves. In what is now Alabama, they captured an Indian chief who led them into an Indian ambush. When the battle was over, hundreds of Indians lay dead. Many Spanish soldiers had been killed. Nearly all the rest were wounded, including De Soto.

Although his men wanted to turn back after this battle, De Soto led them on. In May, 1541, they reached a mighty river. De Soto did not know that he had found one of the longest rivers in the world—the Mississippi.

By the spring of 1542, even De Soto had become discouraged. He and his men had spent a long, cold winter in a valley west of the Mississippi. In all their travels they had found no trace of gold. The weary, ragged band turned back toward the Mississippi. Near the river, De Soto became ill and died. His men buried him in the river he had found. After De Soto's death, his men traveled as far west as what is now the state of Texas. Then, they returned to the Mississippi River. They built crude boats and sailed all the way to a Spanish settlement in Mexico.

De Soto's search for gold ended in failure. However, he had explored much of the region we now call the South.

# The Coming of the Colonists

**The Spanish establish settlements in Florida.** People from Europe tried several times to start colonies in the South during the 1500's, but most of these attempts were not successful. As you have learned, Ponce de León's expedition to start a colony in Florida was a failure. A Spanish colony established in 1526 in what is now South Carolina also failed.

French Huguenots* settled in South Carolina and Florida in 1562, but their colonies, too, were unsuccessful. In 1564 the French founded Fort Caroline at the mouth of the St. Johns River, near what is now Jacksonville, Florida. The next year, the settlement was destroyed by Spanish soldiers, and most of the French settlers were killed.

Soon after the Spanish destroyed Fort Caroline, they founded a new town farther south along the coast. This was St. Augustine, Florida, the first permanent European settlement in what is now the United States.

Although Spain controlled Florida for almost two hundred years, few Spanish settlers came to this area. The only important Spanish settlements were at St. Augustine and Pensacola.

**La Salle claims the Mississippi Valley for France.** At the same time that Spanish explorers were coming to the South, people from France were exploring far to the north, in what is now Canada. A French sea captain named Jacques Cartier sailed up the St. Lawrence River in 1535. In 1608 Samuel de Champlain founded a trading post on the St. Lawrence. This later grew to be the city of Quebec. (See map on page 63.)

In the years that followed, many other French explorers, fur traders, and missionaries came to Canada. Among these men was René Robert Cavelier, Sieur de La Salle. In 1678 King Louis XIV granted La Salle permission to explore the Mississippi River and to claim land for France.

To reach the Mississippi, La Salle and his men traveled up the St. Lawrence River and through the Great Lakes. Then they headed down the Illinois River, which flows into the Mississippi. Along the way, they built three forts—Fort Conti, Fort Miami, and Fort Crèvecoeur. From these forts, La Salle planned to trade with the Indians for furs. In this way he expected to earn money to build additional forts along the Mississippi River.

Early in 1682, La Salle and his men reached the Mississippi. They paddled down the river in birchbark canoes. On April 9 they reached the mouth of the river, at the Gulf of Mexico. La Salle claimed all the territory along the Mississippi for France. He named the land Louisiana in honor of his king.

**New Orleans and other French settlements are established in the South.** La Salle returned to France in 1683. King Louis was pleased with his achievements and gave him permission to establish a colony at the mouth of the Mississippi River. He also named La Salle governor of the newly claimed land.

In 1685 La Salle sailed into the Gulf of Mexico with a large group of colonists. But he was unable to find the mouth of the Mississippi. He landed more than three hundred miles west of the river. There he built a fort. After two years of hardship, only a few of the colonists remained. La Salle led a small group on a march toward Canada to get help, but he was killed by some of his own men.

Although La Salle was not able to establish a colony in the New World, he led the way for other French settlers.

In 1699 the French established a town near what is now Biloxi, Mississippi. (See map on page 114.) This town became the capital of the territory of Louisiana. Later the French founded other settlements. One of these became the great city of New Orleans.

**People from England settle along the Atlantic coast.** England, too, claimed a share of the vast lands in North Amer-

ica. This claim was based on two voyages made by the explorer John Cabot,* in 1497 and 1498. During the late 1500's, an English noble, Sir Walter Raleigh, made two attempts to start a colony on Roanoke Island, off the coast of what is now North Carolina. Although these attempts were not successful, they gave England a much stronger claim to territory in the New World.

In 1607 a group of Englishmen landed in Virginia and founded a settlement called Jamestown. (See map on page 114.) These settlers were sent by merchants in England who hoped to make money by trading with the new colony. Most of the people who settled at Jamestown expected to find gold and other riches. Instead, they found hunger and sickness. By 1610 the

La Salle was a daring French explorer and fur trader. In 1682, he and his men paddled down the Mississippi River in birchbark canoes. When they reached the mouth of the river, La Salle claimed the entire valley of the Mississippi for France. (See the picture at left.) He named this vast territory Louisiana. Why did La Salle choose this name for the lands he claimed?

colonists were ready to abandon Jamestown and return to England. Ships loaded with fresh supplies arrived just in time to save the little colony. Jamestown was the first permanent English settlement in North America.

In the years that followed, many more colonists came to America from the British Isles. By the middle of the 1700's, there were thirteen British colonies along the Atlantic coast between Canada and Florida.

Four of the British colonies were in the part of our country we now call the South. These four were Virginia, North and South Carolina, and Georgia. The Carolinas were part of a huge piece of land that the King of England had given to eight nobles in 1663. Georgia was founded in 1733 by an Englishman named James Oglethorpe, partly to keep the Spanish from moving northward from Florida.

**Black people are brought from Africa to work on plantations in the South.** In the southern colonies, the land and climate were well suited to growing farm crops. (See pages 162-165.) At that time, settlers in America could obtain land either free or at a very low price. Some settlers were able to acquire thousands of acres of rich farmland. They established huge farms called plantations. There they grew tobacco and other valuable crops to sell to people in England.

The plantation owners needed large numbers of workers to help them raise their crops. At first, they tried to hire workers from Europe, but this did not work out very well. Much of the farm work was difficult and unpleasant. Few European laborers were willing to work so hard for the plantation owners when they could easily obtain land and start farms of their own.

Gradually, the European settlers began buying black men and women from Africa to work on their plantations. In those days, slavery was common in Africa and many other parts of the world. European traders would sail along the African coast with cargoes of rum, cloth, and other valuable goods. They would offer these goods to the rulers of African tribes in exchange for slaves. Tribes often went to war against each other in order to capture prisoners to sell to the Europeans. The captives would be loaded onto ships for the long, difficult voyage across the Atlantic. During the journey, many of these people died of hunger or disease. Upon reaching America, the remaining captives were sold at auction to European settlers, who forced them to work on the plantations.

At first, the African people who were brought to America only had to work a certain number of years. Then they were given their freedom. But as time went on, more and more labor was needed in the colonies. As a result, the colonial governments passed laws that took away most of the rights of the black people and forced them to remain slaves for life.

Over the years, hundreds of thousands of black people were brought from Africa to the American colonies. By the middle of the 1700's, more than one third of the people in the South were of African descent.

**Britain and France struggle for control of North America.** By the middle of the 1700's, Great Britain and France

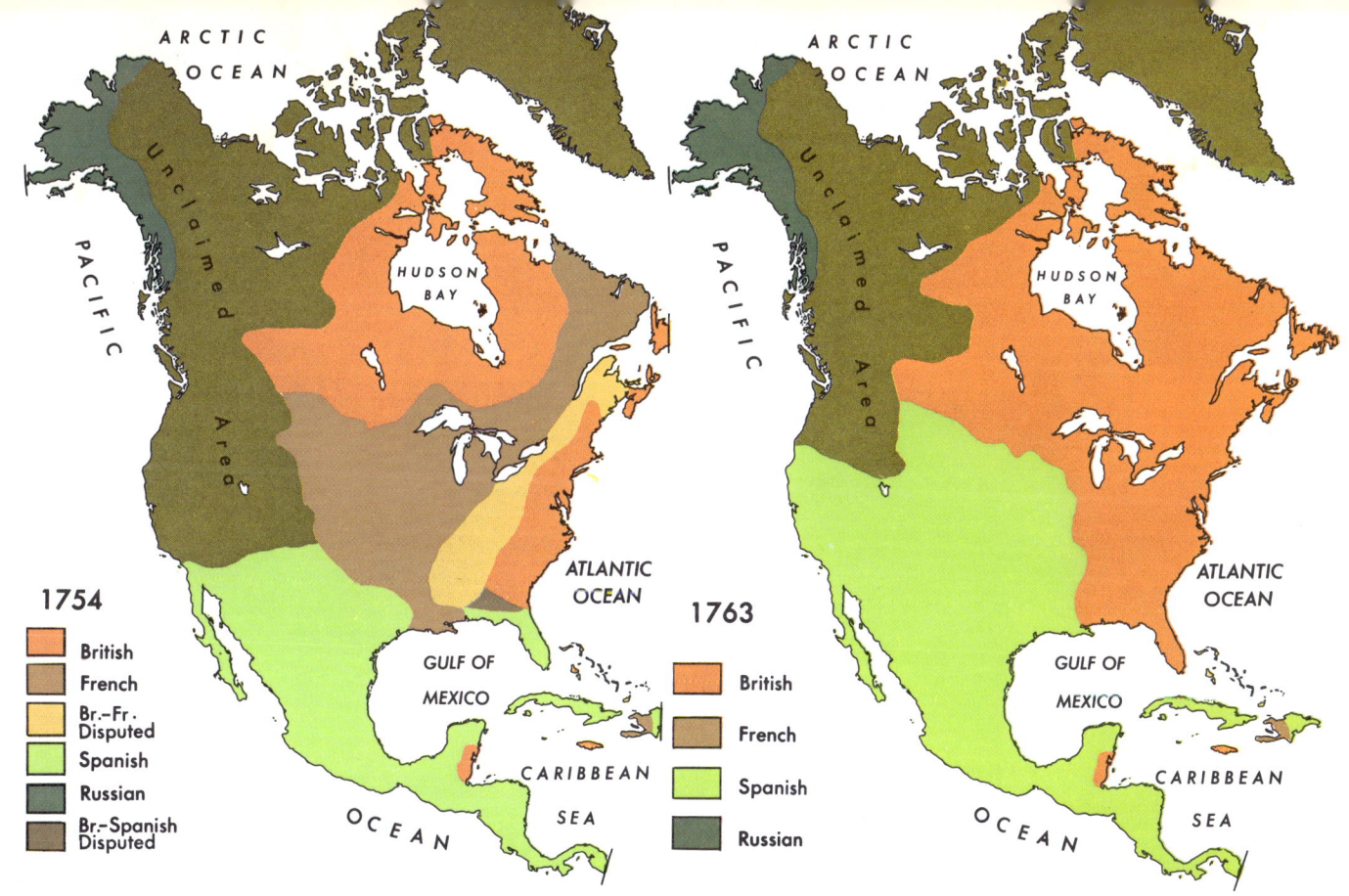

**European claims in North America** before and after the French and Indian War. The treaty that ended this war forced France to give up nearly all its land in the New World. Britain gained all of France's territory east of the Mississippi River except for New Orleans. France also gave Britain almost all the land it claimed in what is now Canada. Spain lost Florida to Britain, but received New Orleans and French territory west of the Mississippi River.

were quarreling over territory in the New World. Britain controlled most of the land along the Atlantic coast of North America. (See map above.) France still controlled much of Canada, as well as the lands in the Mississippi Valley. Some of the land that lay between the British colonies and the Mississippi was claimed by both France and Britain.

This dispute over territory led to the French and Indian War, which lasted from 1754 to 1763. This war was finally won by Great Britain. The treaty of peace gave Britain vast territories in North America. France lost nearly all its lands in the New World. Spain, which had sided with France, lost Florida. To make up for this loss, the Spanish gained possession of New Orleans and all French territory west of the Mississippi River.

**Settlers begin moving west of the Appalachians.** When the French and Indian War was over, the British colonists in America thought they would be free to settle west of the Appalachian Mountains. But the English government was afraid that this might cause trouble with the Indians who lived in

65

The French and Indian War was won by the British, who gained vast territories in North America.

the area. In 1763 the English King issued a proclamation forbidding any colonists to move west of the mountains. In spite of this proclamation, many settlers moved into the territory that lay between the colonies and the Mississippi River.

In the South, colonists began moving westward into the area that is now Tennessee and Kentucky. Since it was difficult to cross over the rugged Appalachians, the colonists had to follow passes through the mountains. Many settlers traveled westward from Virginia over the Wilderness Road. This trail, blazed by Daniel Boone, led through the Cumberland Gap.* In the lands beyond the mountains, the pioneers found pleasant, green valleys in which to make their new homes.

During this war, George Washington (right) served as an aide to the commander of the British troops.

**Make Discoveries About an Explorer**

Three Europeans who explored parts of the South were Ponce de León, De Soto, and La Salle. Do research about one of these explorers to find information for a report. In your report, you will want to answer the following questions.

1. Why did this European explorer come to the part of our country we now call the South?
2. Did he achieve his goals? Explain.
3. How did his explorations affect the history of the South?

**Adventures in Reading**

*Discoverers of the New World,* edited by American Heritage

*Jamestown Adventure,* by Olga W. Hall-Quest

*The Lone Hunt,* by William O. Steele

*Daniel Boone,* by James Daugherty

# 5 The Revolution and the New Nation

Independence

**A Problem To Solve**

When the English colonies were established in America, the people expected to remain loyal to England. <u>Why did they eventually revolt against the mother country?</u> In forming your hypotheses, you may wish to consider the following:
1. taxes paid to England by the colonists
2. prices the colonists received for raw materials sold in England
3. prices the colonists had to pay for goods manufactured in England
4. who made the laws for the colonies

See pages 256-258

**Discontent in the colonies leads to revolution.** After the French and Indian War, the American colonists became more and more unhappy under British rule. As we have seen, the colonists refused to obey the English King's proclamation against settlement of the western lands. (See page 66.) However, this was not the only quarrel. Other conflicts arose because the British expected the colonies to contribute wealth to the mother country. Trade and manufacturing in the colonies were controlled in such a way as to benefit Britain. For

**In Virginia's legislature,** Patrick Henry spoke out against the taxes that the American colonies were forced to pay to Britain.

instance, the colonists were supposed to sell raw materials to Britain at low prices, and to buy manufactured goods from Britain at high prices. Also, the British Parliament* passed several different laws that required the colonists to pay certain taxes to Britain.

Most of all, however, the American colonists resented living under laws they had not helped to make. Although the taxes imposed by Parliament were not especially heavy, the colonists did not believe they should have to pay them. They felt that the lawmakers in the mother country could not possibly understand the problems or needs of the colonies.

Finally, the conflicts between Britain and the colonies led to the Revolutionary War. The first shots were fired in the spring of 1775. On July 4, 1776, the colonies declared their independence from Britain. The new nation, called the United States of America, was not yet free, however. It did not become an independent country until 1783, after it had won the war.

**The new nation grows larger.** By the terms of the peace treaty that ended the Revolutionary War, the United States owned all the land from the Atlantic Ocean to the Mississippi River, and from Canada to Florida. (See map below.) Thousands of pioneers traveled westward to make their homes in the lands beyond the Appalachian Mountains. By 1796 two new states, Kentucky and Tennessee, had been carved out of the western wilderness.

More land was soon added to the United States. (See page 72.) The purchase of the vast territory of Louisiana, in 1803, greatly increased the size of the country. In 1819 the United States

*See Glossary

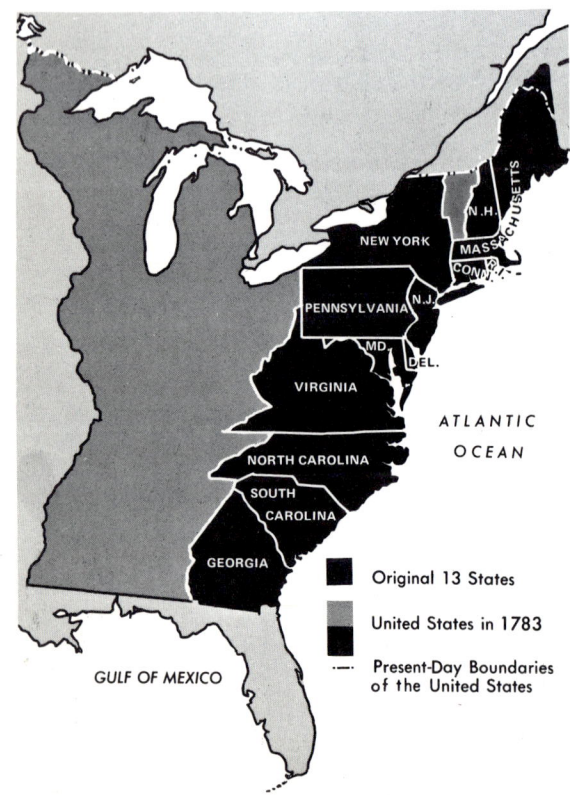

## HOW THE UNITED STATES BEGAN

When the United States first became a country, it had only thirteen states. The story of these states began in 1607. In that year, a group of colonists from England built a settlement on the Atlantic coast of North America. This was Jamestown, located in what is now the state of Virginia. As time went on, more people from the British Isles came to America. People from the Netherlands and Sweden came, also. The British soon took over the colonies these people established.

In 1776 thirteen British colonies in North America declared their independence from Great Britain. They called themselves the United States of America. The new nation had to fight for its freedom, however. This conflict was known as the Revolutionary War.

Finally, in 1783, Britain signed a treaty recognizing the independence of the United States. This treaty also gave to the new country the land that lay between the states and the Mississippi River. As the years passed, the United States gained control of more and more of North America. (See page 72.)

Culture

**Raising the American flag in New Orleans.** In 1803 the United States purchased the vast territory of Louisiana from France. New Orleans and other settlements in Louisiana had been founded by people from France during the 1700's. These people had a culture, or way of life, that differed in certain ways from the culture of the English-speaking settlers. What signs of French culture can still be found in New Orleans today? Do research in other sources to discover information that will help you answer this question.

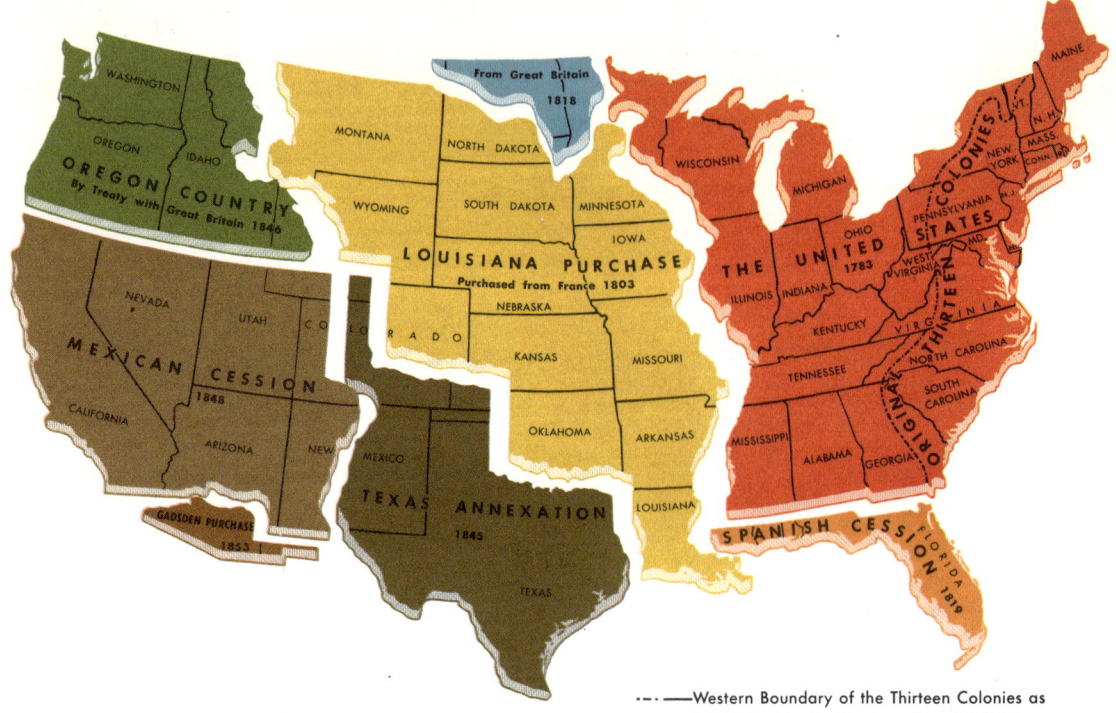

—·—·— Western Boundary of the Thirteen Colonies as Established by the Proclamation of 1763*

## How Our Country Grew

**The United States in 1783.** At the end of the Revolutionary War, our country extended westward from the Atlantic Ocean to the Mississippi River, and southward from Canada to Florida. (See special feature on page 70.)

**Louisiana Purchase.** West of the Mississippi River was a huge area called Louisiana, which was owned by Spain. In 1800, France acquired Louisiana from Spain. Three years later, the United States purchased this territory from France and it became part of our country.

**Treaty of 1818.** In 1818, the United States signed a treaty with Great Britain, which then owned Canada. Under this treaty, the 49th parallel° became the United States-Canadian boundary from the western part of what is now Minnesota to the Rocky Mountains.

**Spanish Cession.** In 1763, the British gained control of Florida, which had belonged to Spain. Twenty years later, the Spanish regained Florida. In 1818, the United States sent troops here to fight Indians who had attacked American settlements. The next year, Spain signed a treaty by which the United States gained possession of Florida.

**Texas Annexation.** American settlers living in Texas revolted against the Mexican government and in 1836 established an independent country. They asked the United States to annex° Texas, which it did in 1845.

**Oregon Country.** Both the United States and Great Britain claimed the Oregon Country, a large area west of the Rocky Mountains. In 1846, the two nations signed a treaty that gave the United States nearly all of the Oregon Country south of the 49th parallel.

**Mexican Cession.** Mexico was angry because the United States had annexed Texas. In 1846, the two countries went to war. The United States won the war in 1848. Mexico was forced to sell us California and other territory shown on the map above.

**Gadsden Purchase.** In 1853, our country bought from Mexico parts of what are now southern Arizona and New Mexico. This was known as the Gadsden Purchase.

**Alaska and Hawaii.** Alaska and Hawaii are shown on the map on page 13. In 1867, the United States bought Alaska from Russia. The Hawaiian Islands were annexed in 1898.

gained possession of Florida, which the British had given back to Spain at the end of the Revolutionary War.

During the first half of the nineteenth century, the United States forced many tribes of Indians to give up their lands. This was because settlers who were now moving into territory west of the Appalachian Mountains wanted more land. The United States government set aside certain areas west of the Mississippi River to be used for resettling the Indians. Few white people had settled in these areas, and the land there was thought to have little value.

During the 1830's, more than seventy thousand Indians had to leave their homes and move to the west. Among these Indians were the Cherokees, who lived in Georgia. They had kept their treaties faithfully and adopted many of the white people's customs. Even so, they were forced to move to a reservation* in faraway Oklahoma. Nearly one fourth of the Cherokees died during this long, difficult journey, which became known as the "Trail of Tears."

Some tribes of Indians fought against the United States in an effort to keep their homes. The Seminole, who lived

**Seminole Indians in Florida.** These people are descended from the Seminole who hid in the Florida Everglades during the 1830's, to avoid being sent to Oklahoma by the United States government.

in Florida, were among the last of the Indians to move to the west. Only after they had been defeated by United States troops in two fierce wars did most of them leave Florida. A few hid in the Florida Everglades, where their descendants live today.

By the middle of the nineteenth century, the United States was a huge and prosperous country. It extended from the Atlantic Ocean to the Pacific, and from Canada to Mexico. (See page 72.) Since the Revolutionary War, its population had grown from about three million to more than twenty-three million. Many new cities and towns had been established, and old ones had grown larger.

The South, however, was still mainly a region of farms. Wherever the land was level and fertile, there were great plantations. Black people did most of the work on these plantations, where crops such as cotton and tobacco were grown. In the hills and mountains, and in areas where the soil was poor, farms were smaller. Nowhere in the South was there much manufacturing, and there were few large cities or towns.

**Change and Continuity**

The picture at left shows the house and gardens at Mount Vernon, George Washington's plantation along the Potomac River in Virginia. For nearly a century after our nation became independent, the South remained a region of farms. There were few large cities, and almost no factories. Some of the farms in the South were large plantations like Mount Vernon. Why do you suppose the South remained a farming region for such a long time? Do research to discover some of the ways in which the South has changed during the last one hundred years. In what ways, if any, has it remained the same?

# 6 The Union Endures

**People in the new nation disagree on two important issues.** From the time the United States was founded, there were issues on which people did not agree. Two of these issues were especially important in shaping our country's later history. One was the issue of states' rights. In the northern part of our country, most public leaders believed that the federal government should be more powerful than the states. They felt that the states had a duty to enforce all federal laws. Many southern leaders, however, thought that the states could limit the power of the federal government whenever they considered it necessary. Some even claimed that the states had the right to leave the Union* if they wished.

Slavery was the other important issue on which people did not agree. Many people in the northern part of our country felt it was wrong for one person to own another as a slave. By 1787 most northeastern states had passed laws freeing their slaves or providing for the gradual ending of slavery. In that year, Congress passed a law prohibiting slavery in any new states that might be formed north of the Ohio River and east of the Mississippi River. In the southern states, slavery was permitted. Many southerners thought slavery was wrong, but they were afraid that plantations in the South could not be run profitably without slave labor.

**These issues divide the nation.** Before the United States was one hundred years old,

*See Glossary

Conflict

The picture at left shows Henry Clay, a senator from Kentucky, speaking in the United States Senate. Clay proposed a plan that he hoped would settle the dispute between the North and the South. His proposal, known as the Compromise of 1850, helped to keep the nation united for a while. But in 1861 the Civil War broke out. What were the causes of this great conflict? Do you think the Civil War could have been avoided? Explain.

the issues of slavery and states' rights had led to a serious dispute between the North and the South. Most people in the North wanted to prevent the spread of slavery into new territories that were being formed west of the Mississippi River. Most white southerners felt the federal government had no right to prevent the spread of slavery.

These different beliefs finally led to the division of the United States into two parts. Shortly after Abraham Lincoln was elected president in 1860, South Carolina seceded* from the Union. This was because Lincoln was the leader of the Republican Party, which wanted to stop the spread of slavery. Almost immediately, six more slaveholding states seceded. In February, 1861, the seven states that had left the Union established a separate country. It was called the Confederate States of America, or the Confederacy.

**The Civil War is fought to preserve our nation.** President Lincoln believed that no state had the right to secede from the Union. He refused a Confederate demand that federal troops be withdrawn from Fort Sumter in Charleston, South Carolina. On April 12, 1861, Confederate troops fired on the fort, and the Civil War began.

Within a few weeks, four more states left the Union and joined the Confederacy. The new nation included Texas and all of the states that make up the South today except Kentucky. The states of Missouri, Kentucky, West Virginia,* Maryland, and Delaware were called border states. Although these states permitted slavery, they remained in the Union. Some of their citizens fought for the Union, while others fought for the Confederacy.

Lincoln declared that the war was being fought to save the Union, and not to end slavery. In this way he kept the border states from leaving the Union. Eventually, however, Lincoln realized that the Union would have to

*Continued on page 83*

## OUR COUNTRY DIVIDED

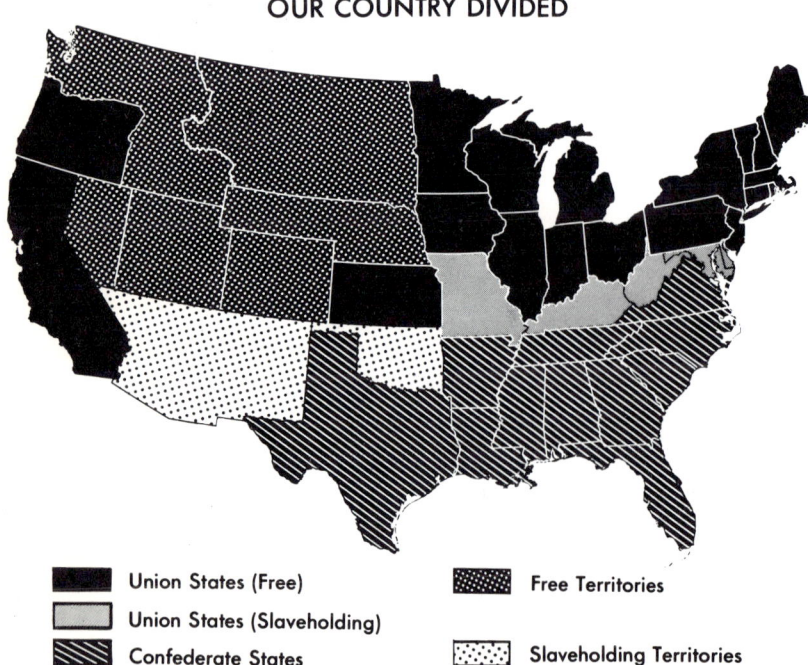

- Union States (Free)
- Union States (Slaveholding)
- Confederate States
- Free Territories
- Slaveholding Territories

From 1860 to 1865, the United States was a divided country. In 1860 Abraham Lincoln was elected president. None of the southern states had wanted Lincoln as president, however, mainly because Lincoln was against slavery in the territories and new states of our country. Shortly after the election, South Carolina seceded from the Union. During 1861 ten more states seceded. These states, together with South Carolina, became a separate nation called the Confederacy. The western part of Virginia remained in the Union, and later became the state of West Virginia. The United States was a divided country until the Civil War ended in 1865.

The Civil War began on April 12, 1861, when Confederate soldiers fired on Union troops stationed at Fort Sumter. The Confederacy was made up of states that seceded from the United States.
1. Do you think the Confederate leaders *wanted* to be disloyal to the United States? Explain why you think as you do.
2. Do you think the people who supported the Confederate states were loyal to their own ideas and beliefs? Why do you think this?

Perhaps you would like to discuss these questions with your classmates.

Loyalty

See pages 240-241

General Robert E. Lee (center) was one of the South's outstanding military leaders during the Civil War. Many well-trained generals and loyal soldiers fought on the side of the Confederacy.

After four years of fighting between the Union and the Confederacy, the Civil War came to an end. What were some of the North's advantages that made victory possible for the Union forces?

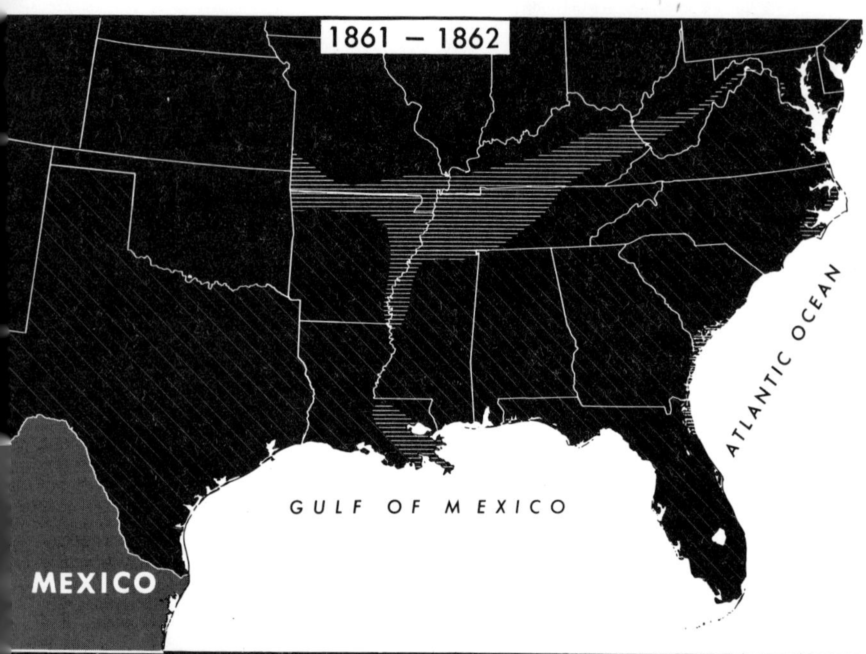

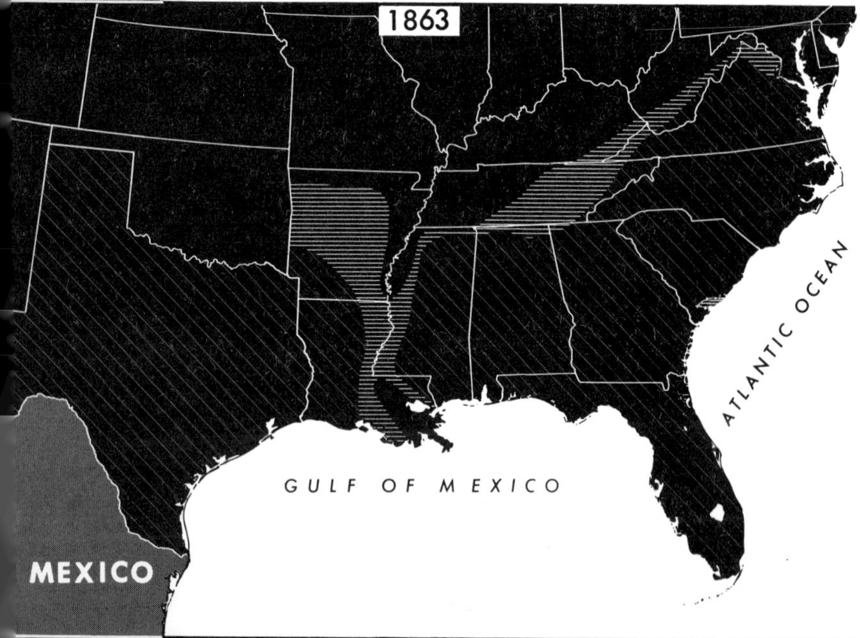

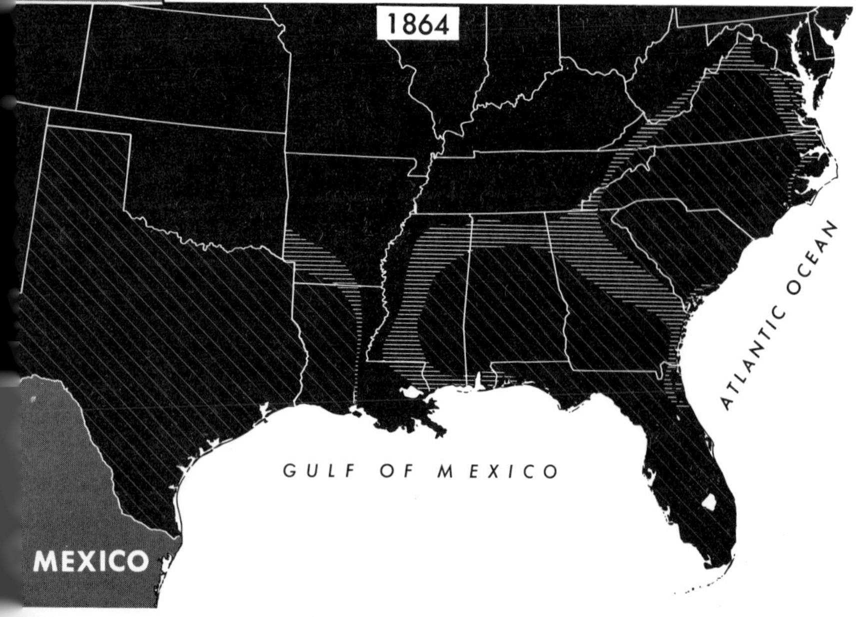

The Civil War was fought between two groups of states in our country, usually called the Union and the Confederacy. The issues on which these groups disagreed are discussed on pages 77 and 78. The Confederacy included Texas and all of the states in the South except Kentucky. These states declared themselves independent from the United States. The Union, made up of the remaining states, was determined to keep the country united. The war lasted from 1861 to 1865.

**1861-62.** In the first years of the war, much of the fighting took place in Virginia, Kentucky, and Tennessee. The Union gained little ground in Virginia. However, Union forces under General Grant gained much of Tennessee. A Union fleet won territory near the mouth of the Mississippi River.

**1863.** For the North, 1863 was a year of triumph. President Lincoln issued a statement proclaiming the freedom of the slaves in areas still held by Confederate forces. At Gettysburg, Pennsylvania, Union armies defeated Confederate troops commanded by General Lee. Farther west, Union armies gained complete control of the Mississippi River.

**1864.** In spite of Union victories, the Confederacy did not give up. During 1864, General Sherman led Union troops through Georgia in a destructive march, and Grant moved his forces into Virginia.

**The war ends.** On April 9, 1865, Lee surrendered to Grant. The Civil War was over, and the United States was no longer a country divided.

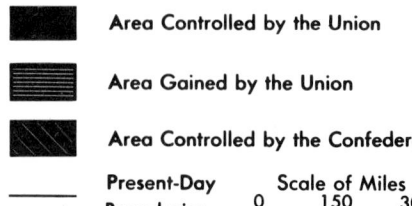

take a stand against slavery. The nation could not remain a democracy unless slavery was abolished. On January 1, 1863, Lincoln issued a statement proclaiming the freedom of the slaves in areas held by Confederate forces. This statement became known as the Emancipation Proclamation.

During the Civil War, the North had certain advantages over the South. It had a larger population, a better transportation system, and much more wealth. Farms in the North produced a wider variety and larger amounts of crops and livestock. There were more factories to produce weapons and other supplies. The North also had the help of nearly 200,000 black troops who fought for the Union. The South, however, had many good soldiers and outstanding military leaders, such as Robert E. Lee and Thomas "Stonewall" Jackson.

The advantages of the North finally made victory possible for the Union. After four years of fighting, Lee surrendered to a Union general, Ulysses S. Grant, at Appomattox, Virginia. The war had cost the lives of many thousands of soldiers. But the nation had been saved.

The Civil War settled the questions of secession and slavery. No state has ever again claimed the right to secede from the Union. After the war ended, all remaining slaves were freed and slavery was prohibited by the Thirteenth Amendment to the Constitution.

## Reconstruction

**A war-torn nation faces serious problems.** At the end of the Civil War, several serious problems remained to be solved. Much of the South had been badly damaged during the war. What was the best way to rebuild the South? How could new governments be established in the southern states? Should the freed slaves be granted all of the same rights and freedoms as other Americans? The period during which the American people dealt with these problems is known as Reconstruction.

President Lincoln had a plan for setting up new governments in the southern states. In April, 1865, however, Lincoln was assassinated by an actor who supported the Confederate cause. Andrew Johnson succeeded Lincoln as president. His plan for establishing new state governments was similar to Lincoln's. By December of 1865, Johnson had approved new governments in all of the former Confederate states except Texas.

Many members of the United States Congress were opposed to Johnson's way of dealing with the southern states. Congress was controlled by northern Republicans, and a number of them felt that Johnson was treating the South too kindly. Also, some Republican leaders opposed Johnson's plan because it did nothing to protect the rights of the newly freed black people in the South. These leaders, as well as many other northerners, became alarmed when the southern states began passing laws known as "black codes." These laws gave some rights to the blacks, but they also imposed many restrictions. For example, black people could not serve on juries. In some states, they could not quit their jobs without permission. For these and other reasons, Congress began taking action to control Reconstruction.

**The Fourteenth Amendment.** In 1866 the members of Congress passed the

**Black people voting after the Civil War.** The Fifteenth Amendment to the United States Constitution helped protect the voting rights of blacks. In what ways did the Thirteenth and Fourteenth amendments to the Constitution affect black people in our country?

Fourteenth Amendment to the Constitution. This amendment included two especially important sections. One section made it clear that blacks were citizens of the United States. It also said that a state could not take away any rights belonging to all citizens. The other section declared that people who had held state or federal offices before the war and had supported the Confederate cause could not hold government office. However, the amendment also said that the right to hold office could later be restored to these people by Congress.

The Fourteenth Amendment was quickly ratified* by most of the northern states. But it could not become part of the Constitution unless some of the southern states would ratify it also. This was because an amendment to the Constitution must be ratified by three fourths of all the states. Most white southerners were strongly opposed to the Fourteenth Amendment. Tennessee was the only former Confederate state that would agree to ratify it.

Northern political leaders were determined that the Fourteenth Amendment should be adopted. As a way of accomplishing this, Congress passed a series of laws called the Reconstruction Acts. These acts divided the former Confederate states, except Tennessee, into five districts under military control. They also abolished the governments of these states. Before a state would be allowed to come back in the

Union, it had to establish a new government that would ratify the Fourteenth Amendment.

**The restoration of the Union.** Under the direction of federal troops, new governments were formed in the southern states. By the summer of 1868, enough of these states had ratified the Fourteenth Amendment for it to become part of the Constitution. The next year, Congress passed the Fifteenth Amendment to help protect the voting rights of black people. To be readmitted to the Union, the remaining southern states had to ratify not only the Fourteenth Amendment but also the Fifteenth. The last of the southern states finally rejoined the Union in 1870.

The Reconstruction governments were largely under the control of whites. Many of the white lawmakers and other officials were northern Republicans who had come to the South at the end of the war. Others were southerners who joined the Republican Party. These people were elected with the help of black voters. Although black people did not actually control any state government in the South, many were elected to state and local offices.

The Reconstruction governments accomplished much good. Most of the new state constitutions recognized the principle of equal rights for blacks and whites. The governments played a large part in rebuilding the South. For example, they provided money for repairing public buildings and roads. Perhaps the most important achievement was expansion of the public school systems. During Reconstruction many thousands of children, both black and white, were able to attend school for the first time.

Unfortunately, there was much waste and dishonesty in the Reconstruction governments. Many officials in these governments had little education or experience, and they often wasted public funds. Some people used tax money for their own purposes. It should be pointed out that there were also many dishonest officials in northern state governments and in the federal government at that time.

**The end of Reconstruction.** The Reconstruction period ended in 1877, when federal troops were withdrawn from the last of the southern states. By that time, white southerners had taken control of all the state governments in the South. These people were generally opposed to giving equal rights to blacks. After Reconstruction ended, most of the southern states passed laws that required people to pay a special tax or pass a literacy* test in order to vote. Such laws helped to keep blacks from voting. Most states also passed segregation* laws. These laws kept black people from sharing schools and other public facilities with white people. Not until the 1950's and 1960's did most blacks in the South begin to regain their basic rights as United States citizens. (See Chapter 9.)

Questions To Guide Your Research
1. Explain the two important issues that divided our nation and led to the Civil War.
2. Explain the words "Confederacy" and "Reconstruction," telling how each is related to the history of the South.

Adventures in Reading
*Harriet Tubman: Conductor on the Underground Railroad,* by Ann Petry
*Jed,* by Peter Burchard
*Journey Cake,* by Isabel McMeekin

A tenant farmer in the 1890's. After the Civil War, most of the South's plantations were divided up and the land was rented to tenant farmers.

# 7 The Growth of the New South

**Tenant farming in the South.** Before the Civil War, most of the work on large plantations in the South was done by slaves. After the war, plantation owners no longer had slaves to do the work. Few of them had enough money to hire laborers. Some planters sold small plots of land to former slaves or to other people who wanted to own farms. But few people in the South had enough money to buy even a small piece of farmland.

In order to put their land into use again, most plantation owners began renting small pieces of land to tenant* farmers. Usually tenant farmers paid for the use of the land by giving the plantation owners shares of their crops. For this reason, most of the tenant farmers in the South were called sharecroppers. Since they had little money, sharecroppers usually had to obtain seed, tools, and food on credit. Many of them were constantly in debt.

Tenant farmers seldom knew how to make the best use of land. Most of them planted the same crop, such as tobacco

*See Glossary

or cotton, on the same land year after year. This removed minerals from the soil, so that the land no longer produced good crops. Some farmers plowed in straight rows up and down the hillsides. When it rained, some of the fertile topsoil was washed away.

The tenant-farming system helped the South get land back into production after the Civil War. But the burden of heavy debts and poor farming methods kept most southern farmers from earning a good living. For many years, the South lagged behind other parts of our country in farming.

**The growth of industry in the South.** After the Civil War, many business people realized that the South needed

**A worker in an early textile mill in the South.** Since cotton and cheap labor were both plentiful in the South after the Civil War, some manufacturers built textile mills.

**Interdependence**

A paper mill in Georgia. Goods produced in the southern states are now used by people throughout the nation and in many foreign countries. Do you think that people in the South depend upon other regions and other countries to supply many of the goods they need? Could any nation or region in the modern world supply its needs entirely by itself? Give reasons for your answers.

more manufacturing and trade. Cotton was plentiful in the South, and there were many people who could be hired to work in factories for low wages. As a result, some manufacturers built textile mills in the South. Many of these mills were located along the Fall Line, where waterpower was available. In the 1870's, an iron and steel industry began to develop at Birmingham, Alabama. Nearby mines provided both

for a variety of raw materials and manufactured goods. With the help of money loaned by northern bankers, railroads in the South were rebuilt and expanded. Seaports such as New Orleans, Louisiana, and Charleston, South Carolina, became great trading cities.

**Problems and progress.** During the first part of the twentieth century, the number of tenant farms in the South decreased greatly. With the growth of industry, many tenants left the farms to take jobs in factories. Workers who were still willing to do farm work demanded higher wages. In order to make a living from their land, the landowners were forced to use more machinery and better farming methods. With the help of various government agencies, many southern farmers learned how to farm their land more efficiently. (See pages 166-168.)

In recent years, the South has made great progress in farming and industry. However, it still faces some of the same problems that are found in every part of the United States. Some of these important problems are discussed in Chapter 9.

iron ore and coal. Large amounts of timber were cut from the forests that stretched across broad areas of the South. As more and more industry developed, towns and cities grew larger. Chapter 13 tells the story of modern industry in the South.

Trade between the South and other parts of the country and the world also increased. Products such as cotton, lumber, and textiles were exchanged

Share Ideas in a Class Discussion

As a class, discuss the following statement.
   A knowledge of the South's history helps us to understand the South of today.
You will need to do research in Parts 3 and 4 of this book, as well as in Part 2. In your discussion, consider how the South's history has affected:
1. farming and industry
2. the growth of cities
3. the various groups of people who live in the South
4. problems facing people in the South today

The suggestions on pages 264-265 will help you carry on a worthwhile class discussion.

About 46 million people live in the South. They are very much like people in other parts of our country.

# Part 3
# People

The people of the South are very much like people in other parts of our country. They share the same basic needs and the same important beliefs about democracy. They also share many of the same problems. As you explore the chapters in Part 3, try to discover answers to these questions.

- Which of the many different needs listed on the chart on page 100 do you have? Are your needs similar to those of schoolchildren in England? In China? Explain your answers.
- What five important principles must people follow in order to make democracy work?
- In what ways, if any, do these principles affect your own life at the present time?
- In what ways may each of these principles affect your life when you are old enough to vote?
- What are some ways in which the people of the South are trying to solve the problems they face?
- Which of the problems discussed in Chapter 9 affect people in your community?
- What are some ways in which southerners have contributed to the arts of our nation?

# 8  People and Cities

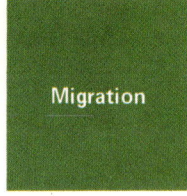
Migration

**A Problem To Solve**

Since the beginning of the present century, many people have left rural areas in the South and moved to cities. What are the reasons for this migration of people from rural areas to urban areas? In forming hypotheses to solve this problem, you may wish to consider the following:

a. ways in which modern farming methods affect agricultural production
b. ways in which cities help individuals to meet their basic needs
c. ideas and ways of living that encourage the growth of cities

Chapter 14 contains additional information that will be helpful in solving this problem.

See pages 256-258

**Modern office buildings near the city of Atlanta, Georgia.** In recent years, urban areas in the South have been growing in population. However, out of the twenty largest metropolitan areas in the United States, only one—Atlanta—is located in the South.

**Arts** — The mansion shown in the picture above was built by English colonists in the South during the eighteenth century. The English built many beautiful houses in the Georgian style of architecture. What other groups of settlers came to the South from Europe during colonial days? In what ways, if any, did these settlers influence the kind of architecture found in the South? Do research in other sources to find information that will help answer these questions.

**More than one fifth of all Americans live in the South.** About 46 million people live in the eleven states that make up the South. This is more than one fifth of the population of the entire United States.

In the South, just as in most other parts of the country, population has been increasing steadily. There are about six million more people in the South today than there were only ten years ago. Some states, of course, have been growing more rapidly in population than others. Florida, for example, is one of the fastest-growing states in our country. Its population has increased by nearly one-third in the last ten years.

The map on the opposite page shows the distribution of people in the United States. Each tiny dot on the map stands for ten thousand people. If you com-

pare this map with the one on page 114, you will notice that the population of the South is distributed quite evenly. There are no large areas where few people live, as there are in the West. Neither are there large areas that are very densely populated, as there are in the Northeast and the Midwest.

For centuries, people have been coming to the South from many parts of the world. Today, people of all races and many different national* origins make their homes in the South.

**People of European descent.** Many southerners are descended from early settlers who came to America from the British Isles. Throughout much of the South, the people still bear the English, Scotch, or Irish names of their ancestors who came here two or three hundred years ago.

The English brought their language and many customs to the colonies. Among the southern cities founded

*See Glossary

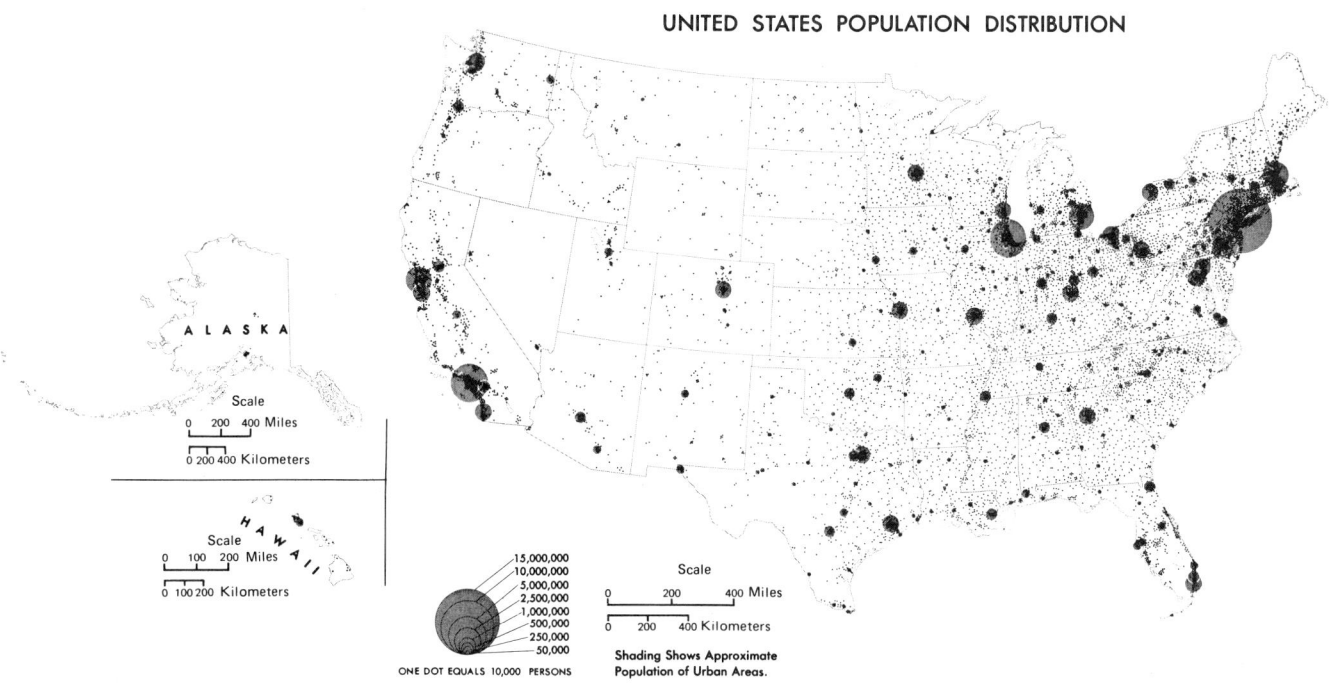

UNITED STATES POPULATION DISTRIBUTION

and named by the English are Charleston, South Carolina, and Richmond, Virginia. Many beautiful Georgian-style* houses built in the South by the English colonists are still standing.

In the South there are also people of French descent. Most of them live in southern Louisiana. Some are descendants of families that came to Louisiana from France early in the eighteenth century. Others are descended from Acadians who settled here later in the same century. The Acadians were people of French descent who lived in a section of Canada called Nova Scotia. They were driven out of Nova Scotia by the British during and after the French and Indian War.

People whose ancestors came from still other parts of Europe also live in

the South. For example, in Louisiana there are descendants of Spanish families that settled here long ago. On Florida's Gulf coast there are people of Greek descent. In Kentucky, many people of German descent live in towns along the Ohio River.

**People of African descent.** More than nine and one-half million black people live in the South today. Nearly all of them are descended from people who were brought from Africa during the 1600's and 1700's to work on plantations in the South. (See page 64.)

Many people of African descent have helped to shape our country's history. During the Revolutionary War, thousands of black soldiers fought bravely against the British. Nearly 200,000 blacks served with the Union armies during the Civil War. President Lincoln believed that if it had not been for these troops, victory for the North might have been delayed.

Black people have enriched life in America in many different ways. For example, black musicians have played an important part in the development of certain distinctive kinds of American music, such as jazz, rock, and "soul" music. Some of our country's leading writers, educators, and government leaders have been black people. Other blacks have been outstanding athletes, entertainers, or scientists.

**People of Latin-American descent.** During the present century, many people have come to the South from Spanish-speaking countries in Latin America. By far the largest number of these are from the island country of Cuba. In 1959 Fidel Castro came to power in Cuba and began to set up a Communist

Freedom

See pages 212-213

The photograph at left shows a southern family enjoying a backyard cookout. Do you think that the members of this family have very much freedom to live as they please? What makes you think this? Are there any people in our country today who do not have as much freedom as other Americans? If so, who are they? What might be done to help these people gain more freedom?

dictatorship. Large numbers of Cubans fled to the United States because they did not want to live under communism. Many of them settled in or near Miami, Florida. Today, more than 250,000 people in Florida are of Cuban descent. People have also come to the South from the island of Puerto Rico, which is a self-governing commonwealth associated with the United States. Still other people in the South are of Mexican descent.

**American Indians.** Nearly eighty thousand Indians, or Native Americans, live in the southern states. Most of them are in North Carolina. This state has a Cherokee Indian reservation, which is located at the edge of Great Smoky Mountains National Park. There are some Choctaw Indians in Mississippi and Seminole Indians in Florida. (See pages 73 and 75.) Most of the Indians in the South no longer live on reservations. Their way of life is similar to that of other people who make their homes in the South.

**People of Asian descent.** Some of the people in the South are descended from people who came from China, Japan, and other countries in Asia. Florida

**Young people of Cuban descent in Florida.** More than 250,000 people in Florida are of Cuban descent. Many of these people have come to the United States since early in 1959, when Fidel Castro began to set up a Communist dictatorship in the island country of Cuba.

and Virginia are the states with the most people of Asian descent.

## Cities of the South

**Urban areas in the South have been growing in population.** At the beginning of the present century, the cities of the South were much smaller than they are today. Most people in this region lived on farms or in small towns. As time passed, however, more and more people moved from rural areas into urban areas. Also, people from other parts of the United States came to urban areas in the South. Today about six out of every ten people in the South live in cities or large towns.

The main reason why urban areas in the South have been growing in population is that they provide many opportunities for people to meet their basic needs. To understand why this is true, you must know about the main kinds of needs that are shared by all human beings.

**What are the basic human needs?** Scientists who study human behavior claim that each person's really important needs are almost exactly the same as those of everyone else. These basic needs are the same whatever your skin color, your national origin, your sex, or your religion may be. Whether you are rich or poor, you have these same needs.

Physical needs. Some of your basic needs are so important that you will die or become seriously ill if they are not satisfied. We call these physical needs. Your need for food is an example of a physical need. If you will compare yourself with an Eskimo and a person who lives in the tropics, you will realize that all three of you have similar physical needs. You must all have air to breathe, food to eat, and water to drink. Each of you may sleep in a different kind of bed, but you must all sleep. The Eskimo wears heavier clothing than you do, in order to keep warm. People in the tropics need less clothing than you do because they live in a warmer climate. Although people meet their physical needs in different ways, these needs are really the same for everyone.

Social needs. A person may have all of his or her physical needs satisfied, yet still not be able to lead a happy, useful life. In order for a person to be completely happy and healthy, certain other needs must also be satisfied. Some of these are called social needs. Your need for your family is an example of a social need. Your social needs, just like your physical needs, are shared by all human beings.

One of your most important social needs is to feel that you belong to a group. This group may be your family, your school, your church, or a group of friends. You need to feel that you have earned the respect of these people, and you need to respect them.

In order to become a happy and useful human being, you must have an opportunity to develop and use your abilities. For example, you were born with the ability to think. To develop this ability, however, you must gain knowledge through new experiences. You must also have opportunities to decide things for yourself. You may have been born with a talent for art, but if you never have a chance to draw or paint, your talent may never

> **All Human Beings Have Similar Needs**
>
> 1. All people have certain physical needs, such as:
>    - ... food to eat
>    - ... air to breathe
>    - ... sleep
>    - ... protection from heat and cold
>    - ... exercise
> 2. All people have certain social needs, such as:
>    - ... belonging to a group of people who respect them and whom they respect
>    - ... a chance to develop their abilities
>    - ... a chance to make decisions
>    - ... goals to work for
>    - ... a feeling of accomplishment
> 3. All people have a need for faith.
>    People may be sustained by different kinds of faith, such as:
>    - ... faith that their lives will be happy and useful
>    - ... faith that they can solve their problems if they plan intelligently and work hard
>    - ... faith that there is order in the universe
>    - ... faith in God

develop. Education helps people make better use of their talents and abilities.

Another social need is to have something important that you want to accomplish. You must have goals. Perhaps you want to do well in your schoolwork or in sports. You may want to learn to play a musical instrument. When you are working toward a goal, you are more likely to make use of opportunities to develop your abilities. Whenever you reach one of your goals, you have a feeling of satisfaction. Then you are ready to choose a new and more important goal.

The need for faith. In addition to your physical and social needs, you also have a need for faith. In order to feel secure, you must have faith that you will be able to do some useful work in the world, and that you will be generally happy. You will still have problems, of course. But it is important to feel that you will be able to work toward solving whatever problems life brings to you. You need to feel that

Developing one's abilities is a basic human need. What are some other needs that all people share?

life is precious, and that the future is something to look forward to.

One kind of faith that helps people to face the future with confidence is faith that there is order in the universe. The more we learn about our universe, the more certain we feel that we can depend on nature. For instance, we know that the sun will rise each day. We also know that water will freeze at a temperature of about thirty-two degrees Fahrenheit.*

Through science, we can learn to predict certain kinds of events. For example, your local weather forecaster makes a report each day on the weather

101

you can expect the next day. Although the forecast is not always right, it is right most of the time. Today, warning systems can tell us when and where a violent storm, such as a hurricane, is forming. The people who live in the path of the storm can protect themselves from harm. Scientists cannot as yet predict when an earthquake will strike. But they can tell where earthquakes are most likely to occur.

Most people have faith in God as the source of the order in the universe. This kind of faith helps them to live better lives, and to face problems with courage and confidence. Throughout history, most people have had some kind of religious faith. Today, as in the past, people express and strengthen their faith by attending religious services.

**How do cities help people to satisfy their basic needs?** In the South, just as in other parts of our country, people who live in urban areas have many opportunities to meet their physical needs. A variety of jobs are available in factories, stores, and offices. People can usually earn more money from one of these jobs than they could by working on farms. They can use the money they earn to buy food, clothing, and shelter for themselves and their families.

The people who live in and near cities also have various opportunities to meet their social needs. For example, there are many clubs and other organizations for people with similar goals and interests. By taking part in club activities, people can develop their own talents more fully and work together to achieve important goals. Sometimes the schools in urban areas are better than those in rural areas. In most large cities there are colleges and various trade schools. These make it possible for young people and adults to continue their education beyond high school if they wish.

In large urban areas, people have many opportunities to express their faith in God by worshiping with others who share their beliefs. Many different religious groups have built churches and other places of worship in these areas.

**What ways of living make it possible for cities to develop?** The cities of the South, like those in other parts of our country, would never have developed if people had not made use of certain ideas and ways of living. Chapter 14 tells about some of the more important of these "great ideas." Let us see how the great ideas have influenced the growth of cities in the South.

**Rules and government.** The people who live in the cities of the South would not be able to meet their needs successfully if they did not follow rules. To understand why this is true, imagine what it would be like to live in a city where there were no traffic laws, or where people could dump their trash or garbage anywhere they pleased. Without rules, or laws, life in cities would be unpleasant and even dangerous.

Every city in the South has people who make the laws and see that the laws are carried out. In other words, every city has some form of government. Usually the laws are made by a group of elected officials called the city council or the city commission. An official such as a mayor or a city manager is in charge of running the city government. Police officers and judges are needed to deal with people who are accused of disobeying the laws.

**Students working in a medical laboratory** at a university in Virginia. In the cities of the South, there are many colleges and universities that train young people for future careers.

Who makes the laws in the community where you live? How do the people of your community select these lawmakers?

**Language and communication.** The people of the South, like those in other regions, must have effective ways of communicating with each other in order to achieve their goals. For example, there are daily and weekly newspapers that provide people with information about important events in the community. News is also communicated through radio and television broadcasts. Without effective means of communication, it would be very difficult to carry on city life.

**Education.** Education is another great idea that has helped the cities of the South to grow. In every community, young people must learn certain skills in order to earn a living. They must also learn certain ideas and attitudes that will help them to live successfully in their community. In the cities of the South, there are many fine grade schools and high schools where young people can receive a good education. For older students, there are colleges and universities, as well as special schools that train people for certain occupations. How do the schools in your community help make it a good place in which to live?

**Using natural resources.** In order for people to live in any kind of community, they must be able to use the earth's resources to meet their needs. Among the most important natural resources are sunshine, water, and fertile soil. Other natural resources include forests and mineral deposits.

What are some of the most important natural resources used by the people of your community?

Some communities in the South have grown into cities partly because they are located near valuable resources that can be used by industry. For example, the city of Birmingham, Alabama, is located near rich deposits of iron ore, coal, and limestone. All three of these minerals are needed in making steel. The use of these natural resources has helped Birmingham become an important steel-manufacturing city.

**Tools.** In order to use the earth's resources to meet their needs, people must have many different kinds of tools and machines. If you were to visit a textile mill in Charlotte, North Carolina, you would be able to see why this is true. Several kinds of complicated machinery are needed to spin cotton into yarn. Other machines are needed to weave the yarn into cloth. Modern industry would not be possible without the use of many different kinds of tools and machines. These tools are also needed to construct houses and other buildings.

**Division of labor.** The people who live in the cities of the South work at many different kinds of jobs. Some people are employed in factories that produce

**Canning shrimp in Biloxi, Mississippi.** The people of Biloxi have made excellent use of the natural resources available to them.

manufactured goods. Others work in stores, banks, or business offices. Still others earn their living by providing various services that people need. Among these workers are doctors, teachers, carpenters, plumbers, barbers, and police officers.

When the work of a city is divided among people who do different jobs, each person can work at a job that he or she enjoys and does best. With the money people earn from doing their jobs, they can buy the goods and services their families need. Do you think it would be possible for people to live in cities if each person had to meet his or her needs all alone? Why do you think this?

**Exchange.** Another great idea that has influenced the growth of cities is exchange. In every city, there are many people who make their living by exchanging goods and services.

One reason why cities have developed is that they are convenient places for people to buy and sell goods. For example, Raleigh, North Carolina, is the trading center for a rich farming area. Farmers send products such as cotton, livestock, and vegetables to Raleigh to be sold. People come from miles around to buy these goods at markets or to purchase other things they need at Raleigh's many stores.

Some of the South's largest cities, such as New Orleans, Louisiana, and Norfolk, Virginia, are seaports. Farm products, minerals, and manufactured goods are brought to these ports for shipment to other ports in the United States or in foreign countries. Goods from foreign lands are shipped to these same ports.

**Cooperation and loyalty.** Two important ways of living that have helped cities in the South to grow are cooperation and loyalty. The people of a community must work together in many different ways to solve their problems and to accomplish important goals. They realize that unfriendly attitudes and lack of cooperation can hurt everyone in their community. Most of the people who live in cities of the South are loyal to their community and to their fellow citizens. They express this loyalty by obeying the laws, paying their taxes, and taking an active part in community affairs. Do you think most of the people where you live are loyal to their community? In what ways do they express their loyalty?

**Freedom.** In the cities of the South, most people enjoy a great deal of freedom. They can choose where they want to live and move freely from one place to another. They are free to work at jobs of their own choosing or to start their own businesses if they wish. They are free to speak and write their opinions on any subject, and to hold public meetings. They can worship God in any way they please, or not worship at all. These freedoms are limited only by the laws that their elected officials have passed. Do you think that freedom has helped the cities of the South to grow? If so, how?

**Great cities of the South.** The map on page 114 shows the location of the main cities in the South. Nearly every large city is surrounded by a number of smaller cities and towns. Together these make up what is known as a metropolitan area. The six largest metropolitan areas in the South include the cities of Atlanta, Georgia; Miami, Florida; Tampa and St. Petersburg, Florida; New Orleans, Louisiana; Louisville, Kentucky; and Memphis, Tennessee.

**A street in Atlanta, Georgia.** More than 1,775,000 people live in the Atlanta metropolitan area. This area has grown rapidly during recent years. Why do you suppose this is so?

**Atlanta** (population 490,000; altitude 1,050 feet). Atlanta is the capital and largest city of Georgia. It is an inland city located on the rolling land of the Piedmont Plateau. The Atlanta metropolitan area has grown rapidly during the last few years, and it is still growing. Today it is the largest metropolitan area in the South, with a population of more than 1,775,000.

Atlanta began as a railroad terminus* and soon became an important transportation city. During the Civil War, Union troops under General Sherman set fire to Atlanta. The city was almost completely destroyed. After it was rebuilt, Atlanta became the state capital. Today, Atlanta is a modern city with many fine parks and schools. It is sometimes called the "Dogwood City" because of the beautiful dogwood trees that border many of its streets.

Excellent transportation and communication facilities have helped Atlanta become an important trading and business city. Railroads and highways stretch out from Atlanta like the spokes of a wheel. A number of airlines also serve the city. Atlanta is a market and distribution center for farm products such as cotton and livestock. Many products manufactured in the South

107

are shipped to northern markets by way of Atlanta. Because it is a major transportation and communications center, Atlanta has attracted banking, insurance, and other business offices.

Thousands of workers in Atlanta are employed in government work or in manufacturing. In addition to the many departments of the state government, Atlanta has more than ninety federal agencies. Factories in the Atlanta area make over three thousand different products. Among these are textiles, furniture, chemicals, and paper. Atlanta also has automobile-assembly plants. A huge aircraft plant near Atlanta employs a large number of workers.

**Miami** (population 357,000; altitude 0 to 20 feet). Miami is located in the southern part of Florida, on the Atlantic coast. (See map on page 114.) To the east of downtown Miami are the sparkling blue waters of Biscayne Bay, an inlet of the Atlantic Ocean. Biscayne Bay is usually dotted with fishing boats, sight-seeing launches, cabin cruisers, and many other kinds of boats. Two and one-half miles east of downtown Miami is the city of Miami Beach. It is located on one of several long, narrow islands that border the coast. Beyond these islands is the open ocean.

Miami and its neighboring communities have grown so close together that it is impossible to tell where Miami ends and other cities begin. There are more than twenty-five cities and towns in the Miami metropolitan area. Among these are Miami Shores, North Miami, Hialeah, and Coral Gables. The island city

**Miami** is the central city of a large metropolitan area in southern Florida. Millions of tourists visit this city each year.

of Miami Beach is also part of the Miami metropolitan area. It is one of the most famous resorts in the world. Here, hundreds of tall hotels and apartment buildings line the Atlantic shore.

The population of the Miami metropolitan area has grown rapidly. Today this metropolitan area is the second largest in the South. It is the home of about 1,415,000 people.

In 1957, residents of the Miami area voted to establish a metropolitan government to deal with problems that affect the whole community. Since then, other metropolitan areas have copied Miami's plan.

Miami's most important industry is the resort business. Each year, millions of tourists visit the city. Many of the people who live in Miami are employed in hotels and restaurants. Some of the others work for transportation companies such as railroads and airlines. Miami is also a manufacturing, trading, and shipping city. Furniture, clothing, and chemicals are among the products made in Miami's factories. Vegetables and citrus fruit grown in rich agricultural areas nearby are sent to packing plants in Miami. Foods and manufactured items produced in Miami are shipped to many other parts of our country.

**New Orleans** (population 587,000; altitude 4 feet below sea level to 15 feet above sea level). New Orleans is the largest city in Louisiana and the chief port of the entire South. It is located on the Mississippi River, near the Gulf of Mexico. The oldest part of the city lies along the north bank of the river. Much of modern New Orleans sprawls along the shores of a body of salt water called Lake Pontchartrain. (Compare map on page 114 with map on page 249.) More than one million people live in the New Orleans metropolitan area.

New Orleans was founded in 1718 by French colonists. The following year,

**New Orleans**, Louisiana's largest city, is located on the Mississippi River near the Gulf of Mexico. More than one million people live in the New Orleans metropolitan area.

the little settlement was severely damaged by floodwaters from the Mississippi River. In order to protect their land from floods, the settlers built earthen levees along the banks of the river. As more and more settlers came to New Orleans, the town spread into nearby areas. Swampland was drained, and more levees were built.

The location of New Orleans near the mouth of the Mississippi River has helped it become a leading port city. Among our country's ports, New Orleans ranks second only to New York in the amount of cargo handled. The docks and piers of the Port of New Orleans stretch for miles along both sides of the river. Oceangoing ships

carry passengers and cargo between New Orleans and other seaports all over the world. Boats and barges also travel between New Orleans and port cities located on the Mississippi River and its branches.

During the twentieth century, industry has grown rapidly in New Orleans. Minerals found nearby, such as petroleum, natural gas, sulfur, and salt, are processed in the city's refineries and chemical plants. Some of the natural gas is used to make the electricity needed for manufacturing. Many of the products of Louisiana's farms, such as sugarcane, cotton, and rice, are sent to factories in New Orleans for processing. Many kinds of manufactured goods, as well as minerals and farm products, are shipped from New Orleans to other states and to foreign countries.

Each year, millions of tourists visit New Orleans. Some people come to visit the historic French Quarter. This is the oldest part of the city, settled by the French early in the eighteenth century. Here, there are narrow streets, quaint shops, and old buildings decorated with lacy, iron grillwork. Many people come to New Orleans for Mardi Gras. This is a famous festival that lasts for about two weeks just before Lent.*

**Tampa and St. Petersburg.** About halfway up the Florida peninsula, a large inlet of the Gulf of Mexico cuts into the coast. This is Tampa Bay. Along the shores of the bay are several cities, the largest of which are Tampa and St. Petersburg. About one and one-third million people live in the Tampa–St. Petersburg metropolitan area.

**Colorful parades** are part of the famous Mardi Gras festival held each year in New Orleans.

# Cities of the South

This map shows the location of the main cities in the South. It is based on populations of central cities rather than on populations of metropolitan areas. All cities with a population of 100,000 or more are included. Smaller cities mentioned in the text are also shown on the map.

Tampa (population 304,000; altitude 0 to 72 feet) is the largest city on Tampa Bay. It is located on a fine harbor at the northeastern end of the bay. Tampa is Florida's most important trading, manufacturing, and port city on the Gulf coast. Ships from other American ports and from foreign countries bring products such as tobacco, petroleum, and sugar to Tampa. The city's leading export is phosphate rock, which comes from mines nearby. Lumber, canned citrus fruit, and other items produced in the Tampa area are also exported.

The tourist business is one of Tampa's most important industries. Many thousands of people come here to enjoy such sports as fishing, sailing, and golf.

St. Petersburg (population 253,000; altitude 0 to 45 feet) is the second largest city in the Tampa Bay area. It is located on the peninsula that separates the Tampa Bay area from the Gulf of Mexico.

St. Petersburg is mainly a resort city. Because the sun shines here almost every day of the year, it is sometimes called the "Sunshine City." Tourists come here to swim, fish, sail, or just to enjoy the sunshine. Many older people live in St. Petersburg after retirement.

**Louisville** (population 347,000; altitude 380 to 540 feet). The largest city in Kentucky is Louisville. It is located on the Ohio River, at the western edge of the Bluegrass. (Compare map on opposite page with map on page 248.) About 890,000 people live in the Louisville metropolitan area, which includes some towns on the other side of the Ohio River, in Indiana.

Louisville is one of our country's leading river ports. At one time, ships traveling on the Ohio River had to stop at Louisville because of a series of rapids, or falls, in the river. Goods were unloaded, carried around the falls, and reloaded onto ships on the other side of the falls. Since 1830, when a canal was opened at Louisville, ships have been able to bypass the falls.

Louisville is one of the South's most important business and manufacturing cities. In addition to whiskey distilleries and factories that make cigars and cigarettes, Louisville has plants that manufacture furniture, electrical appliances, and other products. The largest baseball-bat factory in the United States is located here.

Each year, Louisville attracts large numbers of tourists. Many people come here to watch the Kentucky Derby. This famous horse race is held in May at Churchill Downs racetrack.

About thirty miles south of Louisville is Fort Knox. Here, in huge vaults, the United States government keeps much of our nation's gold reserve.

**Memphis** (population 651,000; altitude 275 feet). The city of Memphis is located in the far southwestern corner of Tennessee, on the Mississippi River. It is near the place where De Soto first saw this river. (See page 60.) Andrew Jackson* helped to found Memphis in 1819. The city soon became a busy river port. Steamboats stopped at its docks to load cotton and other products. Today, Memphis is the largest city on the Mississippi River between New Orleans and St. Louis. About 850,000 people live in the Memphis metropolitan area.

Memphis is an up-to-date city, with modern office buildings, factories, and homes. It also has many fine old houses that were built by wealthy planters before the Civil War.

Memphis is one of our country's leading inland ports. If you were to take a sight-seeing cruise on the Mississippi River, you would see piers, wharves, and warehouses stretching along the waterfront. You would probably notice workers loading barges with lumber, cotton, and other products of the area. These goods are shipped to many parts of the world. On the river, diesel tugboats chug along, pushing strings of barges. Many of these barges are heading downstream toward New Orleans, where their cargoes will be loaded aboard oceangoing ships. (See map on page 29.) Others are bound for St. Louis and other cities upstream.

Memphis is the main trading and business city for western Tennessee and parts of neighboring states. It is one of the world's largest markets for cotton and hardwood lumber. Each year, about four million bales of cotton are sold here. Memphis is also a market for livestock, grain, and other products of farms in the area. The city is one of the major wholesale distributing points of the South. Many drug companies, grocery suppliers, and other businesses have branch offices and warehouses in Memphis.

Manufacturing is also important in Memphis. Many people work in plants where cottonseed, rice, and other farm products are processed. This city is one of the leading meat-packing centers in the South. Other important products manufactured in Memphis include paper, chemicals, farm machinery, and electronic equipment.

**Using Maps To Make Discoveries**

By comparing the map on page 114 with the maps on pages 29 and 208, you will be able to discover additional information about the cities of the South. With the help of these three maps, try to answer the following questions.
1. Which twelve cities in the South have populations of 250,000 or more?
2. Nine of these twelve large cities are main port cities. Which ones are they?
3. Which of these nine large port cities are located on rivers?
4. Which of these nine large port cities are located on the Intracoastal Waterway?
5. One of the South's twelve largest cities is not part of a main industrial area. Which one is it?

**Memphis**, with over 650,000 people, is Tennessee's largest city. Its location on the Mississippi River has helped Memphis become one of our country's major inland ports.

# 9 Citizenship in a Democracy

**All communities have laws.** In every community in the world, the people have rules, or laws, to live by. These laws are generally intended to help people feel secure, lead happy and useful lives, and satisfy their needs. In communities where the laws are just and the people obey them, life is safer and more pleasant for everybody.

Laws are made in different ways in different parts of the world. In some communities, a single person or a small group has the power to make and enforce laws without the consent of the rest of the people.

In other communities the people govern themselves, making and enforcing their own laws. These communities are called democracies. In a very small community, such as a family or a village, people can make and enforce their own laws directly. They can do this by meeting together to discuss their problems and to make decisions.

It is not possible, however, for the citizens of a large community or an entire country to meet together. Therefore, a sensible way has been worked out for large groups of people to govern themselves. The people who make up the large group choose a smaller group to represent them. This group makes the laws and sees that they are enforced. Countries with this kind of government, such as the United States, are called representative democracies.

**The people in a democracy share five important beliefs.** Many people are convinced that democracy provides the best way of making laws and enforcing them wisely. In order to make democracy work, however, the citizens of a country must share five important beliefs, or principles. Most Americans, like other people who live in successful democracies, follow these principles.

With the help of a crossing guard, these schoolchildren can cross the street in safety. In communities where the laws are just and the people obey them, life is safer and more pleasant for everybody.

**Five Important Beliefs Shared by People in a Democracy**

1. Every person is important.
2. People have the right to govern themselves.
3. Decisions should be made by majority vote.
4. All people have certain inalienable* rights.
5. Laws should apply equally to all citizens of a country.

**1. Every person is important.** Most Americans believe that every person is important, whatever groups he or she may belong to. We believe all people are important no matter what their religion may be. All people are important whether they are rich or poor, or whether their skin is black, white, or some other color. All people are important no matter what their sex or national origin may be.

*See Glossary

There are several reasons for believing that every person is important. In the first place, most Americans follow religions that teach the equality of all people under God. Second, we know that all human beings have almost exactly the same basic needs. (See page 100.) Third, we know that problems cannot be solved unless individual human beings think about them. Finally, we know that progress begins with the ideas of individuals.

When we really believe that every person is important, we are more likely to treat other people the way we would like to be treated. We are also more careful not to harm other people in our efforts to satisfy our own needs. For example, if you forgot to bring your lunch to school, you would not take someone else's lunch for yourself.

**2. People have the right to govern themselves.** Most Americans believe that the citizens of a country have the right to govern themselves. We think every person should be able to have some part, no matter how small, in running the government under which we live.

**3. Decisions should be made by majority vote.** Most Americans believe that the best way for people to govern themselves is by majority vote. In our country and other democracies, all qualified citizens have an opportunity to vote for lawmakers and many other government officials. The candidates who receive the most votes are elected.

**The Florida House of Representatives.** The members of this group are elected by the citizens of Florida to help make laws for the state. Most Americans believe that the citizens of a community should have some part in running the government under which they live.

Here in the United States, the people elect some of the government officials for cities, counties, and states, as well as for the nation. In local and state elections, the people often vote not only on candidates, but also on issues. For example, the citizens in a community may have a chance to vote on whether they wish to pay the additional taxes needed for a new school.

Although choices and decisions made by majority vote are considered final, we believe that the opinions held by the minority are also important. We feel that it is the duty and the privilege of those who disagree with the majority to express their opinions. They are free to offer criticisms and suggestions.

**4. All people have certain inalienable rights.** Most Americans and other people who live in democratic countries believe that certain rights are natural and inalienable. This means that they cannot be given up or transferred to the government, even by a majority vote.

A democratic government is expected to protect all of the rights that the people consider inalienable. In our country, we believe that we are entitled to life, liberty, and the pursuit of happiness, which are listed as inalienable rights in our Declaration of Independence. We believe these rights include the freedom to form and express our own opinions and religious beliefs. We believe a person accused of a crime should have a fair trial, and should be considered innocent until proven guilty. We also believe that people should have the freedom to satisfy their needs and to develop their abilities.

**IMPORTANT RIGHTS AND FREEDOMS GUARANTEED BY THE UNITED STATES CONSTITUTION**

| Right or Freedom | Guaranteed by |
|---|---|
| **Freedom of Press** | 1st Amendment |
| **Freedom of Speech** | 1st Amendment |
| **Freedom of Assembly** | 1st Amendment |
| **Freedom of Petition** | 1st Amendment |
| **Freedom of Religion** | 1st Amendment |
| **Security of Person** | Art. I, Sec. IX |
|  | 4th Amendment |
| **Life, Liberty, and Property** | 5th Amendment |
|  | 13th Amendment |
| **A Fair Trial** | 5th Amendment |
|  | 6th Amendment |
|  | 7th Amendment |
|  | 8th Amendment |
| **Voting Rights** | 15th Amendment |
|  | 19th Amendment |
|  | 23rd Amendment |
|  | 24th Amendment |
|  | 26th Amendment |
| **Equal Protection Under the Law** | 14th Amendment |

**5. Laws should apply equally to all citizens of a country.** Most Americans believe that all the citizens of a country should be treated in the same way by their government. Everyone should be required to obey the same laws. Each person's vote should count exactly the same as every other person's. No one should ever gain or lose any rights or privileges on account of religion, skin color, sex, national origin, or income.

**A democratic government is only as good as the people make it.** In a successful democracy, most of the citizens follow the principles discussed above. They help to run their own government by voting in each election. They also encourage other people to vote. This is

**Voting.** In a democracy, every qualified citizen has an opportunity to vote. What important document helps protect voting rights for every person in the United States?

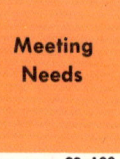

**Meeting Needs**

See pages 99-102

The photograph above shows workers picking oranges in Florida. By working at jobs, most people in the United States earn enough money to meet their physical needs. In addition, their work helps them to satisfy many of their social needs. Do you believe that people in democratic countries are more likely to live happy, successful lives than people who live under other forms of government? Explain why you think as you do.

because they realize that if only a few people vote, the government officials who are elected may not represent the majority of the citizens.

In order to have a good government, the citizens in a democracy must elect honest, capable men and women to public office. People are better able to choose their government officials wisely if they have read about and listened to the ideas of all the candidates. For this reason, education is very important in a democracy. In order to vote intelligently, the people must be able to understand the things they read and hear. They must also be able to think things through clearly.

## Problems for Democracy

**Most citizens of our country are able to satisfy their basic needs.** In the United States today, most people have opportunities for satisfying their basic needs. For example, the opportunity to work usually makes it possible for people to meet their physical needs. Workers are able to exchange their labor for money to buy food, clothing, and shelter.

Opportunities for meeting social needs are also available to most citizens of our country. Our system of free, public education offers most people a chance to develop their abilities. Under our democratic form of government, citizens have a chance to help make decisions on important issues. In every community there are clubs and other organizations that provide opportunities for people to work together toward important goals.

Most of our citizens have the faith they need for a happy and useful life. They may have faith in the goodwill of other people or in the orderliness of the universe. Many people have faith in their own ability to solve their problems and to reach the goals they have set for themselves. Most people also have faith in God.

**Some of our citizens do not have an opportunity to satisfy their basic needs.** Although the United States is a very rich and powerful nation, there are millions of people in our country who do not have an opportunity to satisfy all their needs. Sometimes, through no fault of their own, people cannot provide food, clothing, and shelter for themselves and their families. Some people do not have an opportunity to satisfy their social needs. Others lack the faith that might help them solve their problems.

Conditions that prevent large numbers of people from satisfying their needs may be called social problems. Every country in the world, including our own, has social problems that need to be solved. Let us explore some of these problems to see how they affect people in the United States and what is being done to solve them.

**The Need for Faith**

See pages 100-102

Do you think this girl has faith in herself? Do you think most Americans have faith in their ability to do the things they want to do? To solve problems? Do you have this kind of faith? Explain your answer.

## Five Social Problems

At the present time, the people of the United States are especially interested in finding solutions to five serious social problems. These problems are:
1. lack of jobs
2. lack of education
3. handicaps and illness
4. prejudice
5. discrimination

**Many Americans cannot find jobs.** The most serious problem faced by many people in the United States today is that of earning a living. Some people work at jobs that pay them very little money. Others cannot find jobs at all. According to government figures, about seven out of every one hundred workers in our country are unemployed at the present time. Let us explore some of the reasons why this is so.

Causes of unemployment. Sometimes the United States, like other countries, goes through a time of business troubles known as a recession. When this happens, many stores and factories are not able to operate at a profit. Some of them have to lay off many of their workers, while others may go out of business entirely. As a result, there are not enough jobs for all the people who need them.

Some of the unemployed workers in our country live in areas where few jobs are available. These are known as depressed areas. Many different circumstances have caused these areas to become depressed. For example, in some places, land that was once suitable for farming has been ruined by poor farming methods or by mining operations. Also, certain areas that once employed many workers now

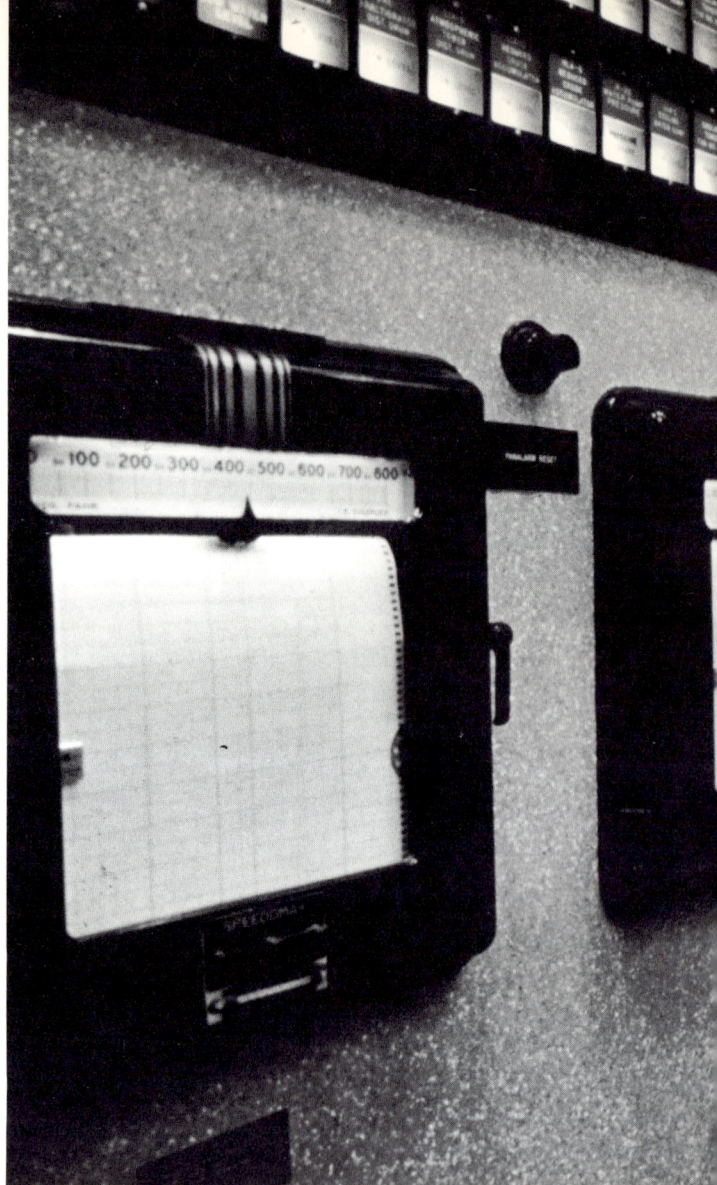

lack industry. This has happened for several reasons. In some cases, mines have been shut down because all the valuable minerals have been removed. In other cases, businesses have moved away because the owners could no longer make a profit in that location. Factories have sometimes closed down because people stopped buying the goods they were making.

Unemployed people who live in depressed areas are often unable to move to places where there are more jobs. They cannot save enough money to pay

A worker in an automated plant. What is automation? How does it affect workers who have no special skills? How does it affect highly trained workers, such as technicians and engineers?

for the cost of moving. Also, many of them are so discouraged by their lack of success at finding a job that they stop searching.

Even when plenty of jobs are available in a certain area, many people have difficulty finding employment. Some are too elderly for certain jobs, or their health is too poor. Others cannot find jobs because of discrimination. (See pages 140-143.) In addition, many people are unemployed because they lack the education or the special skills needed to hold the available jobs.

In the past, many jobs were open to people who did not have much education or who lacked special skills. Today, however, many jobs that used to be done by unskilled or partly skilled workers are performed by automatic machinery. The use of machinery that needs few, if any, human beings to operate it is called automation.

Because automation is increasing, the kinds of jobs that are available are changing rapidly. The number of jobs that can be held by unskilled workers is growing smaller every day. At the
*Continued on page 132*

129

# Inflation Is a Serious Problem

**The cost of goods and services has been rising steadily.** Many Americans find it difficult to meet their needs because they have to pay higher and higher prices for the goods and services they use. This condition is known as inflation. Many kinds of goods and services are much more expensive than they were only a few years ago. In 1966, for example, a loaf of bread cost about fifteen cents. In 1976 the average cost of a loaf of bread was more than twice as high.

When prices go up, the value of money goes down. In other words, a certain amount of money will buy fewer goods and services than it did in the past. For instance, a dollar bought only about half as many goods and services in 1975 as it did in 1956.

**What causes inflation?** Prices increase for a number of different reasons. Sometimes there are many people who want to buy a certain product but only a limited supply is available. Some people are then willing to pay higher prices to make sure of getting this scarce item. For example, in 1973 oil refineries in the United States were not producing enough gasoline to supply all the people who wanted to buy it. This caused the price of gasoline to increase very rapidly.

Sometimes a business firm raises the price that it charges for a certain product in order to make a larger profit. If there are many different firms that make the same product, each company will be slow to raise its prices. Otherwise, it may lose customers to firms whose prices are lower. But in many industries today, only a few companies produce nearly all the available supply of a certain product. If one company raises its prices, the others are likely to do the same.

Labor unions may also bring about an increase in prices. By threatening to go on strike, a union can sometimes force a company to increase the wages of its workers. When this happens, the company may have to raise the price of its product in order to continue operating.

Inflation may also be caused by the federal government spending more money than it receives in taxes. In recent years, for example, wars and space exploration have caused the government to go into debt. Also, enormous amounts of money have been spent to provide our citizens with the health, education, and welfare services that they demand. Whenever the government spends more money than it receives in taxes, it issues new money. When this new money goes into circulation, people have more money in their pockets to buy the things they need and want. This creates a scarcity of goods and services. People are then willing to pay more for these goods and services, and as a result prices rise.

**How does inflation affect people's lives?** Inflation is not a very serious problem for people whose incomes are rising as fast as prices. This has been true of many families in the United States. For example, in 1965 average factory workers in the United States earned about $100 a week, not including the amount taken out of their paychecks for federal taxes. By 1975 the same workers earned about $166. This amount of money bought just as many goods and services as $100 did in 1965.

There are many people, however, whose income has not been rising as rapidly as the cost of living. Some of these people work at jobs that pay little more than they did ten years ago. Others are elderly people who are living on pensions* or on money they saved when they were younger. Although their income remains about the same, they have to pay more money for the goods and services they buy. As a result, their standard of living is lower than it was before.

Inflation is also harmful to many business firms. They must pay higher wages to keep their employees satisfied, and they also must pay more money for the goods they use. If they charge higher prices for their products to meet these rising costs, they may lose some of their customers. As a result, it is often difficult for some business firms to stay in business during times of serious inflation.

In other countries, inflation has sometimes become so serious that it has led to a breakdown of law and order. People have become

*See Glossary

angry and fearful because their standard of living is falling, and they are uncertain about the future. In some nations, the government has been overthrown because it was not able to control the rising cost of living.

**What is being done about inflation?** Today government leaders and other people in the United States are studying ways to solve the problem of inflation. Some people believe the government should try to stop inflation by controlling wages and prices. Workers could not get wage increases and business firms would not be able to raise their prices without the government's permission. Wages and prices were controlled by the government during World War II\* and again in 1971 and 1972. But many Americans strongly oppose price and wage controls. They believe that people should be free to decide on wages and prices without interference from the government.

Some experts think that inflation cannot be avoided if our government continues to provide the many services its citizens demand. These experts say that the government should either spend less money or raise taxes, or both. If the government reduced its spending, less money would be put into circulation and people would have less to spend for goods and services. Raising taxes would have the same effect. In either case, prices would go up much less rapidly, and inflation would be slowed.

There is still much that people need to learn about the causes of inflation and the best methods of preventing it. Only as we gain more knowledge will we be able to make progress toward solving this important problem.

**Citizens protesting high food prices.** Inflation is making it difficult for many Americans to meet their needs today. What are some of the ways in which inflation affects your life?

same time, many new and different jobs are becoming available for highly skilled workers. For example, many people are needed to build the new automatic machines and to keep them running. The available jobs are being filled by people who are well educated or have special training, such as engineers and technicians.

At present, there are many unskilled workers who are unemployed because of automation. The answer to this problem is not to stop using machines, for they make it possible to produce most of the goods that Americans enjoy. Instead, the answer lies in providing more opportunities for education. Our schools must prepare more people to live and work successfully in today's world.

Unemployed people need help. Today various steps are being taken to help unemployed workers get jobs. For example, people in the federal government are studying ways to aid the growth of industry and to prevent recessions. Sometimes the government lends money to business firms that are in trouble. In addition, it has established a number of programs to train unemployed workers in valuable job skills.

Many cities in the South and other regions have started job-training programs to help unemployed workers. A number of private business firms operate programs to retrain workers who have lost their jobs as a result of automation.

Many people who do not have any way of supporting themselves receive help from government agencies. The social security program of our national government provides income for people who are too old or too ill to hold jobs. Unemployment insurance is provided in all of our states. This kind of insurance helps workers during times when they are not employed. Various federal, state, and local government agencies also provide money and other kinds of help for needy families.

People who do not have enough money may also receive help from private organizations in their own communities. Almost every community in our country has an organization that collects money to be used for various welfare, health, and recreation projects. This organization is usually called the United Fund or the United Way. The money it collects is distributed to community agencies. Some of these agencies offer services directly to the unemployed and others who need help.

**Many people do not receive the education they need.** At the present time, many young people in the United

**Education**

See pages 224-225

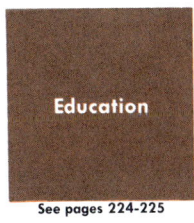

**Children in nursery school.** Many children do better work in regular school if they first attend nursery school. Why is lack of education regarded as one of our country's most serious social problems? In making hypotheses to solve this problem, you will need to consider:

a. ways in which education helps people satisfy their needs
b. the need for educated citizens in a democracy

See pages 256-258

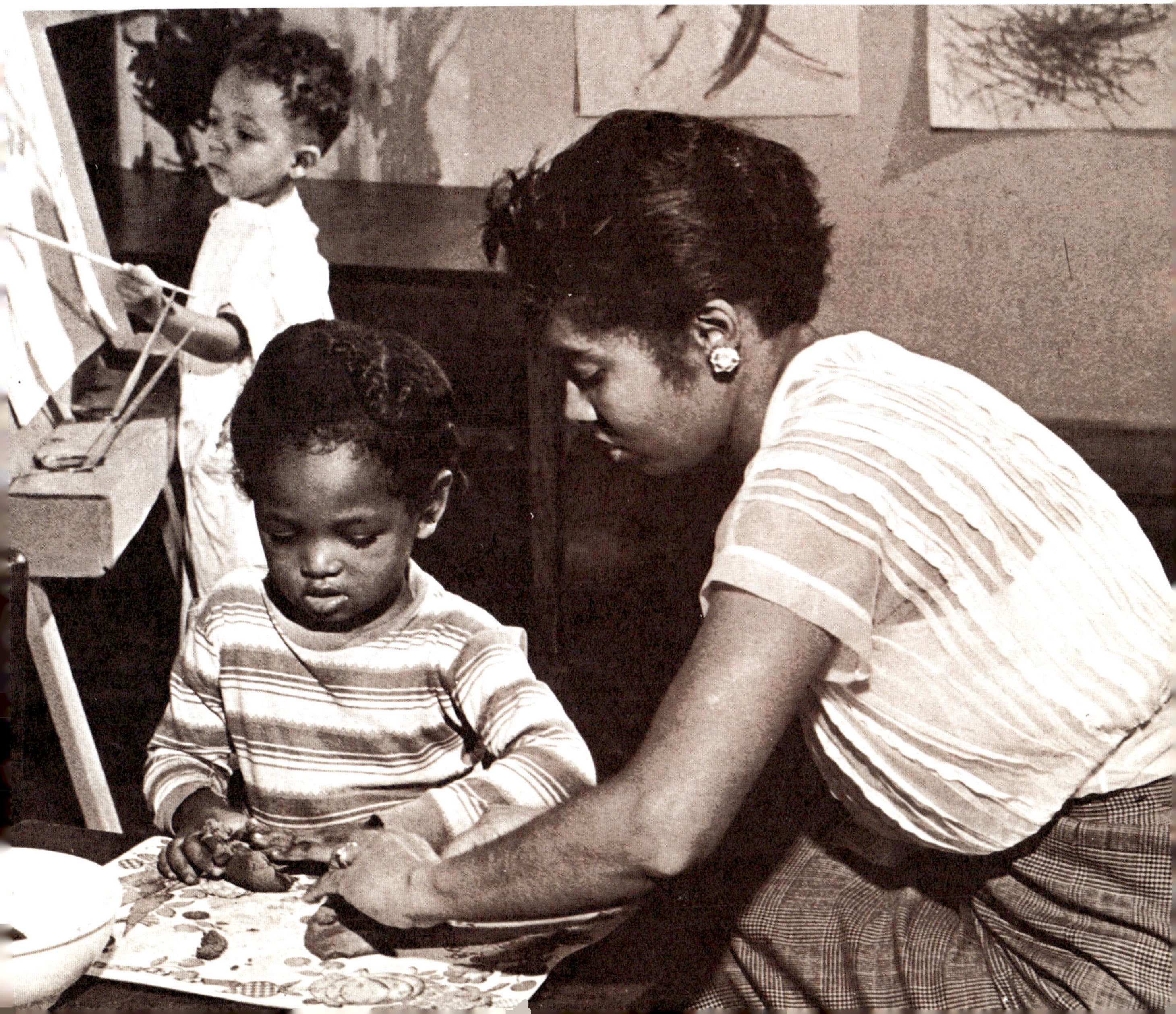

States are not receiving the education they need to develop their abilities and to lead happy, useful lives. There are many reasons for this. Some communities do not have enough tax money to support high-quality schools. Other communities do not provide equally good schools for all the children who live there. For example, although some of our cities spend more money on schools in sections where the people are poor, some spend less. In addition, the quality of our schools varies from state to state.

Many children who live in depressed areas of our country do not receive an education that meets their needs. Because there is less wealth in such areas, less tax money is collected for the support of schools. As a result, schools in

**Signing up for classes** at Georgia State University. More and more opportunities for education are being made available to young people.

these areas are usually not as good as those in other parts of our country. In addition, children in depressed areas often stay home from school. This may be because they are ill or because they do not have suitable clothing to wear.

Most children who live in the poorer sections of large cities do not get as much education as they should, even if they attend good schools. They are usually not as advanced in school as children who live in other sections of our cities. Often they do not score as high on achievement tests as other students of the same age.

One reason why children who live in poor neighborhoods make slower progress in school than children in other sections is that they are not prepared to do schoolwork. Often they come from homes that do not provide the learning experiences necessary for success in school. For example, some children live in homes where there are few toys or books. There may be no pencils, pens, or writing paper. Children from such homes usually do not know many words. Their lack of skills prevents them from doing well in school, even though they may be just as bright as other children.

Studies show that young children from homes with limited learning opportunities may be helped by attending nursery school. In nursery school they can be taught the things most other children learn at home. This experience helps prepare them for kindergarten or first grade.

Many young people leave school before they have fully developed their abilities or acquired the skills they need for life in today's world. Some high school students become discouraged at their lack of progress and drop out. Others leave school to go to work. Many young people who would like to continue their education after high school cannot afford to go to college.

More and more opportunities for education are being made available to the young people in our country. Many

students learn job skills in vocational schools or classes. Others learn skills in on-the-job training programs in offices and factories. Some schools, both public and private, offer special programs for handicapped children or for children who are especially talented.

Each year, millions of dollars in scholarships are awarded to students. Money for these scholarships comes from many different sources. Among these are schools, churches, business firms, labor unions, individual citizens, and federal and state governments.

**Millions of Americans suffer from illnesses and handicaps.** Although Americans are among the healthiest people in the world, sickness is a serious problem for many of our citizens. Millions of people suffer from serious, long-lasting illnesses such as cancer, heart conditions, arthritis, or mental illness. Others have some kind of handicap that makes it difficult for them to lead a satisfying life. For example, there are many people who are blind, deaf, or crippled.

During the present century, our nation has made tremendous progress in helping people to live healthier and longer lives. In 1900, a ten-year-old child could expect to live to about fifty-five years of age. Today, a ten-year-old can expect to reach the age of seventy-four. For most of their lives, people are generally much healthier than they used to be. Since people are now living longer, however, it is only natural that more people suffer from illnesses that come with old age.

Much progress has been made in preventing illness. For example, few people now suffer from rickets.* This disease may be prevented by adding vitamin D to the diet. Diseases such as polio and whooping cough can be prevented by "shots" or other medicines that protect a person from the effects of disease germs. Illnesses caused by impure water or food have almost been wiped out.

Great advances have been made in treating illness as well as in preventing it. Some kinds of pneumonia can be

Using Tools

See pages 230-235

Through research, many scientists and technicians in our country are developing better methods of preventing and curing illnesses. These researchers often use interesting tools. The man at the left, for example, is using an instrument called an electron microscope. The workers shown at right are studying a film made by an X-ray machine. Perhaps you would like to investigate and make a report on some of the scientific instruments and procedures used in modern medicine.

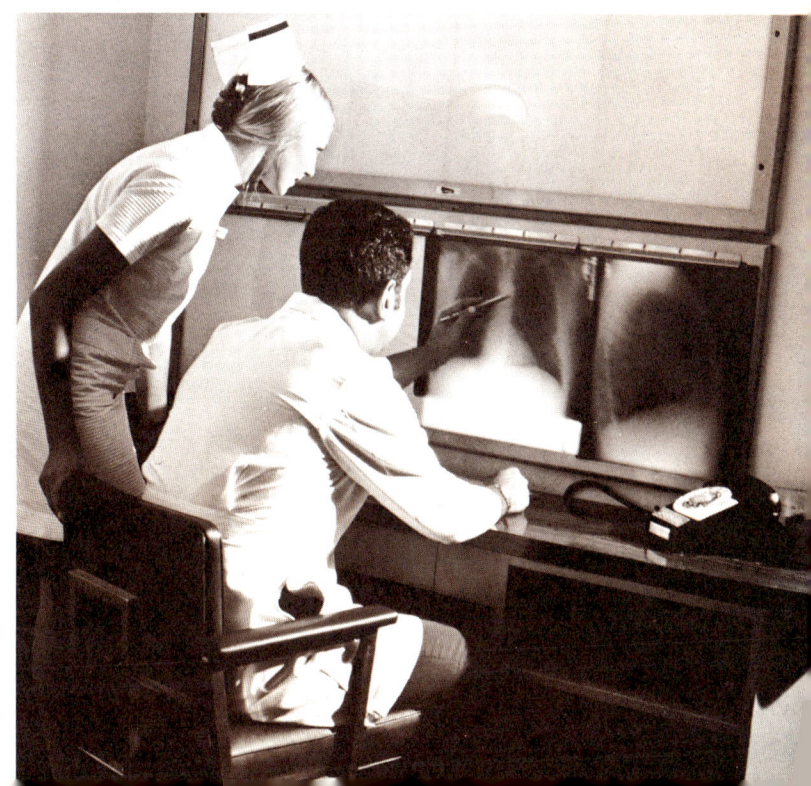

entirely cured with modern medicines. Many other infectious* diseases can also be cured. People with certain diseases that cannot yet be prevented or cured, such as diabetes, are given medicines that allow them to lead fairly normal lives. Much has been done to lessen the suffering of people with crippling diseases and handicaps.

Although these gains are important ones, not all of our country's health problems have been solved. For example, the cost of medical treatment has been rising rapidly. In case of serious illness, a family may have to spend thousands of dollars for doctors' fees and hospital care.

A number of insurance programs are available to help families meet the costs of serious illness. Sometimes individual workers pay for these programs. In other cases, the insurance is provided by employers. An insurance program for older people, called Medicare,* is paid for partly by the federal government. But there are still many medical costs that are not covered by any insurance.

Other health problems also face our nation today. In many rural areas and poorer city neighborhoods, there are not enough doctors to treat all the people who are ill. Some areas also lack modern hospitals. In addition, scientists who have been seeking cures for diseases such as cancer are finding it difficult to raise the money they need for research. Much remains to be done before all Americans receive the kind of medical care they need.

**Some people in our country are the victims of prejudice.** In the United States there are many groups of people who differ in some way from the rest of the population. These are called minority groups. Some groups differ in religion or in national origin. Others differ in physical features, such as the color of their skin.

Sometimes members of minority groups cannot meet all their basic needs because other people have feelings of prejudice toward them. The word "prejudice" means judging people not by their actions but simply by the fact that they belong to a certain group. For example, the Smiths may dislike the Johnsons or feel superior to them, not because of the Johnsons' actions but merely because the John-

Martin Luther King, Jr. speaking at a civil rights rally in Washington, D.C. King was a leader in the fight against racial prejudice and discrimination during the 1950's and 1960's. Do you think the problems of prejudice and discrimination have been completely solved? Explain your answer.

sons differ from them in race, religion, or national origin.

Throughout our country, prejudice is a serious problem. Minority groups that have been affected by prejudice include blacks, Jews, Puerto Ricans, American Indians, Mexican-Americans, and people of Chinese or Japanese descent. Although there are more women than there are men in our country, women sometimes suffer from the same kinds of prejudice that members of minority groups do. For example, an employer may be unwilling to promote a woman worker just because she is a woman.

Most people who are prejudiced do not really intend to hurt other people. In fact, they may not even realize that they have any prejudices. Often they have learned these attitudes from friends or relatives without ever seriously thinking about them. Perhaps people who are prejudiced are not aware that people in other groups have the same basic needs as they do, and that these people, too, have a right to satisfy their needs.

When people share experiences, they are usually better able to judge each other as individuals. Therefore, prejudice nearly always lessens when people work together, play together, or go to school together. As we have more opportunities to get to know the members of many different groups, prejudice in our country will gradually decrease.

**Prejudice often leads to discrimination.** Earlier in this chapter, you read about some of the important rights and freedoms to which all Americans are entitled. Sometimes, people who are prejudiced act in ways that prevent members of minority groups from enjoying all their rights and freedoms. This is known as discrimination.

In the past, many kinds of discrimination were permitted by our state and federal laws. For example, an employer could refuse to hire blacks, Puerto Ricans, Chinese-Americans, or other minority-group members. Very often women received lower wages than men for doing exactly the same kind of work. Throughout the nation, there were many hotels and resorts that refused to admit Jews or blacks. Certain medical schools would accept only a limited number of Jewish students.

In some states, children of different races could not attend the same schools or use the same parks and playgrounds. Buses, trains, and other public facilities were also segregated.* Sometimes various measures were used to prevent members of minority groups from voting. (See page 85.)

Decisions made by the United States Supreme Court are helping to end discrimination in our country. In 1954 the court ruled that segregation in public schools is forbidden by the United States Constitution. In spite of this ruling, many school districts continued to provide separate schools for blacks, especially in the South. Then, in 1969, the Supreme Court ruled that schools would have to

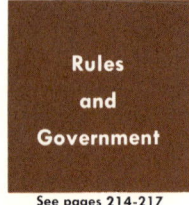

Rules and Government

See pages 214-217

**The United States Congress** has passed several laws to help protect the rights of minority groups. Do you think Congress would have passed these laws if its members did not share the five beliefs of people in successful democracies? Explain your answer.

Freedom
See pages 212-213

The woman in this picture is training for work as a machinist. In recent years, women have been seeking greater freedom to choose the kind of work they wish to do. Do you think women should have this kind of freedom? Should men and women receive the same amount of money for the same kind of work? Give reasons for your answers. Do you think women and members of certain minority groups in our country are ever discriminated against? Explain why you think as you do.

end segregation immediately. As a result of this ruling, many more public schools in our country have been integrated.*

The federal and state legislatures have taken a number of measures to protect the rights and freedoms of people who are often discriminated against. For example, the federal Civil Rights Act of 1964 has helped many women and minority-group members to obtain equal job opportunities. It is also helping to end discrimination in places such as schools, parks, hotels, and restaurants. Another federal law, the Voting Rights Act of 1965, prohibited literacy* tests and other measures that kept blacks from voting. As a result, almost all black citizens now have the opportunity to vote and to be elected to public office. A law passed by Congress in 1968 is helping to end discrimination in housing. In addition, many state governments have passed laws to prevent job discrimination and to end segregation in public places.

In spite of all these measures, discrimination is still a serious problem in our country. For example, black people still find it difficult to buy or rent homes in certain parts of our cities. Sometimes a real estate dealer may try to avoid showing certain houses or apartments to a black family. If a black family does move into a white neighborhood, their new neighbors may make trouble for them.

Because children usually attend the school nearest their home, segregation in housing has often resulted in segregated schools as well. To solve this problem, judges have sometimes ordered school officials to transport black students by bus to schools in white neighborhoods, and white students to schools in black neighborhoods. But busing is strongly opposed by many people who believe that students should attend schools near their homes.

The problem of discrimination must be solved by all Americans, working together. Each person must share the responsibility for finding a peaceful solution. The problem will only be solved when all citizens of the United States learn to live in accordance with the five important beliefs that make our democracy possible.

Police officers investigating a crime. Studies show that serious crime is increasing rapidly, not only in large cities, but also in smaller communities throughout our country.

## The Growing Problem of Crime

**Crime is increasing rapidly in all parts of our country.** Today most Americans are concerned about the large number of crimes committed in our country every year. According to the Federal Bureau of Investigation (FBI), there has been a steady increase in the number of serious crimes such as murder, robbery, and kidnapping. Less serious crimes such as shoplifting and purse snatching are also being committed more often than they were in the past. The graph on the opposite page shows that the amount of serious crime in 1974 was about three times as great as it was in 1960. Studies indicate that crime is increasing rapidly in our cities and also in smaller communities throughout the nation. In fact, the crime rate is now increasing more rapidly in suburbs and rural areas than it is in the larger cities.

**Crime is taking away the rights and freedoms of many people in our communities.** People live in communities in order to

meet their needs more successfully than they could if each person lived alone. To live together happily in communities, however, people must live by laws that protect the rights and freedoms of all the members of the community. (See pages 118 and 214.) A small number of people who break these laws take away the rights and freedoms of the other members of the community.

The increase in crime makes it more difficult for citizens in all parts of our country to meet their needs. Each year, thousands of people are injured or killed in criminal attacks. Billions of dollars in cash, household goods, and merchandise are stolen from homes, factories, and offices. Also, large amounts of money are being spent on various means of preventing crime, such as burglar alarms and other security systems. Many homeowners and business firms are installing stronger locks and buying watchdogs. All people must pay higher prices for the products they buy, because businesses must make up for the losses they suffer and the extra money they spend to combat crime. In addition, people must pay higher taxes when governments have to spend large sums of money for police officers, lawcourts, and prisons.

In areas where there is a great deal of crime, people are constantly fearful and suspicious of each

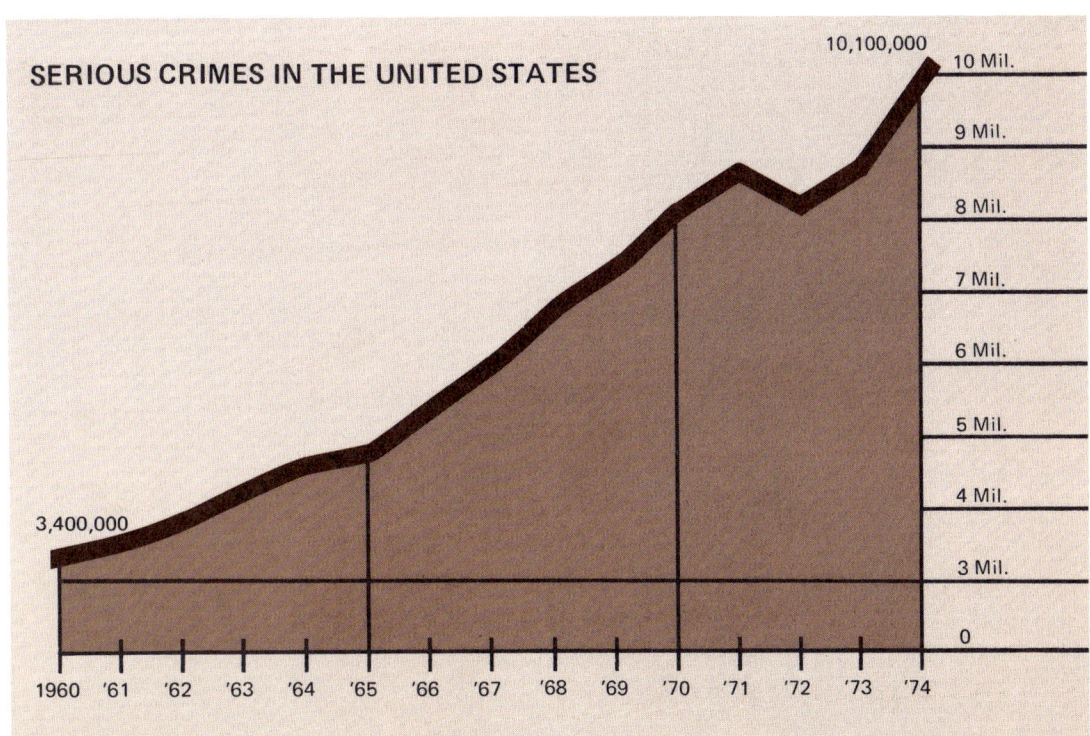

SERIOUS CRIMES IN THE UNITED STATES

other. As a result, they are less willing to make friends with their neighbors or to work together on useful community projects. Crime causes people to have less freedom than they enjoyed before. For example, the people living in a city neighborhood may no longer feel free to walk in a park because they are afraid of being attacked and robbed.

**The battle against crime.** Today, people in the United States are trying in various ways to solve the problem of crime. Many communities are hiring more police officers and buying better equipment for catching criminals. New methods are being used to prevent crimes from taking place. For example, many stores are now equipped with television cameras that allow employees to watch for shoplifters. The United States government is trying to stop the smuggling of heroin and other drugs from foreign countries. This may reduce the number of thefts and other crimes that are committed by drug users.

Many people believe that the best way to prevent crime is to make sure that persons who break the law are punished severely. Criminals who are set free after only a short time in prison often turn to crime again. In fact, about half of all the crimes in our country are committed by persons who have been in prison at least once in the past. Experts believe that changes are needed in our justice system to enable our courts to deal more severely with such "repeaters."

At the present time, it is quite easy for citizens of the United States to buy guns and other weapons for their own use. Some people believe that the number of serious crimes could be reduced by making it illegal or more difficult for a person to own certain kinds of guns. Other people argue that stronger gun-control laws would help criminals rather than law-abiding citizens, since criminals would probably be able to obtain all the guns they wanted illegally.

In many communities today, private citizens are working together to stop the spread of crime. For example, a group of neighbors may take turns patrolling the area in which they live. If they see any

Cooperation

See pages 218–219

**Education helps communities reduce crime.** According to scholars who have made a special study of crime, education is the most important way in which a community can reduce crime. People must build constructive values that will help them decide what is right and what is wrong, and they must learn that crime harms the entire community. What are some other ways in which a community can prevent or reduce crime? What are two important ways in which citizens can cooperate to help solve the problem of crime?

signs of a crime being committed, they report it immediately to the police. Some citizen groups teach homeowners various ways of protecting their property from such criminals as burglars and car thieves.

**Crime prevention through education.** Scholars who have made a special study of crime report that all of the methods mentioned above are helpful in reducing crime. They believe, however, that education is the most important way of fighting crime. According to these scholars, people must build constructive values that will help them decide what is right and what is wrong. They must learn that crime takes away rights and freedoms and harms the entire community. They must also learn that in the long run "crime does not pay," since most criminals are eventually caught.

**Crime prevention through social services.** Specialists in crime prevention also point out that the program of social services in our country reduces crime. These services make certain that no one in any community needs to steal in order to obtain food, clothing, or shelter. However, some scholars argue that communities should also provide better housing in poor neighborhoods and more recreation programs for young people. They say that people should have more opportunities for education and well-paying jobs. According to this point of view, people who are able to earn a good living will be less likely to turn to crime as a means of satisfying their needs.

**Every person in our country shares in the responsibility for preventing crime.** Perhaps the most important way in which a citizen can help solve the problem of crime is to obey all local community laws as well as the laws of our country. But experts tell us there is another important way in which our citizens can help. If every person who observes or has knowledge of a crime would report it, many more criminals could be arrested and brought to trial. Our system of justice depends not only on the police and our courts, but also on the cooperation of our citizens.

**Children in a gym class.** Almost every human being is born with the possibility of achieving a happy, useful life. The South, like other parts of our country, is making great progress in providing people with the opportunities and the freedom to satisfy their needs. Which basic needs do you think these children are satisfying?

## Progress in the South

**The South has the same problems that face the rest of our country.** The people of the South suffer from the same problems that are found in other parts of the United States. They, too, are trying hard to find solutions to the serious problems discussed in this chapter.

Most workers in the South today have jobs that enable them to earn a satisfactory living. During recent years, the growth of industry has provided new jobs for hundreds of thousands of factory workers. With the help of the federal government, many southern farmers have learned how to run their farms more efficiently. The federal government has also helped people in some parts of the South to make better use of their natural resources. (See TVA feature on pages 192-195.)

**Workers in an engineering office.** In the South, as in other parts of the United States, a growing number of well-paying jobs are being filled by members of minority groups. In some places, candidates belonging to minority groups have been elected to important government positions.

Today, the South is providing better opportunities for education than ever before. A greater proportion of young people are finishing high school and attending college.

People in the South have become much more healthy in recent years. For example, as late as the 1940's more than two million southerners suffered from a serious disease called malaria. The germs that cause malaria are carried from one person to another by a certain kind of mosquito. Now, modern methods of controlling mosquitoes have wiped out this disease in the South. With the rise of family incomes,

people in the South are able to afford more nourishing food and better medical care.

Like other parts of the United States, the South is making progress toward ending prejudice and discrimination. For example, citizens are no longer required to pass a literacy test or pay a special tax before they can vote. As a result, the number of black voters in the South has increased rapidly. Some districts have elected black candidates to important government posts. Black people are no longer required to attend separate schools or to sit in separate sections of buses and trains. In addition, a growing number of interesting and well-paying jobs are being filled by women and members of minority groups.

The increase in crime is a serious problem in the South, just as it is in other parts of our country. Today many southerners are working together to prevent crime in their communities. In New Orleans, for example, several thousand persons have joined a group that organizes neighborhood patrols and instructs people on ways to protect their homes from thieves. As a result, the number of burglaries committed in these neighborhoods has dropped sharply. Progress in the fight against crime will come faster if more citizens cooperate in their efforts to solve this important problem.

Thinking Together

As a class, discuss the following statements:

1. Unsolved social problems not only harm individuals, but they also harm our country as a whole.

2. All the citizens in a democracy share in the responsibility of working toward solving their country's social problems.

Before the discussion, think critically about each statement. Do you agree with the statement, or do you disagree? Make a list of the reasons for your belief.

# 10 The Arts

**A Problem To Solve**
<u>How do the arts of the South help us understand the people of this region?</u> In forming hypotheses to solve this problem, you will need to consider each of the following:
1. southern painting and architecture
2. literature of the South
3. music of the South
4. southern crafts

To solve this problem, you will need to do additional research in other sources.

See pages 256-258

Many of our country's great writers, painters, architects, and musicians have lived in the South. Through their works artists express their thoughts and emotions. As you explore various works of art created in the South, you will not only gain a better understanding of this area's history, but you will also discover some of the values important to the people of the South.

**Architecture.** Southerners have created many fine examples of architecture. During colonial times southern planters built handsome Georgian-style homes, which were modeled after a style of architecture popular in England.

After the Revolutionary War, classical Greek and Roman styles of architecture became popular in the United States. Our third president, Thomas Jefferson, borrowed ideas from the classical Roman style in designing his own home, Monticello. Jefferson also designed the Capitol at Richmond and several buildings for the University of Virginia.

**Monticello,** Thomas Jefferson's home, is located near Charlottesville, Virginia.

*Daniel Boone Coming Through the Cumberland Gap* is one of George Caleb Bingham's best-known paintings. Bingham, who grew up in Virginia, became famous for his paintings of early American life.

Wealthy cotton planters in Mississippi, Alabama, and Georgia built elaborate homes in a style known as Greek Revival. Outstanding features of these homes are stately white columns and two-story porches, built to shield the rooms from sun and allow space for outdoor living. Many such homes can still be seen in Natchez, Mississippi, on the banks of the Mississippi River. In some parts of Louisiana, beautiful wrought-iron balconies and gates show the influence of the early French settlers.

**Painting and sculpture.** Many American painters have made their homes in the South. Perhaps the best known is George Caleb Bingham, who was born in Virginia. He was one of our country's outstanding nineteenth-century painters and is well known for his paintings of subjects from American history. One of his most famous pictures is entitled *Daniel Boone Coming Through the Cumberland Gap*. In his later years, Bingham lived in Missouri and painted many pictures showing life in the Midwest.

Frank Duveneck was a Kentucky-born artist who spent much of his life in Europe. Duveneck's style of painting influenced many other American artists. He used broad, flat strokes to show everyday scenes. Duveneck was also a sculptor and an etcher.*

**Literature.** In the early days of our country, some of the leading writers in the South were also well-known statesmen. Thomas Jefferson wrote the Declaration of Independence and many papers on political and scientific subjects. James Madison, who also lived in Virginia, was one of the authors of *The Federalist*. This was a series of papers about the United States Constitution.

By the end of the nineteenth century, several southern writers of fiction had become widely known. Joel Chandler Harris wrote a series of delightful animal tales known as the "Uncle Remus" stories. His quaint characters such as Brer Rabbit, Brer Fox, and Tar Baby are still popular today.

Many of America's major twentieth-century novelists were born in the South. William Faulkner used his home state of Mississippi as the setting for many novels, such as *The Sound and the Fury* and *Light in August*. In 1949 he was awarded the Nobel Prize for literature. Faulkner and several other southern writers have received Pulitzer prizes for fiction. Among these are Margaret Mitchell, for *Gone With the Wind*, and Harper Lee, for *To Kill a Mockingbird*.

Another important southern writer was Thomas Wolfe. He wrote several long novels that include descriptions of the beautiful countryside in North Carolina, where he was born. His best-known work, *Look Homeward, Angel*, is based on his own experiences.

Many novelists born in the South have written realistically of the problems faced by rural and small-town southerners. Among these are Erskine Caldwell, Carson McCullers, and Eudora Welty. Another is Richard Wright, one of America's first major black novelists. Other southern-born novelists include Truman Capote, Frank Yerby, and Du Bose Heyward.

Short-story writer William Sydney Porter wrote under the pen name of O. Henry. Eudora Welty and Truman

*See Glossary

**William Faulkner,** a great American author, lived in Mississippi. He used his home state as the setting for many of his novels, such as *The Sound and the Fury* and *Light in August*.

See pages 220-223

**Try this experiment.** Imagine you are walking down a street in Tokyo, Japan. Write a paragraph describing the things you see, hear, and smell. Now write another paragraph describing a walk down the street you live on. Which of your descriptions is more complete? Why is this true?

William Faulkner, like many writers who have lived in the South, used southern characters and places to express his own feelings to his readers.
1. Why do you think Faulkner used southern people and places in his novels?
2. Do you think Faulkner could have written convincingly about the South if he had not lived there? Give your reasons for thinking so.

Capote are famous for their short stories as well as their novels.

The South has also produced many fine poets and dramatists. Important poets born in the South include Sidney Lanier, John Gould Fletcher, John Crowe Ransom, and Robert Penn Warren. Warren has received Pulitzer prizes for both poetry and fiction. Tennessee Williams, one of our leading playwrights, has twice received the Pulitzer Prize for drama. Many of his plays are about people in the South.

**Music.** Much of our country's popular music originated in the South. In fact, New Orleans is often called the "cradle of jazz," although no one knows exactly where or when jazz began. Around 1890-1910 young musicians in New Orleans and other parts of the South combined elements from Negro spirituals, marching tunes, and gospel songs to create a new rhythmic form of music called jazz. Louis Armstrong, an internationally known jazz trumpeter, was born in New Orleans and started his career in that city. W. C. Handy, a jazz composer best known for his "St. Louis Blues," was born in Alabama, but spent part of his life in New Orleans.

The Negro spirituals that influenced early jazz musicians were often sung by field hands as they worked in the cotton fields of southern plantations.

Louis Armstrong, one of the best-known jazz performers in the world, was born in New Orleans. Jazz originated in the South sometime around the beginning of the twentieth century.

"Swing Low, Sweet Chariot" is an example of one of these spirituals.

Many well-known folk songs have come from the mountains and valleys of the South. The lovely ballad "Down in the Valley," once heard only in the mountains of Kentucky, is now known throughout the United States.

The style of popular music known as "country and western" developed mainly in the South. For many years, the radio program "Grand Ole Opry," which features country-and-western music, has been broadcast from Nashville, Tennessee. This city also produces most of the country-and-western recordings made in the United States. Many leading singers and composers live in Nashville.

**Crafts.** Pioneers who settled in the Appalachian Highlands of the South made nearly everything they needed by hand. Using native materials they skillfully fashioned clothing, furniture, pottery, and other household items. Even after machine-made goods became readily available, many mountain people took pride in tanning their own leather, dyeing their own wool, spinning their own cloth, and making their

**Chet Atkins** is one of our country's most popular country-and-western artists. Like jazz, this type of music originated in the South. Perhaps you would like to play a country-and-western record and a jazz record. Then, as a class, discuss the following questions.
1. Do you think country-and-western music and jazz are both "arts"? Why do you think this?
2. Which of these kinds of music do you like better? Why?

**A North Carolina woman weaving cloth** on a handloom. Skilled workers throughout the South create beautiful handicrafts such as bedspreads, pottery, and furniture.

own dishes. In recent years, community leaders have encouraged mountain people to make and sell their handicrafts, not only as a source of income, but also to assure that knowledge of these arts will not be lost. Throughout the South, people are able to express their creative ability by producing beautiful and useful objects.

In North Carolina, for example, skilled workers make sturdy rocking chairs and tables by hand, out of hickory or walnut wood. Others carve graceful stringed instruments called dulcimers from maple or cherry. In the western part of the state, potters shape native clay into attractive teapots, candlesticks, bowls, and other items, using their own designs. Many mountain people raise and shear their own sheep, spin the wool, and dye it with native bark. Then they design and weave beautiful woolen bedspreads. Collectors are willing to pay good prices for these homespun spreads. Other craft workers create patchwork quilts or cornhusk dolls.

**Investigate Arts and Crafts in Your Community**

As a class, do research to discover what kinds of arts and crafts are carried on in your own community. Then make a bulletin-board display showing newspaper and magazine articles about local artists and craft workers. Perhaps an artist or craft worker in your community would be willing to talk to your class about his or her work.

# Part 4
# Earning a Living

In the South, as in other parts of our country, people do many different types of work. For example, the man shown in the picture at left earns his living by farming. In what other ways do you suppose people in the South earn their living? Make a list of the kinds of jobs you think people in the South might have. The following questions will suggest some of the types of work you may wish to include on your list.

- What are the main types of farming in the South?
- What natural resources are found in the South? In what ways do people in the South use these resources?
- What types of industry are there in the South?
- What are some of the ways in which tools and machines help people in the South do their work?

# 11 Farming

**Early colonists found the South well suited to agriculture.** The first Europeans to arrive in the South discovered that much of the land would produce good crops. In some areas, the soil was very rich. The climate of the South was warm, and rain was plentiful. People in Europe heard about the fertile land in the South and came to this part of the New World in great numbers.

Many of the southern colonists began to grow crops that could be shipped to England and sold there for high prices. By raising a single cash crop, such as tobacco, some southern planters became very wealthy. In the eighteenth century, huge plantations spread over the most fertile parts of the Coastal Plain in Virginia, the Carolinas, and Georgia. Where the land was hilly or less fertile, there were many smaller farms.

In Virginia and North Carolina, tobacco was the most valuable crop. By 1772 Virginia was exporting more than 70 million pounds of tobacco to Great Britain each year. Raising tobacco was so profitable that some southern planters used almost all of their land for this one crop. These planters had to purchase much of their food from colonies farther north.

The main cash crops produced in South Carolina and Georgia were rice and indigo. Planters grew rice in hot, marshy lowlands. On sandy uplands, farmers raised indigo. The indigo plant was used to make a valuable blue dye. In the year 1773, more than 80 million pounds of rice and more than a million pounds of indigo were exported from these two colonies.

Little cotton was produced in the southern colonies. This was mainly because the preparation of cotton for market was such a slow process. The fluffy fibers in cotton bolls are attached to many

**Farmlands in Virginia.** A warm climate, plentiful rainfall, and large areas of fertile soil have helped make agriculture important in the South. List some of the major farm products of the South. Which of these products can be produced in other parts of the United States?

Exchange

See pages 238-239

**The New Orleans cotton market** is shown in this 1873 painting by the French artist Edgar Degas. During the 1700's and 1800's, many southern farmers grew a single crop, such as cotton or tobacco, which could be sold to people in other parts of the United States and in foreign countries. What are some of the advantages and disadvantages of raising a single cash crop?

seeds. These seeds must be removed before the fibers can be used to make cloth. In colonial times, the seeds had to be removed by hand. It took twenty-five workers one hundred days to clean the cotton grown by one field hand in a single season.

Near the end of the eighteenth century, textile factories in England began using new machines that could produce cotton cloth quickly and cheaply. The owners of these factories needed large amounts of cotton fibers and were willing to pay high prices for them. Southern planters knew that cotton would grow well on their land. If a fast, easy way could be found to clean the cotton, the planters would be able to export huge amounts of cotton fibers to England. They could become rich.

In 1793 a young American named Eli Whitney invented a machine called the cotton gin. Using this machine, a worker was able to clean fifty times as much cotton as he or she could by hand. Now the seeds were easily removed from all the cotton that southern planters raised. The cotton was sold at a good profit. Most of the planters who had been growing rice or indigo began to raise cotton instead.

After producing large amounts of cotton for several years, many plantations in the Carolinas and Georgia no longer produced good yields. Cotton farmers began to move to fertile new lands in Alabama, Mississippi, and Louisiana. By 1849 cotton had become the main crop in a wide belt that stretched across much of the South. Tobacco had remained important in Virginia and North Carolina, and was now also a leading crop in Kentucky.

**Poor farming methods were used in many parts of the South.** Until the present century, many farmers in the South continued to raise a single crop on most of their land. On some farms, the main crop was cotton. On others, it was tobacco. Although some farmers made large profits from one-crop farming, this method had disadvantages.

One disadvantage for one-crop farmers was that they could not earn steady incomes. Cotton was often damaged by the boll* weevil or other insects, or by disease. Tobacco, too, was often attacked by insects or disease. In a year when the crop was badly damaged, one-crop farmers would have little to sell. Even when their crop was large, they could not depend on good incomes. The demand for farm products such as cotton and tobacco was not steady, and prices varied greatly from year to year.

The farmer who raised only tobacco or cotton faced another disadvantage. When one of these crops was planted on the same land year after year, the soil became less fertile. This was because both cotton and tobacco take large amounts of plant food from the soil.

In some parts of the South, poor farming methods caused the soil to wash away, or erode. Before the land was settled, it had been covered with grass or trees. This kept the soil from being washed away by rainwater. When the land was cleared and used for growing crops, rainwater washed away the fertile topsoil and cut deep gullies in the earth. After a few years, the land could no longer be used for growing crops. Some farmers were forced to move to new land.

**Better methods and new equipment have helped southern farmers.** For many years, agricultural experts have been teaching farmers better farming methods. These improved methods help conserve natural resources and also help farmers produce better crops.

Most southern farmers no longer grow cotton or tobacco on the same land year after year. Instead, they grow a variety of crops. One year cotton or

*See Glossary

**Contour farming in Louisiana.** Many farmers who live in hilly areas plant their crops in rows that curve around the hillsides, rather than in straight, up-and-down rows. Why do they do this?

tobacco may be planted in a field. The next year, the field may be used for growing a crop such as soybeans or clover. These crops require less plant food than cotton or tobacco. Sometimes they are plowed into the soil to help restore its fertility. Fertilizer may also be added. In one or two years, the land is ready to grow cotton or tobacco again. The practice of raising different crops on the same land at different times is called crop rotation.

Good conservation practices have also lessened erosion. Farmers plant crops in rows that curve around the hillsides, instead of in straight, up-and-down rows. This is called contour farming. Land too hilly or not fertile enough for raising crops is used for pasture or growing trees.

New equipment has also changed southern farming. Modern farm implements such as tractors and mechanical cotton pickers are doing work that was formerly done by human labor. A mechanical cotton picker can harvest cotton fifty times faster than a person can harvest it by hand.

Today, the South is still an important farming region. It produces many different kinds of crops and livestock. These farm products are used by people throughout the United States and in a number of foreign countries.

**Livestock.** In recent years, southern farmers have been raising more livestock than ever before. The warm climate and plentiful rainfall in the South are good for growing hay and grass, which provide food for cattle and other farm animals. Many areas that are hilly or that have poor soil can be used more profitably for raising livestock than for growing crops.

Poultry and eggs rank first in value among the farm products of the South.

**Beef cattle in a southern feedlot.** Livestock raising is an important kind of farming in the South.

In this region are many farms where chickens are raised for their eggs and for meat. Arkansas, Georgia, and Alabama lead the nation in the production of broiler chickens. There are also many turkey farms in the South, especially in North Carolina, Arkansas, and Virginia.

The raising of cattle is another important kind of farming in the South. Large herds of beef cattle graze on rich, green pastures in Kentucky, Tennessee, Mississippi, and other states. Some of these cattle are later sent to

**Using Natural Resources**

See pages 226-229

Farmers in the South, like those in other parts of the world, make use of several different natural resources. List these resources, and explain how each of them is used in growing crops and raising livestock. Do you think it is important for farmers to be careful in their use of natural resources? Why? Why not? What can happen when any of these resources are used wastefully? Sometimes nature does not provide all the resources farmers need to grow crops in a certain area. Do research about agriculture to discover ways in which farmers are able to make up for natural resources that are lacking.

Areas that are not well suited to growing crops can often be used as pastures for livestock.

### Exploring the Growing Season

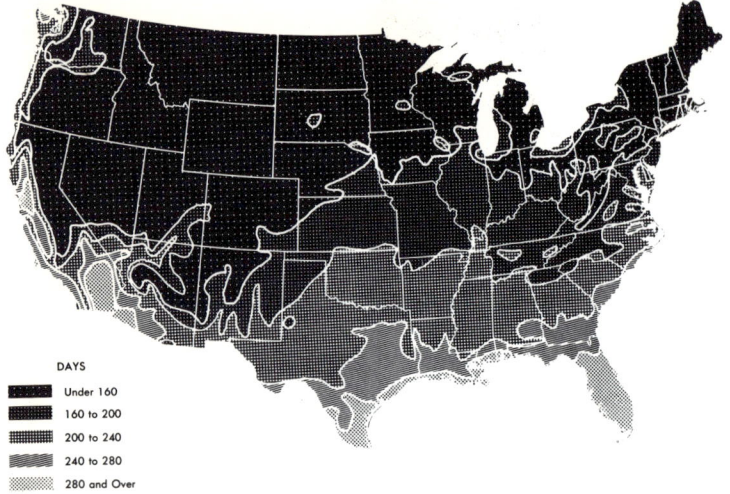

### Cotton Harvested

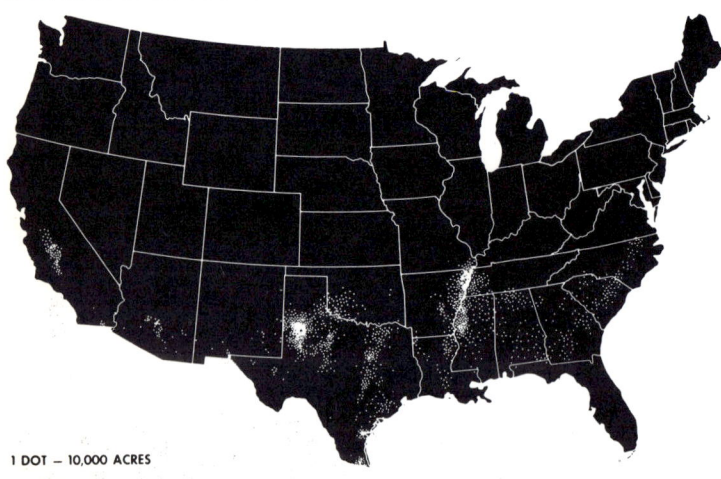

1 DOT = 10,000 ACRES

The growing season is the period of time when crops can be grown outdoors without danger of being killed by frost. Most of the South has a growing season of 200 days or more.

Some crops can be raised only in areas where the growing season is fairly long. One of these crops is cotton, which needs at least 200 days in a row without frost. If you will compare the two maps on this page, you will see that the cotton-growing areas of the South have a frost-free period of 200 days or more. Other crops raised in the South that need a long growing season are oranges, rice, and sugarcane. The South also produces many crops that do not require such a long growing season.

feedlots, where they are fed corn and other grains to fatten them for market. Large numbers of dairy cows are also raised in the South. Many of the dairy farms are located near the larger cities, to supply fresh milk to the people who live there.

Southern farmers also raise several other kinds of livestock. Although hogs are raised throughout this region, the main hog-producing states are North Carolina and Georgia. Sheep farming is especially important in Virginia and Kentucky. Valuable horses are raised on large farms in the Bluegrass area of Kentucky and in the Nashville Basin of Tennessee.

**Cotton.** Cotton has been a leading crop in the South for almost two hundred years. Today, large amounts of cotton are grown in Texas and states farther west. But the southern states still produce nearly half of all the cotton grown in our country.

Most of the South's cotton grows along the Mississippi River in an area that stretches from northern Louisiana to northern Tennessee. (Compare the map on pages 14 and 15 with the cotton map on this page.) This area is well

**Picking cotton by machine in Mississippi.** Nearly half of all the cotton grown in our country comes from the southern states. Which two states lead the South in the production of cotton?

suited to raising cotton. The land is level and covered with a deep layer of fertile topsoil. Rainfall is moderate, and the growing season lasts two hundred days or more. Mississippi and Arkansas are the South's main cotton states.

Let's visit a cotton farm near the Mississippi River. It is September, and the cotton is ready to be harvested. Rows of cotton plants covered with snowy-white bolls stretch as far as the eye can see. Huge cotton-picking machines rumble slowly through the fields, stripping the cotton bolls from the plants. The bolls are taken to buildings where gins separate the seeds from the cotton fibers. Then the fibers are pressed into giant bales, which are taken to a nearby railroad for shipment to textile mills. Not all cotton farms are as large or well equipped as this one. Some cover only a few acres and are tended by "one man and a mule."

**Tobacco.** About nine tenths of all the tobacco produced in our country comes from the South. This crop grows especially well in the light, sandy soil of the Coastal Plain. It is also raised on the Piedmont Plateau and the Interior Plains. The leading tobacco-producing states are North Carolina and Kentucky.

Tobacco must be carefully prepared for market. In June or July, the tobacco plants ripen. The leaves are picked and hung on racks in barns. Sometimes the leaves are allowed to dry, or cure, without the use of artificial heat. But many curing barns today are heated by oil or gas burners. The heat turns the leaves a rich, golden brown. After the leaves have been cured, they are sorted and taken to warehouses. There they are sold to buyers from tobacco companies. During a tobacco auction, a warehouse is a noisy, exciting place. As the buyers make offers, an auctioneer shouts out the bids in a rapid, singsong chant. Farmers usually make a good profit from growing tobacco.

**Soybeans.** Years ago, farmers in the South began planting soybeans as a rotation crop for cotton and other crops. The soybean is a legume, as members of the pea family are called. When legumes are rotated with other crops, they help to keep the soil fertile. This is because legumes can make use of nitrogen* in the air, instead of taking this substance from the soil as most plants do.

Today southern farmers earn more money from soybeans than any other

crop. The beans are used in making both meal and oil. Soybean meal is a good feed for livestock, and soybean oil is used in making margarine, paint, and many other products.

Although soybeans are grown in various parts of the South, the main producing area is the level, fertile Mississippi Valley. Arkansas and Mississippi produce more soybeans than any other states in the South.

**Fruits and vegetables.** On a snowy day in February, we enter a grocery store in New York City. A clerk is unpacking boxes of fresh oranges, celery, and tomatoes. "They just came in from Florida," she says. In some parts of the South, the long growing season makes it possible for farmers to raise crops in all seasons of the year.

Much of Florida has the warm climate needed for growing oranges and grapefruit. This state produces more than three fourths of the citrus fruit grown in the United States.

Other parts of the South also specialize in growing certain fruits or vegetables. Choice apples are grown on the western part of the Piedmont Plateau in Virginia, and in parts of the Great Valley. In South Carolina, Georgia, and other states there are huge orchards of peach trees. Sweet potatoes thrive in the light, sandy soil of the Coastal Plain. Such vegetables as celery, beans, tomatoes, cabbages, and peppers are

**Harvesting tomatoes in Florida.** During the winter months, the South supplies northern markets with tomatoes, oranges, celery, and other fresh produce grown out of doors. Explain why this is possible.

**Peanuts** grow in pods that develop under the ground. At harvesttime, the plants are plowed up and left to dry in the sun. Later, machines called combines are used to remove the pods from the dried plants.

grown on truck* farms along the Atlantic and Gulf coasts.

**Rice and other grain crops.** Many farmers in the South raise grain crops. Rice is grown in parts of Arkansas and Louisiana where the soil is heavy and the land is low and easily flooded. Rice plants must be kept standing in four to six inches of water during the time they are growing. Corn is grown in every southern state. It is used in many processed food products, such as cornmeal and hominy grits. Corn is also important as a feed for animals. Only small amounts of wheat and oats are grown in the South, because other regions have a more favorable climate for raising these grain crops.

**Other farm crops.** The sandy soil and warm climate of the Coastal Plain are excellent for growing peanuts. Georgia leads the entire nation in peanut production. Large quantities are also grown in North Carolina, Alabama, and Virginia. Cooking oil, peanut butter, and dozens of other products are made from peanuts.

Some areas in the South are especially well suited to raising certain crops. Sugarcane is grown in the Florida Everglades and in parts of southern Louisiana, where the soil is very moist and rich. Orchards of tung* trees can be found near the Gulf coast. The tung tree, which originally came from Asia, grows well in the warm, rainy climate here. Tung nuts contain a quick-drying oil that is used in making paints and varnishes. There are many large orchards of pecan trees on the Coastal Plain of the South. Georgia produces more pecan nuts than any other state in our country.

**Harvesting sugarcane.** Florida and Louisiana produce more sugarcane than any other state except Hawaii. This crop grows best where the climate is hot and the soil is very moist and fertile.

Explore Farming in the South

Imagine that you are going to buy land in the South and start a farm. Before you purchase land, you want to find out where you could grow the following crops:

    peanuts    rice    sugarcane
    cotton    tobacco    oranges

Do research to discover what the best location for growing each crop would be. You will need to find information about both the land and climate. You will also want to consider who your customers might be and how your crop could be transported to market. Summarize your findings in a written report.

Thinking Together

1. What facts help to explain why many farmers in the South began growing cotton in the late 1700's and early 1800's?
2. At first, cotton was grown mainly in the Carolinas and Georgia. After several years, however, cotton farmers began moving westward. Explain why.
3. Explain the farming methods listed below, and tell why each is important.
    crop rotation    contour farming

# 12 Natural Resources

The South has many valuable natural resources. In this part of our country are rich mineral deposits and dense forests that provide raw materials for modern industries. Some minerals found in the South are used not only as raw materials, but also as fuels for the production of electric power. In some areas, swiftly flowing rivers are used to generate hydroelectricity.

**Petroleum and natural gas.** There are large deposits of petroleum, or oil, and natural gas in the South. Oil is an important resource in Louisiana, Mississippi, Florida, and Arkansas. Most states in the South have deposits of natural gas. Louisiana leads the nation in the production of natural gas, and is second only to Texas in the amount of petroleum produced.

Petroleum is usually found deep under the ground. Most scientists believe that petroleum was formed millions of years ago, long before people lived on the earth. Much of the earth that is now dry land was then covered by shallow seas. Billions of tiny plants and animals lived in the water. As they died, they sank to the bottom. Over a period of millions of years, the remains of these dead plants and animals were covered by sand and soil carried down to the sea by rivers. Gradually, the sand and soil turned into rock. The pressure of the layers of rock helped change the plant and animal matter into petroleum.

**Using Natural Resources**

See pages 226-229

**Drilling for oil.** Petroleum is one of the South's most important mineral resources. At huge refineries, oil is changed into many useful products, such as gasoline and airplane fuel. Petroleum also provides raw materials for the chemical industry. Do research to discover what chemicals are made from petroleum. You may wish to write a report about these chemicals, called petrochemicals. Include information about how they are made and how they are used.

**A floating oil derrick** off the coast of Louisiana. Why do you think Louisiana leads all the southern states in the production of petroleum and natural gas?

To obtain petroleum, wells are drilled with special equipment. The drills are supported by tall towers called derricks, which are usually built of steel. The petroleum is brought to the surface by means of powerful pumps. It is sent to refineries, mainly through pipelines. At the refineries, the petroleum is changed into many useful products. The gasoline we use in our cars, the fuel burned in jet airplanes, and asphalt used to pave streets are a few of the many petroleum products.

Some of the South's oil deposits lie beneath the Gulf of Mexico. In many places along the coast of Louisiana, oil derricks tower above the waters of the Gulf. Some of the derricks are attached to floating platforms that can be moved from place to place. Others are anchored permanently to the floor of the Gulf. Although many oil wells are located close to shore, others are as far as eighty miles from land.

Natural gas is usually found along with petroleum. Sometimes, however, it is found alone. Pipelines carry natural gas produced in the South to cities and towns in the eastern part of our country. Natural gas is used in many homes for heating, cooking, and other purposes. It is also used as a fuel in factories.

Petroleum and natural gas provide the raw materials for making many valuable chemicals. These are called petrochemicals. Products manufactured from petrochemicals include synthetic rubber, medicines, plastics, and fertilizer.

**Four important mineral resources of the South** are iron ore, limestone, oil, and natural gas.

Iron Ore Deposits

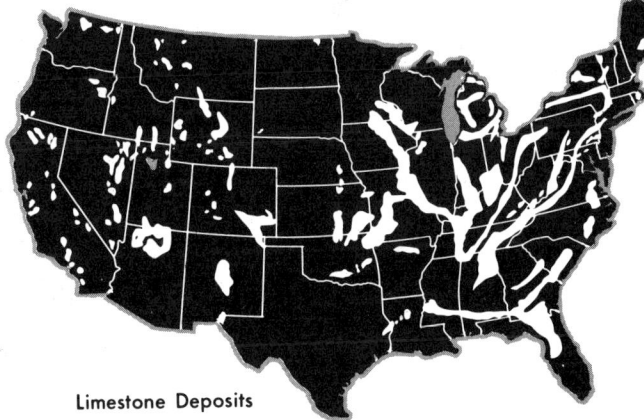

Limestone Deposits

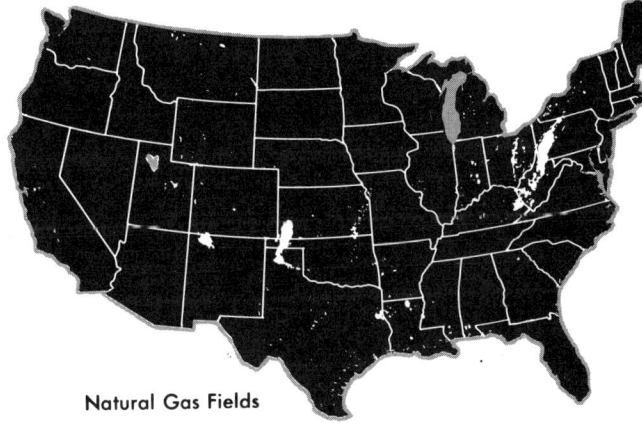

Natural Gas Fields

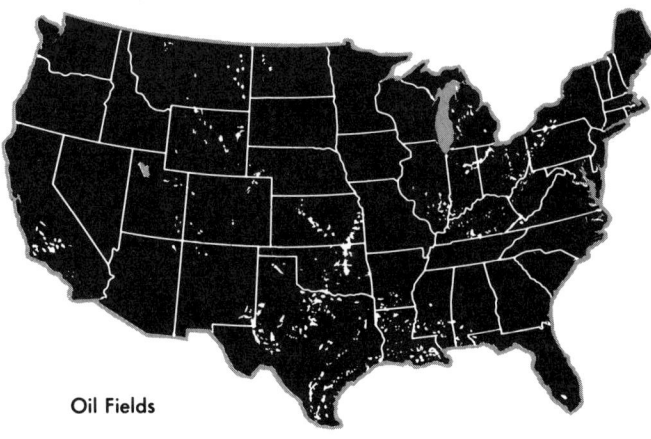

Oil Fields

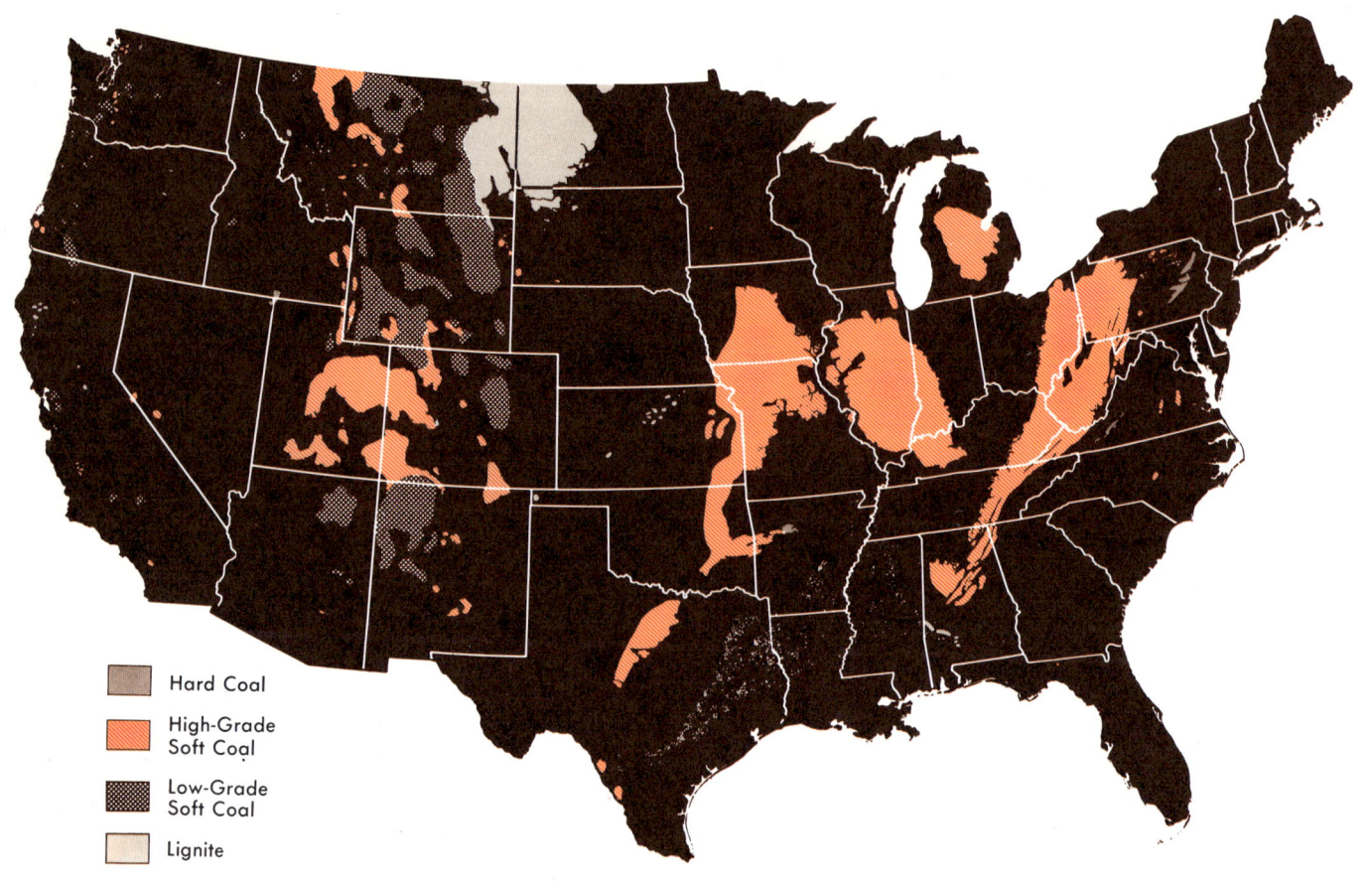

## Coalfields of the United States

The map above shows the main coal deposits in the conterminous United States. Deposits of high-grade soft coal are found in several states of the South. The most important of these are part of a huge coalfield that stretches through much of the Appalachian Highlands region. Kentucky, Virginia, Alabama, and Tennessee are among our country's leading coal-producing states.

Coal is one of our country's most important natural resources. It is burned as a fuel in homes, factories, and steam power plants. Coal also provides raw materials for industry. Iron and steel mills use large amounts of coke, which is made by roasting coal in large, airtight ovens. From the gases driven off during the coking process, thousands of different products are manufactured. Among these are medicines, dyes, and synthetics.*

Coal is a rocklike substance composed mainly of carbon* and water. It was formed millions of years ago from decayed plant matter under the pressure of overlying layers of sand, mud, and water. Different kinds of coal resulted from different kinds of plants and different amounts of pressure. The best coals are those that contain the most carbon, since they give off the most heat when burned.

There are four main kinds of coal. Hard coal, or anthracite, is a high-quality coal that burns without much smoke. Formerly, anthracite was often used for home heating. This type of coal is not very plentiful, however, and little is now mined. High-grade soft coal has a high carbon content, but it gives off large amounts of smoke. This type of coal is also called bituminous coal. Low-grade soft coal, or subbituminous coal, is poor in quality. It is about three-fourths carbon and one-fourth water. Lignite is a soft, brown coal that contains large amounts of water. It is a still poorer quality coal.

*See Glossary

**Coal**. The South has large deposits of high-grade soft coal. (See map on opposite page.) Most of these deposits are in the Appalachian Highlands. They are part of the huge Appalachian coalfield that stretches from northwestern Pennsylvania into Alabama. Almost one third of the coal mined in the United States comes from Kentucky, Virginia, Alabama, and Tennessee. Kentucky ranks second among all the states in the value of coal produced.

Coal produced in the South is used in many ways. Much of it is burned as fuel in homes and factories. Iron and steel plants in Alabama and Tennessee use large amounts of coal from nearby mines. Much of the coal used by these

**Ecology**

**Strip mining coal in Kentucky.** Much of the South's coal is mined by this method. Huge power shovels remove the top layers of soil and rock to expose the coal deposits that lie underneath. Then the coal can be broken up and removed. Many people object to strip mining because they feel it is harmful to the ecology of an area. What is the meaning of the term "ecology"? Why is strip mining considered so harmful? To answer these questions, you may wish to refer to the ecology entry in the Glossary and do research in other sources.

plants is made into coke, which is needed for smelting* iron ore. Certain chemicals are obtained from gases given off during the coking process. They are used in making paints, detergents, dyes, and other useful products.

Trains carry some of the coal from southern mines to ports on the Atlantic coast or Lake Erie. From Atlantic port cities such as Newport News, Virginia, and Charleston, South Carolina, coal is shipped to other seaports in the United States, Canada, and western Europe. From port cities on Lake Erie, large freighters take coal to other ports on the Great Lakes.

**Iron ore.** There are valuable deposits of iron ore in the Appalachian Highlands. The most important deposits in the South are in Alabama, near Birmingham. Alabama is one of our country's leading states in the production of iron ore. It is the only state in the South that produces much of this min-

*See Glossary

Operating a loading machine in an iron mine. Iron ore is one of many valuable minerals found in the South. The most important deposits are near Birmingham, Alabama, in the Appalachian Highlands.

## IRON AND STEEL

The three main minerals needed for making iron and steel are iron ore, coal, and limestone. As the map at left shows, these three minerals are found near the city of Birmingham, Alabama. This is one of the few areas in the world where deposits of iron ore, coal, and limestone are located close together. Trucks and trains carry raw materials to steel plants in the Birmingham area.

To make iron, large amounts of iron ore, coke,* and limestone are placed in a giant blast furnace. Then a blast of extremely hot air is blown into the furnace. The air makes the coke burn with an intense heat that melts the iron ore. The limestone combines with waste materials in the ore to form slag, which rises to the top. Molten iron containing carbon collects at the bottom of the furnace.

To make steel, some of the carbon and other unwanted materials must be removed from the molten iron. This may be done in various ways. Most of the steel made in the United States is produced by a fast, modern method called the basic oxygen process. In this process, oxygen is blown into a special furnace through a tube, at an extremely high speed. The oxygen helps burn out the unwanted materials in the molten metal. In less than an hour, the refined steel is poured out of the furnace. Sometimes small quantities of other metals are added to the molten steel to make special kinds of steel, such as stainless steel.

ALABAMA

Coalfields
Iron Ore Deposits
Limestone Quarries
Scale of Miles
0   20   40

eral, although small amounts have been mined in Georgia and Tennessee. Two important metals, iron and steel, are made from iron ore at huge plants in or near Birmingham. The special feature above gives more information about this industry.

**Bauxite.** Bauxite, the chief ore from which aluminum is made, is also a valuable resource. All of the bauxite mined in our country comes from the South, mainly from Arkansas. The bauxite is mined from huge open pits. Then it is sent to processing plants to be made into alumina.* The finished metal, aluminum, is produced from the alumina. More aluminum is used in the United States than any other kind of metal except iron and steel.

The large quantities of bauxite mined in the South are not nearly enough to meet our country's need for aluminum. Most of the aluminum produced here is made from bauxite or alumina imported from other countries.

**Zinc and pyrites.** The South also has deposits of zinc ore and pyrites.* The largest deposits of these minerals are found in the Appalachian Highlands in Tennessee. This state is a leading producer of zinc ore and pyrites. Zinc ore is shipped from Tennessee to smelters in other parts of our country for processing. Copper and sulfuric acid are produced from pyrites at plants located near the mines. Sulfuric acid is used in manufacturing many industrial chemicals and chemical products.

**A phosphate mine in Florida.** About nine tenths of all the phosphate rock produced in the United States comes from the South. Most of this rock is made into fertilizer. Name three other minerals produced in the South that are used to make chemicals and chemical products.

**Other mineral resources.** The South has several other minerals that are important to chemical industries. Florida is our nation's leading producer of phosphate rock. Smaller amounts are mined in North Carolina and Tennessee. Most of the phosphate rock is made into fertilizer. This is done by heating the rock or by treating it with a chemical such as sulfuric acid. In Louisiana, large amounts of sulfur are mined. Most of the sulfur is combined with other chemicals to make sulfuric acid. Louisiana also has large deposits of salt. This important mineral is used not only in food processing, but also in many other industries. Chemical companies use salt in making hundreds of different chemical compounds.

Quarries in the South yield several types of stone. Tennessee, Georgia, and Alabama produce fine marble, much of which is used as building stone. The finest marble is used for monuments and statues. Georgia produces more granite than any other state in our country. Granite is often used in the construction of large buildings and bridges because it can withstand great pressure. In several states of the South, limestone is quarried. Limestone is a good building stone because it can be cut easily and does not split. It is also used in making cement, and in the production of iron and steel. (See special feature on page 183.)

Several types of clay are found in the South. Georgia and South Carolina are leading producers of kaolin, sometimes called china clay. Most of the kaolin is used as a filler in paper or as a coating to make it smooth. It is also used as a filler for rubber products. Some kaolin is used to make fine china and pottery.

Another clay produced in the South is fuller's earth, which is used to remove impurities from oils. Clays used in making bricks are found in every state in the South.

**Forest resources.** More than half of the land in the South is covered with forests. (See map on page 188.) The warm climate, long growing season, and plentiful rainfall in the South help trees to grow rapidly. Huge forests of pine trees grow on much of the Coastal Plain and on the mountain ranges in the Appalachian Highlands. Hardwoods such as oak, hickory, gum, and walnut are also found in the South, mainly in the highland regions. In addition, many farmers in the southern states raise pine trees on plantations called tree farms.

In order to learn how the forests of the South are used, let's watch a logging crew at work. The lumberjacks have driven to work from their homes a few miles away. They live in a logging camp in the forest only when they are working far from home in rugged areas that are hard to reach by car. Before the lumberjacks begin work, a forester marks the trees that will be cut. Only large trees or diseased trees are marked. The healthy young trees will not be cut. As we watch the lumberjacks at work, the whine of their saws and the crash of the falling trees are so loud that we can hardly hear each other talk. The fallen trees are cut into logs and sent to sawmills. There the logs are cut into lumber, which is used in the construction of buildings and in the manufacture of furniture and other wood products.

**Cutting trees in a southern forest.** More than half of the land in the South is forested.

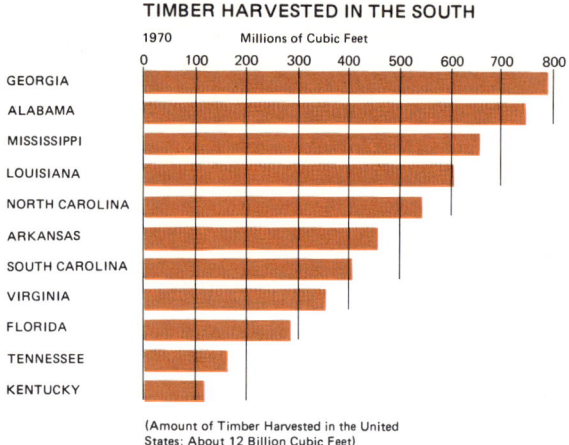

The graph above shows the estimated amounts of timber harvested in 1970 by the states of the South. Nearly one half of all the timber harvested in our country comes from the South.

The map below shows the distribution of forests in the southern part of our country. Notice that every state in the South has many thousands of acres of forest land. More than half the land in the South is wooded.

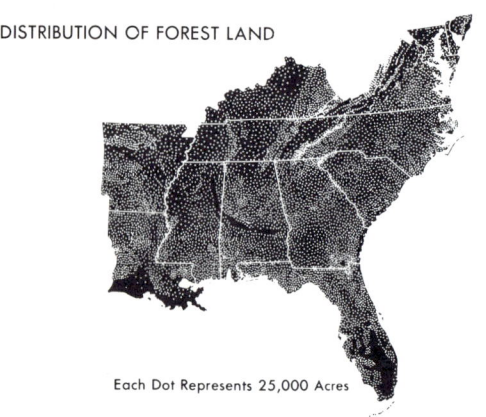

Nearly one half of our country's timber comes from southern forests. Georgia, Alabama, Mississippi, Louisiana, and North Carolina are among the leading states in our country in the amount of timber harvested.

Large amounts of lumber are cut from the timber harvested in the South. Most of this lumber is cut from pine trees, but oak, cypress, and other trees also provide lumber.

Several other products come from the forests of the South. Valuable oils are obtained from the sap of living pine trees or from dead pinewood. These oils are distilled to produce turpentine and rosin. Turpentine is used mainly as a paint thinner. Rosin is used in the manufacture of paint, paper, soap, and many other products. Some of the wood from southern forests is made into wood pulp, which is used in making paper and other products. There are many pulp and paper mills in the South.

**Fish and sponges.** Each year, fishing boats bring hundreds of millions of

**Shrimp fishermen.** Shellfish such as shrimp and crabs are taken in great numbers from the waters that border the coasts of the South. Red snapper, mullet, and other fish are also caught in the South.

pounds of fish to ports in the South. Most of the fish come from the Atlantic Ocean or the Gulf of Mexico. The value of the fish caught in the South is almost one third of the value of our country's total catch.

Louisiana, Florida, and Virginia lead the South in the amount of money received for their fish catches. (See graph on this page.) Louisiana not only leads the South in the value of its catch, but also leads the nation in the pounds of fish caught.

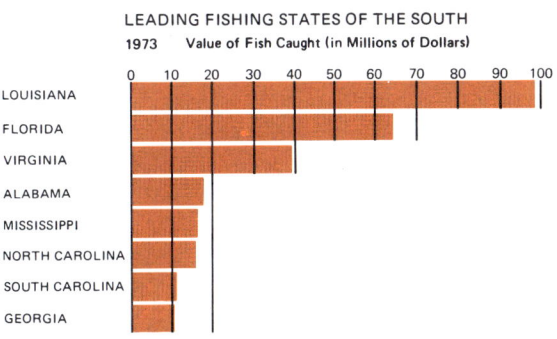

LEADING FISHING STATES OF THE SOUTH
1973  Value of Fish Caught (in Millions of Dollars)

(Total Value of Fish Caught in the United States $907,400,000)

This graph shows the value in dollars of the 1973 fish catch in eight states of the South. The figures include money received for both finfish and shellfish.

Many different kinds of fish are caught in the South. These include red snapper, mullet, and groupers, all of which are used for food. Large amounts of menhaden are also caught. These are made into fertilizer, fish oil, and meal. Shellfish such as shrimp, oysters, and crabs are taken in great numbers from the waters off the coasts of the South. Most of the shellfish are canned or frozen and shipped to different parts of the country. Shrimp bring more money to people in the South than all other kinds of fish combined.

**A sponge diver at Tarpon Springs, Florida.** Tarpon Springs is one of the world's leading sponge-fishing ports. Sponge divers may go down a hundred feet or more to find the sponges on the ocean floor.

In Florida there are divers who bring up valuable sponges from the ocean floor. These people usually wear diving suits, and may go down a hundred feet or more to find the sponges. They use special hooks to pry the sponges loose from the rocks, shells, or other objects to which they are attached. Tarpon Springs, on Florida's Gulf coast, is one of the world's leading sponge-fishing ports.

**Waterpower.** The South has many rivers that can be used to produce hydroelectric power. Most of these rivers begin in the Appalachian Highlands, and their waters flow into the Atlantic Ocean or the Gulf of Mexico.

Let's find out how hydroelectric power is produced. First, a dam is built on the river to hold the water back. The water forms a large lake behind the dam. Then water from the lake is allowed to flow downward through large pipes, usually located inside the dam. In a powerhouse at the foot of the dam, the rushing water turns engines called turbines. The turbines run machines called generators, which produce electricity.

Many hydroelectric power plants have been built on the Tennessee River and its tributaries. A government agency called the Tennessee Valley Authority operates most of these power plants. You can learn more about the TVA on pages 192-195.

Dams and powerhouses have been constructed on a number of other rivers in the South. However, only a small part of the electricity produced in this region comes from hydroelectric power plants. Most of the electricity is generated in steam power plants that burn coal, oil, or natural gas.

**Thinking Together**

Use the following questions to guide your research about the natural resources of the South.

1. How is each of the following resources important to industry in the South?

   petroleum       bauxite
   coal            pine trees
   iron ore        shellfish

   You may wish to do research in Chapter 13 as well as in this chapter.

2. Explain the differences between:
   a. anthracite and bituminous coal
   b. coke and coal
   c. alumina and aluminum
   d. iron and steel

   In doing your research, be sure to refer to the Glossary and Index. You may also wish to do research in other sources.

3. How is hydroelectricity produced? Draw a diagram to illustrate your explanation. You may need to do additional research.

**Share Ideas in a Discussion**

1. What natural resources are found in the area where you live?

2. In what ways, if any, do these resources affect your life? How have they affected the development of your community?

3. Does your community depend on any resources brought in from other parts of the United States? If so, in what ways?

4. Do you believe that you should be concerned about the conservation of natural resources? Why, or why not?

5. What can you and other people in your community do to help conserve natural resources?

# Tennessee Valley Authority

The Tennessee Valley Authority is an agency of the federal government. It was established in 1933 to help people living in the watershed* of the Tennessee River. This area, usually called the Tennessee Valley, includes parts of seven states. (See map on pages 194 and 195.)

At the time TVA was founded, the people in the Tennessee Valley had a number of serious problems. Long before this, most of the forests in the area had been cut down. With few trees on the steep slopes, rainwater drained away very rapidly. This caused the Tennessee and the other rivers in the area to rise and overflow their banks. Sometimes these floods caused millions of dollars' worth of damage. Another problem was that much of the land in the area had been damaged by poor farming methods. For this reason, it was difficult for many farmers to earn a living. (See page 166.) Few other jobs were available because the Tennessee Valley did not have much industry.

TVA went to work to solve these problems. It was given control of Wilson Dam in Alabama and two nearby chemical plants, which had been built by the government in World War I. Then it began building other dams and power plants. These helped to control floods, to produce electric power, and to improve transportation on the Tennessee River. (See pages 194-195.) New industries settled in the Tennessee Valley because they could get electric power at a low price.

TVA has helped develop the resources of the Tennessee Valley in other ways also. For example, it has developed new fertilizers at its chemical facilities near Wilson Dam. It has planted trees on steep hillsides and taught people better farming methods. These measures have helped to conserve soil, water, and forests.

*See Glossary

**TVA's Wilson Dam** and chemical plants near Muscle Shoals, Alabama. Wilson Dam is one of TVA's nine dams on the Tennessee River. More hydroelectric power is generated at this dam than at any other TVA dam on the Tennessee River or its branches.

TVA has built more than twenty-five dams on the Tennessee River and its branches. Other dams have been built by the Army Corps of Engineers and the Aluminum Company of America. Behind each dam an artificial lake, or reservoir, has been created. This system of dams and reservoirs is used by TVA in carrying out several of its main programs.

During the winter and spring months, heavy rains and melting snows cause the rivers to rise. Large amounts of water are stored in the reservoirs behind the dams. This helps prevent flooding on the Tennessee River. It also lessens the danger of floods on the lower Ohio and

**Pickwick Landing Dam**, on the Tennessee River.

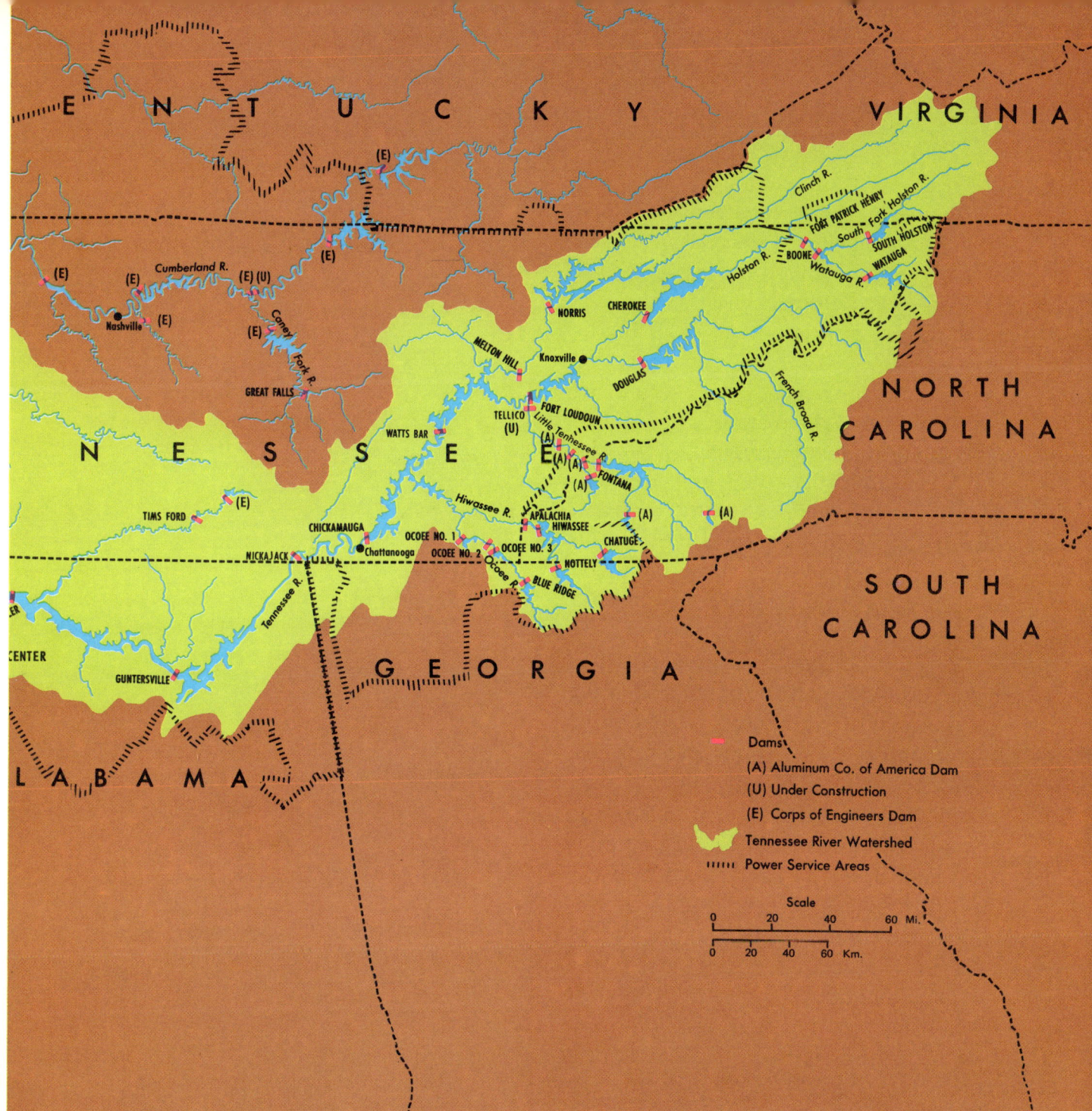

Mississippi rivers, which receive much water from the Tennessee River. In the drier months of summer, much of the water stored in the reservoirs is released into the rivers. This keeps the rivers from becoming so shallow that boats cannot travel on them safely.

The Tennessee River is now used as a water highway all year round. Boats can travel up the river about 650 miles, from Paducah, Kentucky, at the river's mouth, to Knoxville, Tennessee. They travel through a chain of lakes created by nine TVA dams on the Tennessee. At each dam, there are locks* to raise or lower the boats from one level to the next.

Large amounts of electric power are produced by TVA. About one fifth of this power is generated at hydroelectric plants. (See page 191.) The rest is generated at steam power plants that burn coal or at nuclear* plants. Electricity produced by TVA is used in most parts of the Tennessee Valley and in certain nearby areas. Some of TVA's power is used by the federal government for atomic energy research at Oak Ridge, Tennessee, and Paducah.

The reservoirs behind the TVA dams are used for recreation also. Many people come to these lakes to enjoy water sports such as swimming, boating, and fishing.

# 13  Industry

**During the early nineteenth century, the South had few industries.** Imagine that you are traveling on horseback from Boston, Massachusetts, to Savannah, Georgia, in the year 1830. In the northeastern part of the country, the cities and towns are close together. As you ride through the cities, you notice clouds of gray smoke pouring from the chimneys of many factories. Farther south, in Virginia and the Carolinas, you see sprawling fields of cotton and tobacco. You ride for many miles between cities, and in the cities you see very few factories.

In 1830, and for many years afterward, the South was mainly a farming region. Southern planters were making large profits from cotton and tobacco. They were not interested in manufacturing. Most of the other people in the South had little money to use for building factories. The cotton grown in the South was sold to textile mills in Europe or the northern part of the United States. From these same areas, the South bought manufactured goods.

During the Civil War, factories were set up in the South to make weapons, uniforms, and other supplies for the Confederate forces. By the end of the war, however, many of these factories had been destroyed.

**Gradually, new industries were attracted to the South.** Toward the end of the nineteenth century, many business firms began to realize that there were advantages in locating factories in the South. The southern states were rich in raw materials such as cotton,

**A paper mill in Mississippi.** Papermaking is one of the many growing industries in the South. At the end of the nineteenth century there were few factories in the southern states. Today, however, nearly every kind of modern industry can be found in this part of our country. What are some of the reasons for the development of industry in the South during the present century?

tobacco, iron ore, coal, and timber. Rivers on the Piedmont Plateau could furnish waterpower. Many workers were available for factory jobs, and taxes were low.

Soon many factories were rising in the South. Among these were sawmills and chemical plants. Iron and steel mills were built in Birmingham, Alabama. A number of textile mills were established, some by new companies and some by northern manufacturers who moved their businesses to the South. During World War I and World War II, factories were built to produce war materials.

The growth of industry helped many people in the South. Men and women who went to work in southern factories earned good wages. They were able to buy more goods than before. As sales increased, stores hired more clerks and bought more foods from factories. New plants were built to meet the demand. These factories bought more of the farm products and other raw materials produced by southern workers.

**Today, southern industry is still growing.** In recent years, industry has continued to grow in the southern states. Some state and local governments encourage businesses to build factories in the South by offering certain advantages. Among these advantages are assistance in obtaining land and buildings, and favorable tax laws. Today, nearly four times as many southern workers are employed in manufacturing as are employed in farming. In the future, many more industries will make use of the rich resources of the South.

**Textiles and clothing.** Textile manufacturing is one of the most important industries in the South today. More southern workers are employed in the manufacture of textiles and clothing than in any other industry.

Most of our nation's cotton cloth is made in textile mills that are scattered along the Fall Line and on the Piedmont Plateau in the South. Large amounts of hydroelectric power for running machinery are available in this area. Although much of the cotton used by the mills is grown nearby, some of it comes from states to the west.

**Inspecting fabric in a textile mill in North Carolina.** Inspecting the finished product in a factory is only one of the many different kinds of jobs available in most communities in our country. Dividing up the work in a community helps people provide more goods and services than could be provided if each person had to meet all of his or her needs alone. Why do you suppose this is true? Perhaps you would like to discuss this question with your classmates.

Division of Labor

See pages 236-237

Let's visit two textile mills in North Carolina. At the first mill, we see whirring machines that spin cotton fibers into thread. This thread, which is called yarn, is woven into cloth by giant power looms at the second mill. Instead of cotton, some mills use rayon, nylon, or other synthetic fibers.

Some southern factories manufacture clothing from textiles made in the South. In the past thirty years, many apparel factories have been built in this part of our country, especially in Georgia and North Carolina. These factories make dresses, shirts, overalls, hosiery, and many other items.

**Other products made from raw materials supplied by southern farms.** Cotton grown in the South provides raw materials for several manufacturing industries in addition to the textile industry. When cottonseeds are separated from the cotton lint* by machines called gins, some tiny fibers cling to the seeds. These fibers are used in making such products as camera film and

*See Glossary

phonograph records. Oil is squeezed from the cottonseeds and used to make food products such as margarine, cooking oil, and salad dressing. After the oil has been removed from the seeds, the remaining material is made into fertilizer and cattle feed.

The manufacture of food products is an important industry throughout the South. Oil for cooking is made from corn, peanuts, and soybeans, as well as from cottonseeds. In many places, fruits and vegetables are processed in canneries and freezing plants. Large amounts of citrus fruit are processed in Florida. Meat-packing plants are located in Memphis and other large cities. In Louisiana, sugarcane is processed to make the snowy-white crystals that you sprinkle on your breakfast cereal.

The South produces most of the pipe tobacco and cigarettes used in our country. The factories are located near tobacco-farming areas, mainly in North Carolina, Virginia, and Kentucky.

Food processing is an important industry throughout the southern states. The picture at the far left shows workers cutting and packaging pork in a meat-processing and freezing plant in Alabama. The worker shown at left is packing cans of frozen orange juice in a Florida freezing plant. Large amounts of citrus fruits are processed in Florida. What are some of the other foods that are processed in the South?

**An oil refinery in Louisiana.** The processing of petroleum and natural gas is one of the important industries in the South. Some refinery products are used as raw materials in nearby chemical plants.

**Products from petroleum and natural gas.** One of the South's important industries is the processing of petroleum and natural gas. At refineries, crude* oil is made into gasoline, fuel oil, and other products. Impurities are removed from natural gas at processing plants. Certain valuable substances called natural-gas liquids are extracted from gas. Louisiana leads the southern states in the manufacture of petroleum products and natural-gas liquids.

**Chemicals.** The South produces vast quantities of chemicals and chemical products. It has plentiful supplies of many raw materials used by the chemical industry. Among these are coal, sulfur, salt, and phosphate rock. Petroleum and natural gas provide raw materials for chemical plants located near oil refineries. The chemicals made in these plants are called petrochemicals.

Other factories use petrochemicals in the manufacture of chemical products such as synthetic rubber and certain plastics. Some of these factories, which require large amounts of fresh water, are located near the Mississippi River. The river provides a constant supply of water, and also serves as a convenient transportation route.

Chemical plants in the South produce enormous quantities of fertilizer. Plants in Florida and other states make fertilizer out of phosphate rock. In several states, chemical plants make nitrogen fertilizers from ammonia.* Many of the modern processes used to make fertilizer were first developed at TVA's experimental fertilizer plant near Muscle Shoals, in northern Alabama.

Factories in the South make a great variety of other chemical products.

Plants in Tennessee and North Carolina produce chemicals from which various plastics and other synthetic materials are made. Among the many synthetic fibers manufactured in the South are rayon, nylon, orlon, and dacron. Much of the sulfur mined in Louisiana is made into sulfuric acid. Large amounts of this acid are also manufactured in Tennessee, where pyrites provide the raw materials. (See page 183.) Sulfuric acid is used in making products such as paper, glass, steel, paint, fertilizer, and photographic film.

**Products made from wood.** There are vast pine and hardwood forests in many parts of the South. Timber cut from these forests has helped the southern states become leaders in the manufacture of paper, lumber, and a variety of other wood products.

To learn about the paper industry in the South, let's visit a pulp mill near a pine forest in southern Alabama. Here we see wood chips and chemicals being cooked together to make wood pulp. Later, this pulp will be made into the heavy brown paper used in grocery bags. Factories in the South also make newsprint* and other kinds of paper.

Building materials are produced by many factories in the South. At some

**A lumber mill in Florida.** Sawmills in many parts of the South produce large amounts of lumber.

**A furniture factory in North Carolina.** The South has a large forest-products industry. Vast forests of pine and hardwood trees provide raw materials for the manufacture of paper and wood products. Many furniture factories are located on the Piedmont Plateau in North Carolina.

plants, workers tend machines that glue together thin sheets of wood to form plywood. At other plants, wood fibers are pressed together to make a building material called fiberboard. Sawmills scattered throughout the South produce large amounts of lumber.

The South has a large furniture industry. North Carolina is the leading furniture producer in this region. In fact, more household furniture is manufactured in North Carolina than in any other state in our country. Many of North Carolina's furniture factories are in the city of High Point, on the Piedmont Plateau. These factories use lumber supplied by sawmills in the area. The sawmills produce this lumber from hardwood logs cut in the great forests of the Appalachian Highlands.

**Metals.** The South is well supplied with the three main raw materials needed to make iron and steel. Limestone is found in many parts of the South, and there are large deposits of coal and iron ore in the Appalachian Highlands. However, the only area where large amounts of all three are available close together is near Birmingham, Alabama. Plants in this area help to make Alabama the leading producer of iron and steel in the South. Birmingham does have one serious disadvantage for the making of iron and steel. It is far from northern factories that use large amounts of steel. But as more industries move into the South, Birmingham will probably have more buyers for its steel.

Aluminum is another important metal produced in the South. It is made from an ore called bauxite. The bauxite is first processed to obtain a substance called alumina, which contains both aluminum and oxygen. To produce aluminum, the oxygen must be removed from the alumina. Great amounts of electric power are needed to do this.

In Louisiana, there are several plants that make alumina out of bauxite imported from the West Indies and South America. A large plant in southern

Using Tools

See pages 230-235

The South has many industrial plants that make metals or metal products. The workers in the picture at left are operating machines in an aluminum rolling mill. The worker in the picture below is using a machine in a metal-products factory in Tennessee.

1. All machines are tools but not all tools are machines. Explain. You might like to discuss this with your classmates.
2. During the 1700's, certain changes occurred in the way goods were produced in England. These changes, which we call the Industrial Revolution, included the invention of many new machines. What were some of these machines? Who were their inventors? To discover answers to these questions, you will need to do research in other sources as well as in Chapter 14.

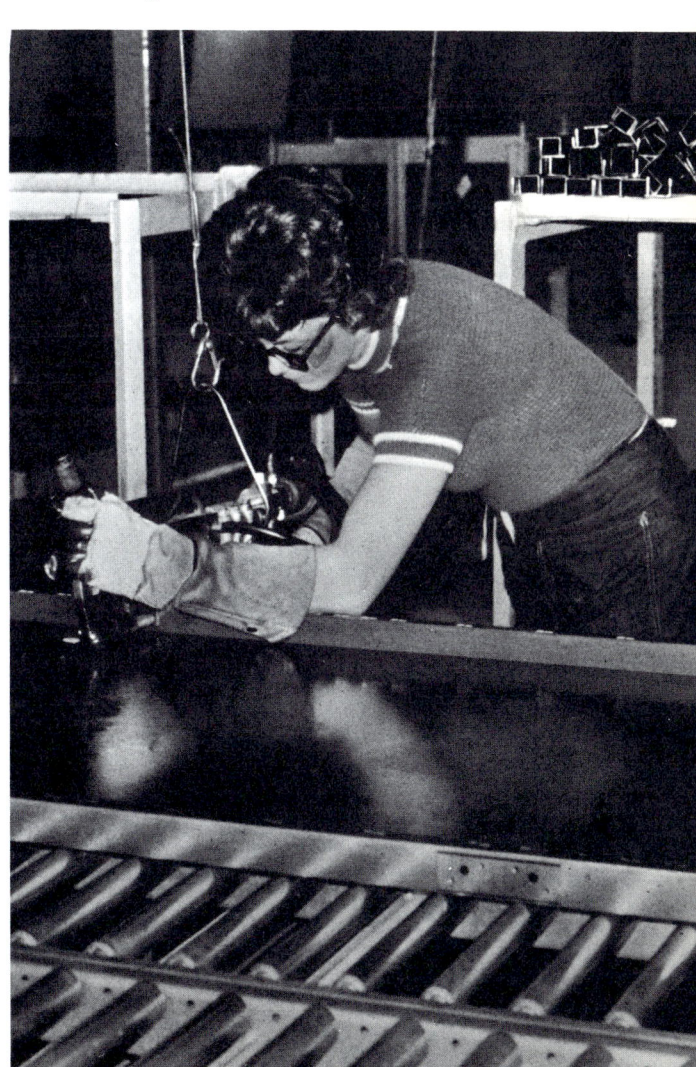

Alabama also makes alumina from imported bauxite. Other alumina plants are located in Arkansas near mines that supply bauxite. (See page 183.)

Several states in the South have factories where alumina is made into aluminum. Some of the alumina comes from alumina plants in the South and some is imported. Aluminum factories in northern Alabama and eastern Tennessee are located near dams and power stations that supply the large amounts of electricity needed by these factories. Aluminum factories in Louisiana use electricity produced mainly at power plants that burn natural gas.

**Transportation equipment.** The manufacture of transportation equipment is a major industry in the South. The largest shipyard in the United States is located at Newport News, Virginia. Many large naval ships, passenger liners, and freighters have been built here. There are other large shipyards along the Atlantic and Gulf coasts. The South also has several aircraft plants and a number of factories where automobiles are assembled.

**Other manufactured products.** Nearly every kind of modern industry can be found in the South today. Among the many household appliances made here are stoves, refrigerators, and sewing machines. The South also produces farm equipment, air conditioners, and many other kinds of machinery. There are factories that make a variety of electrical and electronic devices such as guidance systems for spacecraft. Huge plants in Kentucky, Tennessee, and South Carolina supply plutonium* and other materials used to produce atomic energy.

Many of the South's new industries are unlike the older ones such as the manufacture of textiles. They do not depend so much on a nearby source of raw materials. Their most important "resources" are the skills and ideas of southern workers.

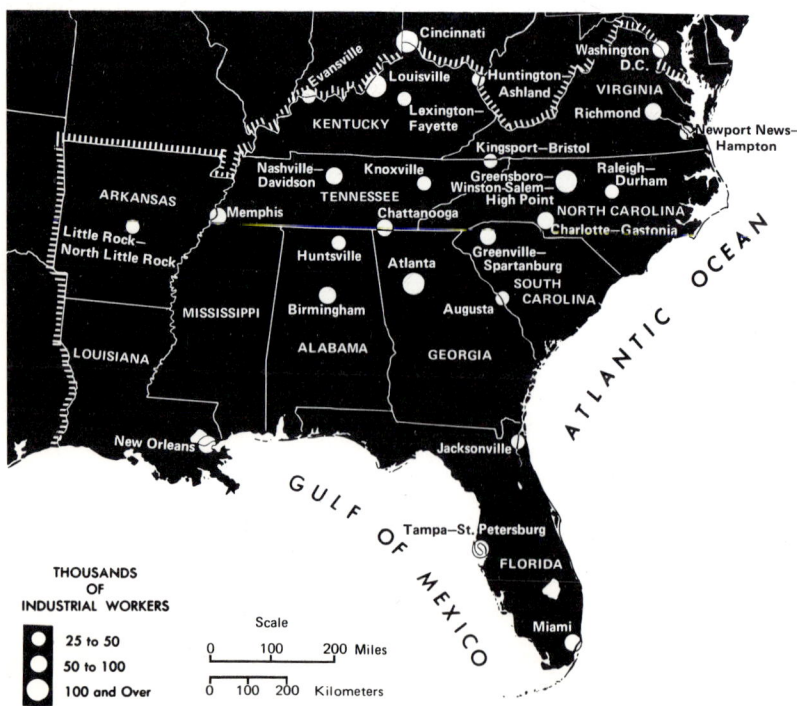

## Main Industrial Areas

The map on the left shows the areas of the South that have the largest number of industrial workers. Use this map, the map on page 29, and information in Chapter 8 to help you answer the following questions.

1. Which of the South's main industrial areas include important seaports or river ports?
2. What are some of the main industries in Atlanta? Miami? New Orleans? Tampa and St. Petersburg? Louisville? Memphis?
3. Which southern state has no large industrial area?

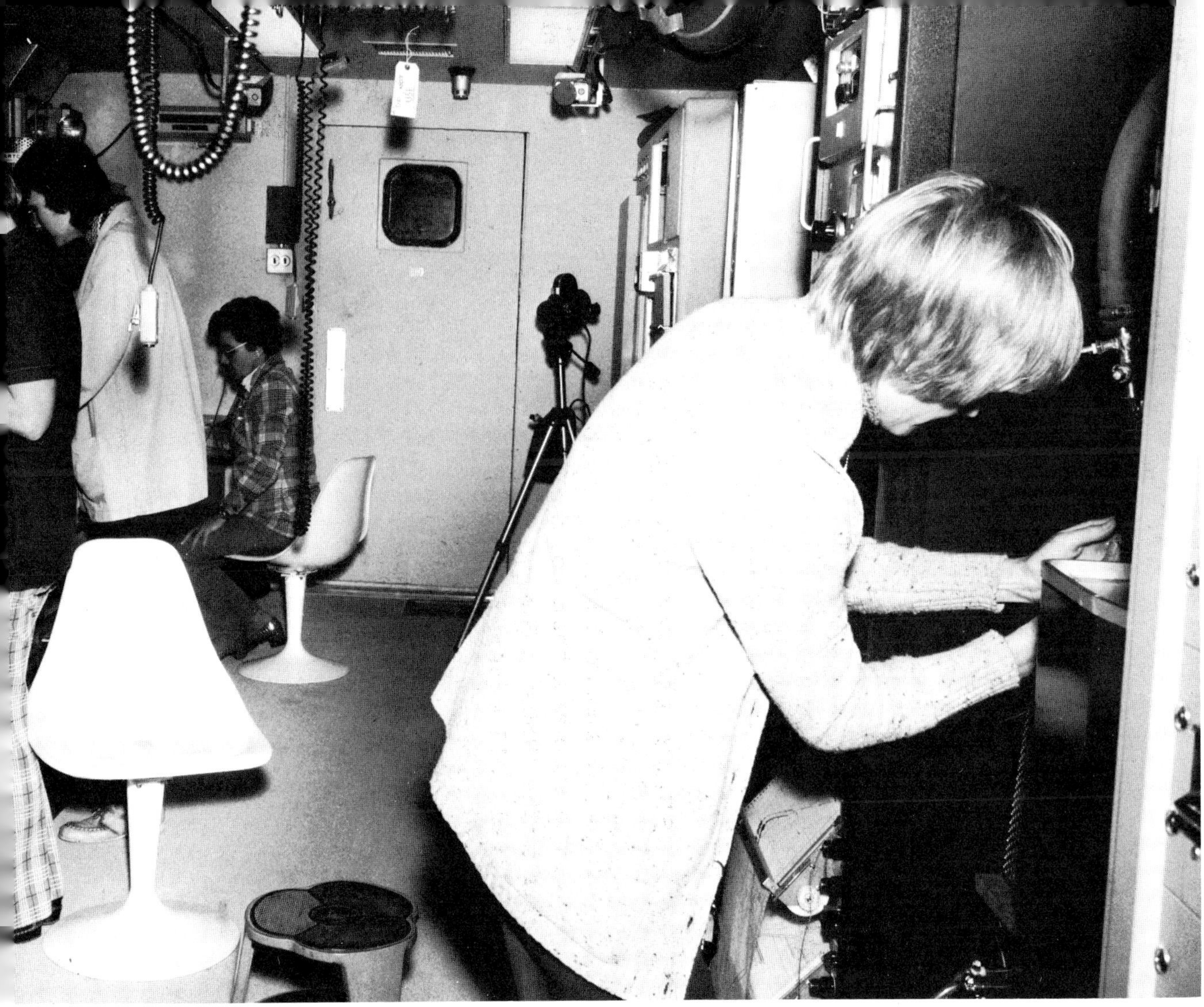

**Researchers at a space flight center in Huntsville, Alabama.** These women are working in a laboratory designed to resemble a spacecraft that is being developed for space flights in the 1980's. Space research has helped to encourage the growth of new industries in the South.

## Develop Your Skills

Graphs are important sources of information, because they can help you "see" relationships. Develop your skill in making and interpreting graphs by doing the following.

1. Make a graph showing the total value of manufactures in each state of the South in 1972. First, to obtain the information you need, refer to each of the state fact tables provided in Part 6 of this book. Then set up your graph like the sample one shown at right. (See also the graphs on pages 188 and 189.)
2. When you have completed your graph, use it to answer the following questions.

a. Which state in the South ranked first in the total value of manufactures?
b. How much was the total value of North Carolina's manufactures? About how many times greater was this amount than the total value of Mississippi's manufactures?
c. What was the approximate total value of all manufactures in the South?

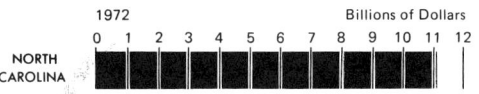

# Part 5
# Great Ideas That Built Our Nation

People have been living in what is now the United States for many thousands of years. During this time, they have always met their needs in communities. No one can meet his or her needs all alone. Only by living and working with other people can a person have a happy, satisfying life.

In order to make community life successful, people have developed certain ideas or ways of living. We call these the "great ideas." This part of the book provides information about ten great ideas that have been especially important in the history of our country. As you do research about these great ideas, try to answer the following questions.

- How did the Native Americans, or Indians, use the great ideas before Europeans settled in America?
- What were some ways in which the American colonists used the great ideas?
- Do people in the South and other parts of the United States still organize their lives around these concepts or great ideas? Explain your answer.
- What might happen to a modern community if the people failed to organize their lives around these concepts or great ideas? Explain your answer.

This picture shows a street in the old section of Williamsburg, Virginia, which has been restored to look much as it did in colonial times. During the seventeenth and eighteenth centuries, many people from Europe founded settlements in America. Can you think of some important ways in which these communities were different from the communities in Europe that the colonists had left behind? In what ways were they similar?

**Preparing the Declaration of Independence.** From left to right in this painting are Benjamin Franklin, John Adams, and Thomas Jefferson. What was the purpose of the Declaration of Independence? What are some of the great ideas that influenced the men who prepared this document?

# 14  Ten Great Ideas

## Freedom

### A Great Idea

The idea of freedom has been important to Americans since the early days of our country's history. Long before Europeans came to North America, the Indians who lived on this continent enjoyed a great deal of freedom. Many of the settlers who came to America from Europe during the 1600's and 1700's were seeking more freedom than they had had in their homelands.

By the middle of the 1700's, there were thirteen British colonies along the Atlantic coast of North America. During the 1760's and early 1770's, Britain began to take away some of the freedoms the colonists had enjoyed. On July 4, 1776, representatives of the thirteen colonies approved the Declaration of Independence. In this famous document, the colonists declared their freedom from British rule and set up a new nation called the United States of America.

At the time our country was founded, there were many people who did not enjoy all the same rights and freedoms as other Americans. For example, most of our country's black people lived in slavery. They were forced to work all their lives for white masters. Chapter 6 of this book tells how the Civil War finally led to the ending of slavery throughout the United States.

For a long time after the founding of our country the freedom of women was limited in certain ways. For instance, women could not vote in elections or testify as witnesses in a court of law. A married woman had no right to any property of her own. Any wages that she earned became the property of her husband.

Gradually women began to gain more rights and freedoms. One state after another passed laws giving married women the right to own property. The Nineteenth Amendment to the Constitution, which became law in 1920, guaranteed women throughout the United States the right to vote.

Do you believe that women today enjoy as much freedom as men do? Explain your answer. If you believe women should have more freedom than they do, what steps do you think they could take to achieve this goal?

**Marchers for woman suffrage** in the early 1900's. "Suffrage" means the right to vote. If you had been a young person at that time, would you have supported woman suffrage? Why? Why not?

## Rules and Government
### A Great Idea

People in every community need to follow rules in order to live together successfully. Why is this true? What kinds of rules do people in your own community follow? How do these rules make life safer and more pleasant for everyone? What would it be like to live in a community that had no rules?

In every community, there must be a person or a group of persons to make the rules and see that they are carried out. In other words, all communities need some form of government. Who makes the rules in your local community? Who enforces the rules that these people make?

Although every successful community has some form of government, not all governments are alike. The United States is a democracy. This means that its citizens have a share in governing themselves. To understand how it happens that we have a democratic form of government, let's look at some important events in history.

More than twenty-five hundred years ago, people in the Greek city of Athens developed certain ideas about democratic government. Every male citizen of Athens belonged to a governing body called the Assembly. A meeting of this body is shown in the picture at left. Members of the Assembly discussed important problems and voted on proposed laws. They also chose officials of the government. Not all the people in Athens had a voice in the government, however. Women and slaves could not vote or hold public office. Do you think Athens was a true democracy? Explain.

Over the centuries, Athenian ideas about government were often forgotten. In Athens itself, democracy came to an end during the second century B.C. Throughout Europe, powerful rulers gained control

In 1619, the first lawmaking body in the English colonies met in Jamestown, Virginia. (See picture at right.) This assembly was called the House of Burgesses. It served as a model for many lawmaking bodies established in the colonies, and later in our states. Without a government to make laws and carry them out, no community can be successful.

over lands and people by force. These rulers handed down their kingdoms to sons or other relatives. People had to obey the laws made by their ruler whether or not they believed the ruler was fair or wise. In England, however, a lawmaking body called Parliament eventually became more powerful than the king. But Parliament was made up partly of nobles and partly of persons chosen by landowners and wealthy merchants. Most people in England still had no voice in governing themselves.

During the eighteenth century, the people's desire for a voice in government became very strong in many parts of Europe, as well as in the English colonies in America. Many people came to believe that all the citizens of a country should have equal rights. They felt it was wrong for rulers and nobles to be born with special privileges. They also believed that every person has certain natural, inalienable* rights, such as freedom of speech.

Toward the end of the century, these beliefs helped bring about an important event. This was the American Revolution, which led to the founding of a new nation based on the principles of democracy. (See page 70.)

Although the United States was founded on democratic principles, not all people had the right to vote at first. Only white men who owned a certain amount of property could take part in elections. By about 1830, however, most states no longer required a person to own property in order to vote. Few black people could vote until after the Civil War. (See Chapter 6.) Women did not gain the right to vote until 1920.

Democracy has now spread to many parts of the world. Most countries in western Europe and North America are democracies, as are Australia and New Zealand. The governments of several countries in South America, Asia, and Africa are based on democratic principles.

In some parts of the world, democratic principles have had little effect. This is true in two of the world's largest countries—China and the Soviet Union. The present leaders in these countries do not give the people much voice in government affairs.

*See Glossary

The picture above shows American citizens preparing to vote by machine in an election. People in many parts of the United States use voting machines. In other parts of our country, paper ballots or computer punch cards are used. Do research to find answers to the following questions.

1. In your state, what qualifications must a person meet in order to vote?
2. How is the president of the United States chosen?

Voting in the Soviet Union is shown at right. The Soviet people may vote for their leaders, but there is only one candidate for each office. Why do you suppose elections are held if the people really have no choice? Do you think you would want to live in a country where you could never have much voice in the government? Why? Why not?

The English settlers who founded Jamestown needed to work together in order to establish a colony.

# Cooperation
## A Great Idea

The first permanent English settlement in the New World was established at Jamestown, Virginia, in 1607. (See pages 63 and 64.) As the picture above shows, the settlers worked hard to build a fort on the site they chose near the banks of the James River. Soon, however, many of the settlers became ill and discouraged. Some refused to do any work at all. Then a bold leader named Captain John Smith took charge of the settlement. He forced the settlers to cooperate with him and with each other by declaring that those who did not work would not be given food to eat. In spite of great hardships, Jamestown survived. During the years that followed, many more English settlers came to America.

The picture on the opposite page shows engineers at Kennedy Space Center in Florida testing equipment used in our country's Apollo space program. Do you think our country could have succeeded in sending astronauts to the moon if people were unwilling to cooperate with each other? Explain why you think as you do.

# Language

## A Great Idea

Look at this picture and study the caption below. Do you think the town crier was an important person in colonial times? Why do you think this? Can you think of some other ways in which the colonists received news? How did they learn about happenings in other colonies? How did they learn about events in England? Perhaps you would like to do research about some of the different ways in which the people of colonial America communicated with one another and with people in other parts of the world.

Throughout history, people have felt the need to communicate with each other. In order to work together, people need to express their ideas and feelings. Early people communicated in various ways. For example, they probably smiled, frowned, made gestures with their hands, and drew pictures. Their most important way of communicating, however, was by speaking. Scientists who have studied the origins of language believe that all human beings—even those who lived in earliest times—have had some form of spoken language.

Each day of your life, you use language to communicate with other people. You talk with your family and your friends. On school days, you talk with

This man is a town crier in Colonial Williamsburg.° He is posting a notice for people to read. Sometimes he walks through the town ringing a bell to get people's attention. As they gather around him, he tells them important news.

your teachers and your classmates. You write notes and letters, and you write out much of your schoolwork. Do you think it is important to use spoken language in such a way as to communicate clearly with other people? Why do you think this? Do you think it is important to express your thoughts and feelings clearly in writing? Why? Why not? Is it important for young people and their parents to communicate effectively with each other? Why do you think as you do?

Human beings did not develop written language until about five thousand years ago. Writing made it possible for people to store information so that it

This boy and his father enjoy talking with each other. Do you think all human beings enjoy sharing ideas and feelings with one another? Why do you think this?

could be used at a later time. Writing also enabled people to communicate over long distances. Today, almost every language in the world can be written as well as spoken.

Much of our knowledge about early civilizations has come from written records. The people of ancient Egypt and Mesopotamia* recorded information in three main ways—by carving on stone, by making marks on moist clay tablets, and by writing on paperlike materials with ink. Do you think the invention of writing may have encouraged the development of great civilizations? Why do you think this? You may wish to do research to discover which civilizations of ancient times left written records and which ones did not.

About five hundred years ago, an important change occurred in the way information was stored. Until then, records had to be written out by hand. Each copy of a book was an individual work of art, requiring many hours of work. During the fifteenth century, a printing press using movable type was invented. This invention made it possible to produce a number of identical copies of a book in a short time.

During the past one hundred and forty years, many new ways of communicating and storing information have been developed. Some of these new methods, such as the telephone and radio, send spoken words over long distances. Others, such as the telegraph, transmit symbols. Methods of recording music and speech on discs or tapes have been developed and are in common use. A special kind of photography called microfilming has been developed. Entire books can now be photographed and stored in a very small amount of space. One of the most interesting modern inventions is the computer. This machine can not only store large amounts of information, but it can also solve problems and provide new data.

The Picturephone permits people who are carrying on a telephone conversation to see each other on small television screens.

Language is one of the most useful of the great ideas. Every day of your life, you use language to express your thoughts and feelings. Without your knowledge of language, you could not understand the thoughts and feelings of other people. Perhaps you would like to write out answers to the following questions. You will probably need to do research to answer some of them.

1. Do you think language helps you to solve problems? Explain why you think this.
2. How does language help you to meet your needs?
3. Do you think that people could live together successfully in communities without language? Why? Why not?
4. How do you think the invention of the printing press in the fifteenth century affected community life in Europe? Explain your answer.
5. In what ways are modern inventions such as the computer affecting community life today? Why do you think this?
6. Do you think the invention of modern methods of communication has encouraged the growth of cities? Explain your answer.

**A painting on a Greek vase,** showing teachers and students in a school in ancient Athens.

# Education
## A Great Idea

The picture above shows teachers and students in a school in Athens about 2,500 years ago. Why do you suppose the citizens of ancient Athens wanted their children to be educated? Do you think the Athenians could have created a great civilization if they had not used the idea of education? Explain why you think as you do.

In all early communities, some of the older members tried to pass on ideas and skills to the younger people. For example, a man might teach his son how to stalk a deer. A woman might show her daughter how to cook and sew. Grandparents would tell stories to the children, who would tell the same stories to *their* grandchildren.

Today, children in most parts of the world obtain a large part of their education in school. In the United States nearly all children attend elementary school, and most of them go on to high school. Many also attend college.

The picture below shows students in an elementary school. They are examining a globe to discover information about the world for a social studies project. What are some of the things you have learned in school? What are some things you have learned outside school? Do you think the things you learned outside school are part of your education? Why do you think this? Do you think education is important for everyone? Why? Why not?

**Elementary school students.** In most parts of the world, children obtain much of their education in school.

# Using Natural Resources

## A Great Idea

By "natural resources" we mean any gifts of nature that people use to meet their needs. Some important natural resources are the following:

>sunshine
>air
>soil
>water
>wild animals
>wild plants
>minerals

Human beings have always depended on the earth's resources to help them meet their needs for food, clothing, and shelter. Early people hunted wild animals for food and for skins to make clothing. Sometimes they added to the food supply by gathering the fruits, seeds, and roots of wild plants. These early people lived in caves or built crude shelters from tree branches, mud, or animal skins. They used wood, stones, bones, and shells to make tools and weapons. Compared to people who lived later, however, the people who lived in early times made very little use of the natural resources around them.

The first major change in the use of natural resources began to take place about nine thousand years ago. People who had formerly obtained their food by hunting and gathering began to use soil, sunshine, and rain to grow crops. They also began to raise animals for food. These people were the world's first farmers.

Scientists who study the past are not sure just when or where people first began to farm. However, they believe that farming probably began somewhere in southwestern Asia, between 8000 and 7000 B.C. Gradually, farming spread from southwestern Asia to Europe and northern Africa. Some scientists believe that people in eastern Asia and western Africa may have developed the idea of farming independently. Scientists generally agree that farming began independently in the New World.

Beginning about six thousand years ago, another important change occurred in the use of natural resources. People began to make tools and weapons out of metals. The first metal used in this way was copper. Later, tin was combined with copper to make bronze. This metal was more useful than copper because it was harder. About 3,500 years ago, people began to produce iron from iron ore. This metal was even better than bronze for many purposes.

Over the centuries, people in various parts of the world learned how to make greater use of the earth's resources. Farmers developed new varieties of plants and animals that were more useful than the older varieties. In addition to food crops, they learned to grow flax* and cotton to provide fibers for making cloth. Farmers also learned how to irrigate their land with water from streams and wells, and how to enrich the soil with fertilizers.

This picture shows logging operations in the South. Do you think trees are an important natural resource? Why do you think this?

Important materials used in construction and for making household goods included stone, clay, wood, and reed. People continued to use the metals that had been discovered earlier, such as gold, silver, tin, copper, and iron. They also learned how to use many additional metals, such as zinc and antimony.* By the fifteenth century A.D., the people of Europe, Asia, and northern Africa had made great advances in the use of natural resources.

The Indian peoples who lived in North America were also using natural resources to meet their basic needs. Some Indian tribes met their needs mainly by hunting wild animals. Other tribes grew crops such as corn, tobacco, squash, and melons.

In the sixteenth century, a man named Théodore de Bry made engravings from some watercolor paintings of Indians and Indian life. A portion of one of his engravings, showing an Indian village in the South, is reproduced below. What were some of the important natural resources used by the Indians in this picture?

The European colonists who settled in the New World soon began to use many of the natural resources around them. The picture at right shows how barrels were made in colonial times. What important natural resource is this cooper, or barrelmaker, using? Do research in this book and other books to discover some of the important natural resources used by the colonists.

The Indians of the South lived in villages of well-constructed houses. Most of these Indians were peaceful farmers, who raised crops such as corn, squash, melons, and tobacco.

A barrelmaker at work in Colonial Williamsburg. What is another word for barrelmaker?

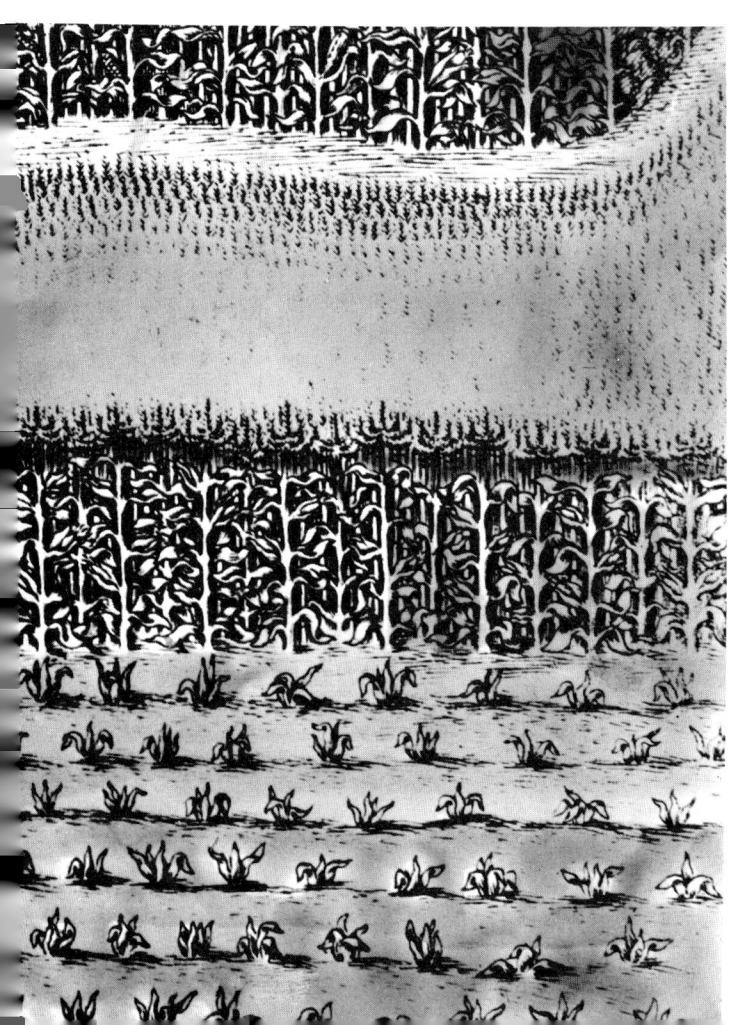

Today, we use hundreds of natural resources in meeting our needs. For example, stone and wood are just as important to us as they were to people long ago. Large amounts of these materials are used in construction and manufacturing. Modern farmers are just as dependent on sunshine, soil, and water as the first farmers who lived thousands of years ago. Iron ore is still one of our most valuable resources. Along with coal and limestone, iron ore is processed in huge furnaces to make iron and steel. Steel is then used to make automobiles, refrigerators, farm machinery, and thousands of other products. Chapter 12 of this book provides information about ways in which natural resources found in the South are being used.

# Using Tools

## A Great Idea

Anything that people use to help them do work may be called a tool. Scientists believe that people first began to make and use tools more than two and one-half million years ago. Early hunters made knives and other hand tools from stone, wood, and animal bones. Later, they began to make arrows and spears by fastening stone points to wooden shafts.

This picture shows an Indian chipping one stone with another to make a tool—perhaps a blade for a tomahawk. Many early people made tools in this way, and a few people still do. Would it be easy to make a tool by this method? Why do you think this?

For hundreds of thousands of years, tools remained much the same. Although they were often beautifully made, they were very simple. About nine thousand years ago, people began to invent new kinds of tools to help them plant and harvest crops. At first, most farming tools were made of wood or stone. Later, however, people discovered how to make tools of metal. In what ways do you think metal tools were an improvement over tools made of wood and stone?

Life changed very little during the centuries that followed the development of farming. Most people produced their own food and clothing with the use of simple tools. Gradually a few machines (tools with a number of moving parts) were developed. These

**Public demonstration of the McCormick reaper,** at Steeles Tavern, Virginia, in 1831. Cyrus Hall McCormick's invention of a machine for cutting grain made it possible for a person to harvest six acres of wheat or oats in a day instead of only one acre by hand. The invention of new machinery for doing farm work was part of the Industrial Revolution, which began in England during the 1700's.

included various kinds of pumps and looms. Even after machines were developed, however, most work was still performed by the muscle power of human beings and animals. Wind and waterpower were used to run certain machines such as mills for grinding grain.

Beginning about the middle of the eighteenth century, three important developments occurred in the way goods were produced. First, many new machines were invented to help people make things more quickly. Second, steam and other new sources of power came into use. Third, factories were built to house the new machines. Together, these three main developments are known as the Industrial Revolution.

The Industrial Revolution began with changes in the way textiles were manufactured in England. In the early 1700's, workers produced cloth in their own homes. They used spinning wheels to make thread and handlooms to weave the thread into cloth. Then, in the 1760's, a spinning machine was invented that could be run by waterpower. Later a power loom was developed. And a new source of power—the steam engine—was introduced for running machines in the textile industry.

As machines became larger, heavier, and more complicated, they could no longer be placed in the workers' homes. Special buildings called factories were constructed, where the workers came to operate the machines.

The new ways of producing goods soon spread from England to other parts of the world. The United States, Belgium, France, and Germany were among the first countries to adopt the new methods.

The Industrial Revolution has continued to spread. Today, it is in different stages in different parts of the world. (See map below.) The United States and several other highly industrialized countries are now moving into a new stage of the Industrial Revolution. This new stage includes automation, which is the development and use of automatic machines. Through automation, it is now possible for an entire industrial plant to be run with only a few human operators.

Do you think the standard of living is higher or lower in nations that have experienced the Industrial Revolution? Why do you think this? You may wish to do research in other sources to check your answer.

**The spread of the Industrial Revolution.** The world's most highly industrialized countries are generally referred to as developed nations. Countries in which the Industrial Revolution has as yet had little effect are said to be developing. In the partly developed countries, industrialization is well under way.

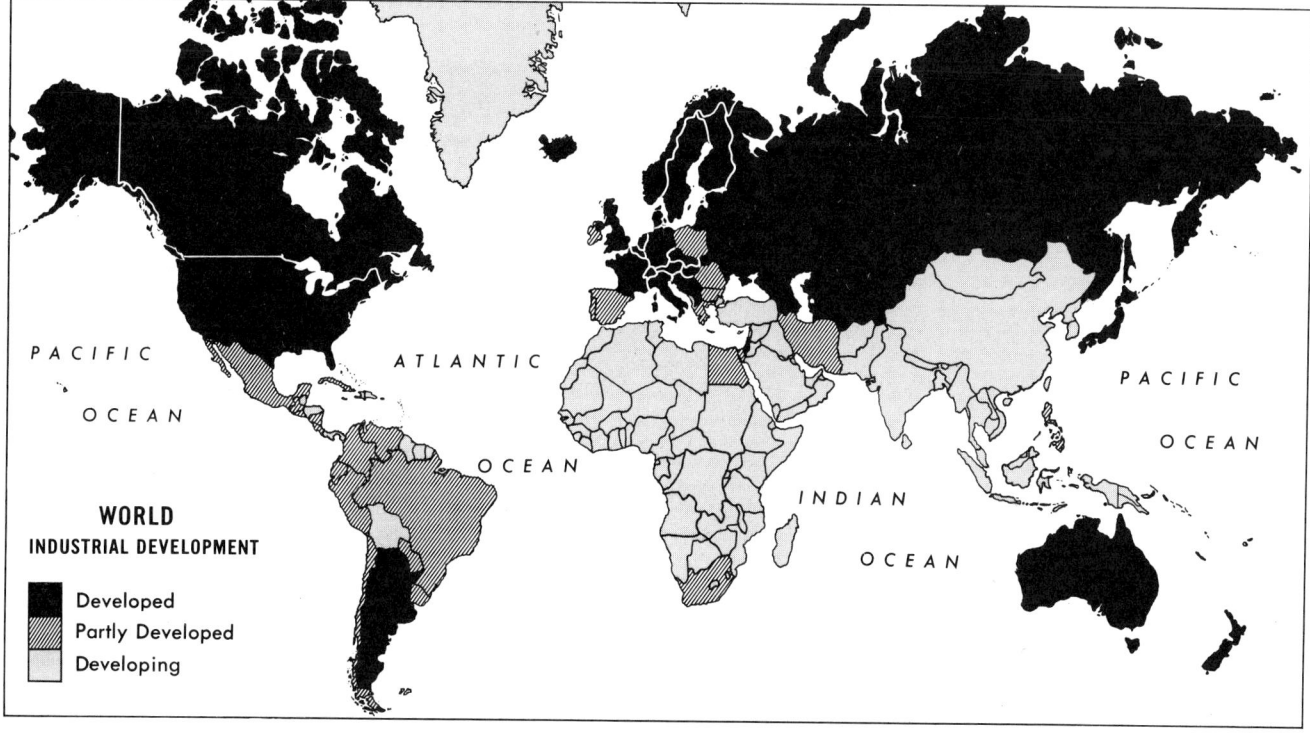

## Do Research To Solve a Problem

During the present century, industry has grown rapidly in the South. The picture at left shows a factory in North Carolina where machines are being used to make lighting fixtures. The picture below shows a worker at a control panel in an automated plant in Kentucky. In many parts of the world, however, there is little industry. Most work is done with the help of simple tools rather than complicated machines. Countries with little industry are generally referred to as "developing" nations. (See map on page 233.) Why has industry grown faster in some parts of the world than in others? To solve this problem, you will need to do research about industry in the South and in one of the developing countries. Then you will need to consider ways in which the following affect the growth of industry:

a. the location of an area
b. the history of an area
c. available natural resources
d. the skills of the people and opportunities for gaining additional skills
e. markets for manufactured goods

See pages 256–258

## Division of Labor

### A Great Idea

The people shown above lived in ancient Egypt. (The dot on the globe at left marks the place where they lived.) The man with the coil of rope is surveying a field of grain, and a man and two boys are helping him. A man and a woman have brought food for the surveyor and his helpers. The men at the bottom of the picture are scribes, who are recording information about the harvest. Do you think it would have been better for the same people to survey and also act as scribes? Why? Why not?

Dividing up the work of a community among people who do different jobs is known as division of labor. By using this great idea, people are able to obtain more goods than they could if each person tried to meet his or her needs all alone.

This man works in a plant where computers are assembled. He and his family do not need the product he is helping to make. He works to earn money, which he uses to buy the things he needs. This man is skillful at his job, and enjoys it very much. He would not like to work on a farm, or to do some kind of work that does not require his special skills. On the other hand, the people who produce the food, clothing, and other things he buys probably could not do this kind of work as well as he does it, and would not enjoy it.

Division of labor makes it possible for each person to work at the job he or she can do best. By dividing up the work, people can produce a larger amount of goods than they could if each person had to produce everything she or he needed. Also, one person could not possibly make and use all the tools needed to produce a complicated machine such as an automobile or a computer. Division of labor helps people produce many things that one person working alone could not make.

The picture at right shows an X-ray technician in a hospital. Instead of helping to manufacture a product, this woman provides a service. Other people who perform services include teachers, doctors, and police officers.

Perhaps you would like to do research in other chapters of this book to discover some of the many jobs that are done by workers in the South. How do the products and services provided by these workers help the people of the South and other parts of the United States to meet their needs?

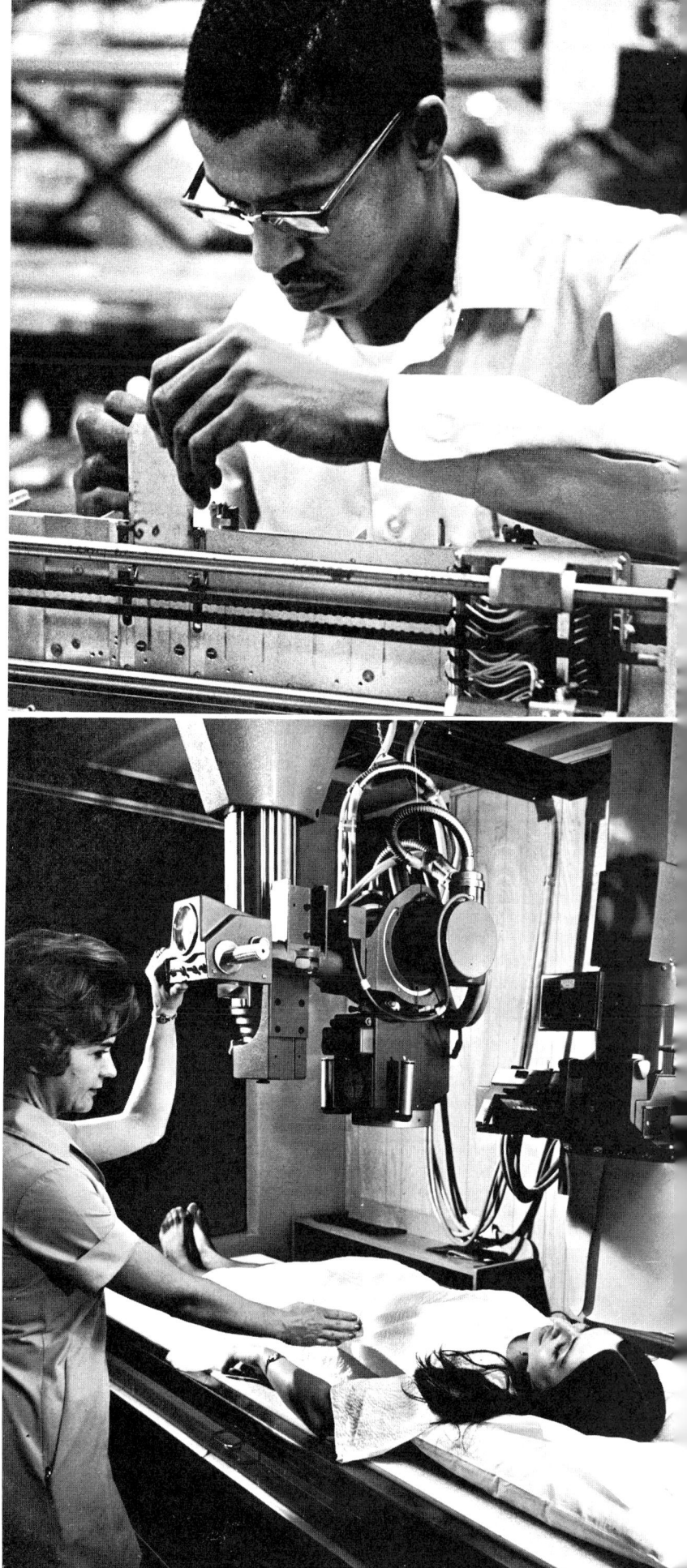

The busy port of New Orleans in the 1880's. New Orleans is both a seaport and a Mississippi River port.

## Exchange

### A Great Idea

In every community, people obtain some of the goods they need through exchange. This results from the fact that every community has some division of labor. For example, even in the simplest communities of early times, not all the people did the same kind of work. Wherever people divide up work, they exchange goods and services with each other.

People in early times did not carry on as much exchange, or trade, as people do today. Why do you think this is true? We not only exchange products and services within our own communities, but we also carry on trade with

Today, it ranks first in the South and second in our country in the amount of cargo handled at its docks.

people who live in many faraway communities.

Since colonial days, New Orleans has been one of our country's main trading cities. In the 1800's, steamboats brought goods such as lumber, sugar, and cotton down the Mississippi River to the wharves that lined the city's harbor. Many of these goods were reloaded onto oceangoing vessels for shipment to other seaports. Sugar, coffee, heavy machinery, and a variety of other products were carried upstream to river ports such as St. Louis and Memphis. Today, New Orleans is still an important trading city. In what ways has trade helped the people of the South to have a better living? Do you think that trade helps all people on earth to live better? Explain your answer.

# Loyalty
## A Great Idea

The picture above shows George Washington with some of his troops at Valley Forge during the Revolutionary War. The winter of 1777-1778, when Washington and his army camped at Valley Forge, was extremely severe. Most of the American soldiers did not have enough clothing to protect them against the cold weather. They were also hungry, for food supplies were inadequate.

In spite of the hardships at Valley Forge, the American soldiers did not give up. Do you think they were showing their loyalty to George Washington? Why do you think this? Do you think they were also showing their loyalty to certain ideas, such as freedom and justice? Explain your answer.

People discovered long ago that to live together successfully in a community they had to be loyal to each other. People were willing to do unpleasant or difficult tasks simply because they felt a strong sense of loyalty to their community. Members of families had to be loyal to each other in order to have a happy family life.

In every truly successful community on the earth today, most of the people are loyal to each other. They are loyal to the laws of their community and their country. They are loyal to their leaders, and their leaders are loyal to them. The people who live in successful communities are also loyal to their ideas and beliefs. Most people in our country, for example, are loyal to the principles of democracy. They are loyal to the ideas of freedom, justice, and equality. In addition, they are loyal to their religious faith.

This picture shows the members of a family enjoying music together. Do you think a family is a community? Why? Why not? Do you think it is important for all the members of a family to be loyal to each other? Why do you think this? What are some of the ways in which parents and children can show their loyalty to each other?

# Part 6

# States of the South

In Part 6 you will be learning more about the eleven states that make up the South. These states have much in common, but there are also many differences among them. During your study of Part 6, you may wish to do research about the following.

1. Choose three southern states. Then compare the land features of these states with the land features in your state. In what ways are the areas alike? In what ways are they different? This book provides much of the information you will need. The suggestions on pages 259-261 will help you locate additional information.
2. The fact tables on the following pages provide much valuable information about the states of the South. Use these tables to answer the following questions.
   - Which state in the South has the largest population?
   - Which state is the largest in area?
   - In which state is cotton one of the leading farm products?
   - Which state leads the South in the value of minerals produced?

**A view from Lookout Mountain.** Visitors to this mountain near Chattanooga, Tennessee, can see seven of the South's eleven states.

243

# Alabama

About three fifths of Alabama lies in the Coastal Plain region of the South. The rest of the state is in the Appalachian Highlands and the Interior Plains regions.

**The Coastal Plain.** Alabama's Coastal Plain includes areas of level land and low hills. Forests, pastures, and fields of crops cover much of the land here. The

Alabama lies in three main regions of the South. These are the Coastal Plain, the Interior Plains, and the Appalachian Highlands.

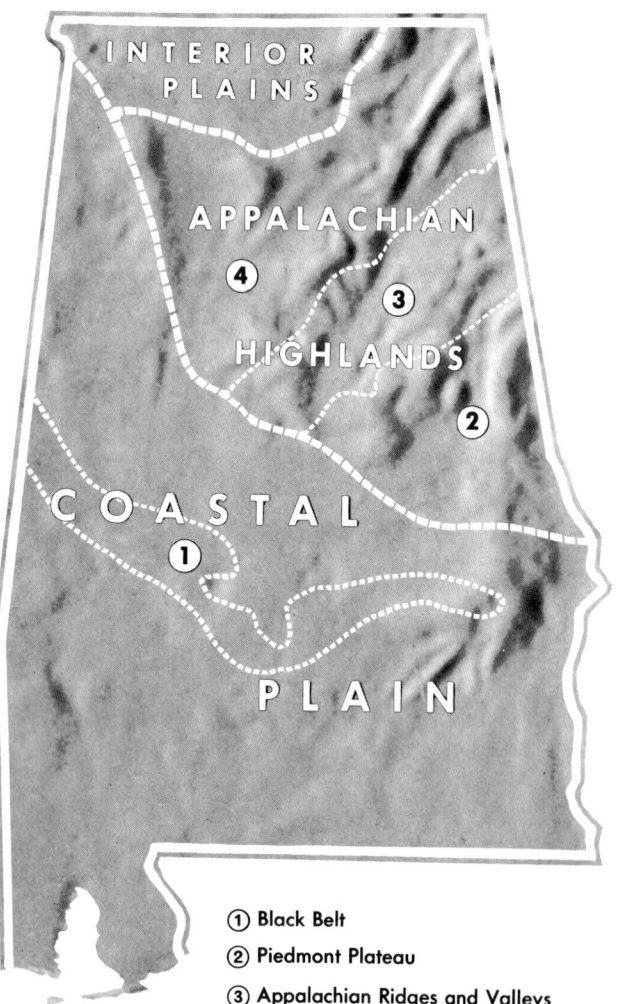

① Black Belt
② Piedmont Plateau
③ Appalachian Ridges and Valleys
④ Appalachian Plateau

GULF OF MEXICO

| Facts About Alabama | | |
|---|---:|---:|
| | Number or Value | Rank |
| Area (square miles) | 51,609 | 29 |
| Population | 3,614,000 | 21 |
| Capital—Montgomery | | |
| Admission Date: December 14, 1819 | | 22 |
| Colleges and Universities | 51 | 20 |
| Farm Products | $1,313,331,000 | 26 |
| Poultry and eggs | 476,561,000 | 5 |
| Cattle and calves | 248,636,000 | 26 |
| Hogs | 103,300,000 | 16 |
| Fish | $ 18,080,000 | 14 |
| Timber Harvested (cubic feet) | 744,829,000 | 5 |
| Minerals | $ 413,056,000 | 21 |
| Coal | 211,695,000 | 7 |
| Cement | 68,894,000 | 8 |
| Petroleum | 41,772,000 | 19 |
| Manufactures* | $5,048,500,000 | 21 |
| Primary metal industries | 797,100,000 | 9 |
| Paper and allied products | 471,100,000 | 11 |
| Textile-mill products | 442,100,000 | 7 |

Black Belt, a narrow strip of prairie with fertile, black soil, extends eastward from Mississippi into this region.

**The Appalachian Highlands.** Three sections of the Appalachian Highlands extend into Alabama. One is the Piedmont Plateau. Much of the Piedmont is covered with low, wooded hills. The Tallapoosa and the Coosa rivers flow through this area. Another section, the Appalachian Ridges and Valleys, has rich deposits of minerals. The southern part of the Appalachian Plateau also extends into Alabama. The fertile valley of the Tennessee River cuts through this area.

**The Interior Plains.** The valley of the Tennessee River also extends through the Interior Plains region of Alabama. There are many small farms and industrial towns and cities in this valley.

*See Glossary

# Arkansas

Arkansas lies in two main regions of the South. These are the Coastal Plain region and the Interior Highlands.

**The Coastal Plain.** Along the Mississippi River, the Coastal Plain region of Arkansas is low and almost level. In the past, the Mississippi overflowed its banks time after time. When the floodwaters withdrew, a layer of rich, dark soil was left behind on the lowlands along the river. For many years, these fertile alluvial* lowlands have been used for farming. Formerly, crops were often damaged by floods. Today, paved riverbanks and levees* protect fields from destructive flooding. In the southwestern part of Arkansas, the Coastal Plain is a little higher and more rolling than it is near the Mississippi River. The soil is sandy and less fertile. Much of this area is covered with pine forests.

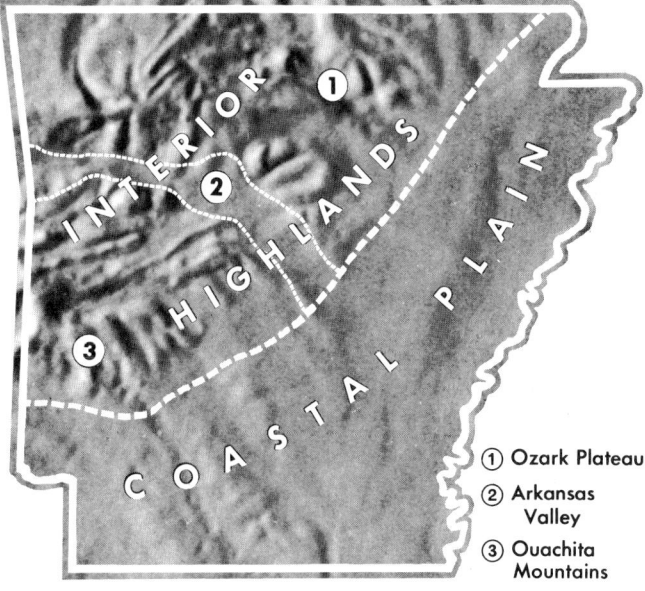

① Ozark Plateau
② Arkansas Valley
③ Ouachita Mountains

**Arkansas** lies in the Coastal Plain and the Interior Highlands regions. In Arkansas, the Interior Highlands may be divided into three sections.

**The Interior Highlands.** In Arkansas the Interior Highlands is divided into three sections. The Ozark Plateau forms the northernmost section. This is an area of rolling tablelands broken by deep valleys. Dense forests cover much of the land. In the northwest are many pastures, vineyards, and orchards. Along the southern edge of the plateau are steep ridges separated by narrow river gorges.

South of the Ozark Plateau is the Arkansas Valley. Here, many farms are located on the fertile lowlands along the Arkansas River, which flows through this section.

The Ouachita Mountains form the southernmost section of Arkansas's Interior Highlands region. Between the wooded ridges of this rugged area are deep river valleys and sparkling lakes.

| Facts About Arkansas | | |
|---|---:|---:|
| | Number or Value | Rank |
| Area (square miles) | 53,104 | 27 |
| Population | 2,116,000 | 33 |
| Capital—Little Rock | | |
| Admission Date: June 15, 1836 | | 25 |
| Colleges and Universities | 19 | 37 |
| Farm Products | $2,366,072,000 | 11 |
| Soybeans | 719,654,000 | 5 |
| Poultry and eggs | 657,565,000 | 2 |
| Rice | 364,635,000 | 1 |
| Fish | $ 2,030,000 | 23 |
| Timber Harvested (cubic feet) | 460,907,000 | 9 |
| Minerals | $ 273,705,000 | 29 |
| Petroleum | 70,618,000 | 16 |
| Bromine | Not available | |
| Natural gas | 28,985,000 | 11 |
| Manufactures* | $2,767,100,000 | 30 |
| Food and kindred products | 353,700,000 | 29 |
| Electrical equipment and supplies | 321,800,000 | 22 |
| Lumber and wood products | 263,300,000 | 12 |

*See Glossary

# Florida

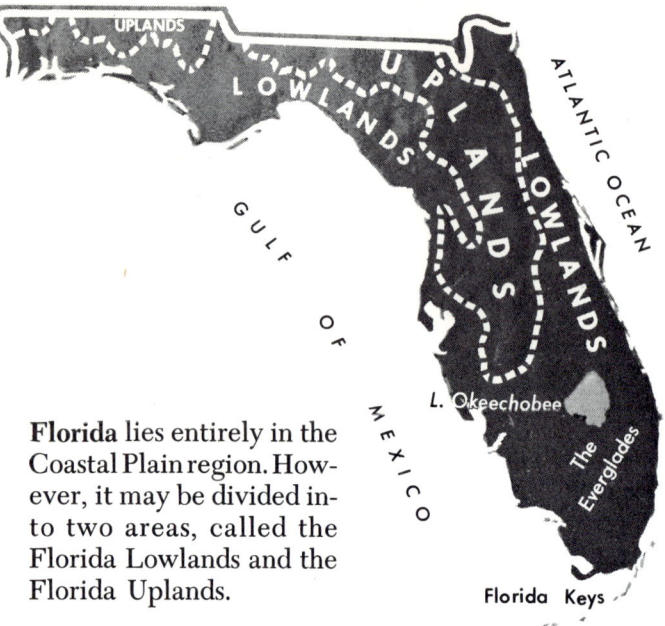

Florida lies entirely in the Coastal Plain region. However, it may be divided into two areas, called the Florida Lowlands and the Florida Uplands.

| Facts About Florida | | |
|---|---:|---:|
| | Number or Value | Rank |
| Area (square miles) | 58,560 | 22 |
| Population | 8,357,000 | 8 |
| Capital—Tallahassee | | |
| Admission Date: March 3, 1845 | | 27 |
| Colleges and Universities | 66 | 12 |
| Farm Products | $1,921,390,000 | 18 |
|   Fruits and nuts | 604,170,000 | 2 |
|   Vegetables | 367,247,000 | 2 |
|   Cattle and calves | 223,376,000 | 29 |
| Fish | $ 64,103,000 | 5 |
| Timber Harvested (cubic feet) | 285,233,000 | 15 |
| Minerals | $ 601,100,000 | 17 |
|   Phosphate rock | Not available | |
|   Petroleum | 150,070,000 | 11 |
|   Stone | 103,595,000 | 3 |
| Manufactures* | $5,477,300,000 | 20 |
|   Food and kindred products | 973,200,000 | 12 |
|   Electrical equipment and supplies | 566,000,000 | 16 |
|   Chemicals and allied products | 501,400,000 | 18 |

Most of Florida is a peninsula, which extends about four hundred miles from north to south. Stretching westward from the northern part of the peninsula is a long, narrow strip of land that is sometimes called the panhandle.

All of Florida lies in the Coastal Plain. Most of this state is a flat lowland. However, about one third of Florida consists of uplands that rise between one hundred and three hundred feet above sea level.

**The Florida Uplands.** Uplands extend along nearly all of the northern border of Florida, and reach over two hundred miles southward down the center of the peninsula. The part of the uplands that extends into the peninsula is covered with broad plains, rolling hills, and lakes. There are many farms and orange groves in this area. Some land is used for grazing cattle. In the panhandle, the uplands are made up of wooded hills and fertile river valleys.

**The Florida Lowlands.** The rest of Florida is made up of flat lowlands that lie along the Atlantic Ocean and the Gulf of Mexico. Wide, sandy beaches stretch along the coast in many places. In some parts of the Florida Lowlands, farming is important. Lake Okeechobee, located in the southern part of the lowlands, is one of the largest lakes in the United States. To the south of Lake Okeechobee is a large, swampy area known as the Everglades.

A group of small islands extends off the southern tip of the Florida peninsula. These are the Florida Keys. Many tourists come here to swim and fish.

*See Glossary

# Georgia

Georgia lies in two of the main regions of the South. These are the Coastal Plain and the Appalachian Highlands.

**The Coastal Plain.** Part of Georgia's Coastal Plain region is bordered by the Atlantic Ocean. Just off the coast are many flat, marshy islands that are part of a chain known as the Sea Islands. Near the Atlantic Ocean, Georgia's Coastal Plain is low and level. Much of the land here is covered with pine forests. Okefenokee Swamp, a giant swamp that extends into Florida, is located in southeastern Georgia. To the north and northwest of Okefenokee Swamp, the land is higher and gently rolling. Here there are many fields of cotton, tobacco, and other crops.

**The Appalachian Highlands.** Four sections of the Appalachian Highlands region extend into Georgia. (See map on this page.) The Piedmont is a rolling plateau. Streams have carved deep gullies in the red clay soil of this section. Cotton fields, orchards, and forests cover much of the countryside here. The border between the Piedmont and the Coastal Plain is called the Fall Line. This is because waterfalls are formed here as rivers flow from the highlands to the lowlands. Most of Georgia's large cities are on the Piedmont or along the Fall Line. The three other highland sections of Georgia are much smaller than the Piedmont. Forests cover hills and ridges in these areas. Cotton, fruit, and other crops grow well in the broad fertile valleys of the Appalachian Ridges and Valleys section.

① Piedmont Plateau  ③ Appalachian Ridges and Valleys
② Blue Ridge  ④ Appalachian Plateau

**Georgia** is the largest state in the South. More than half of Georgia lies in the Coastal Plain. The rest of the state is in the Appalachian Highlands.

| Facts About Georgia | Number or Value | Rank |
|---|---|---|
| Area (square miles) | 58,876 | 21 |
| Population | 4,926,000 | 14 |
| Capital—Atlanta | | |
| Admission Date: January 2, 1788 | | 4 |
| Colleges and Universities | 62 | 13 |
| Farm Products | $1,984,657,000 | 17 |
| Poultry and eggs | 664,850,000 | 1 |
| Cattle and calves | 231,066,000 | 27 |
| Peanuts | 217,430,000 | 1 |
| Fish | $ 10,615,000 | 19 |
| Timber Harvested (cubic feet) | 789,008,000 | 4 |
| Minerals | $ 305,479,000 | 26 |
| Clays | 160,419,000 | 1 |
| Stone | 97,506,000 | 5 |
| Cement | 30,250,000 | 13 |
| Manufactures* | $7,362,200,000 | 15 |
| Textile-mill products | 1,541,600,000 | 3 |
| Transportation equipment | 901,300,000 | 13 |
| Food and kindred products | 822,100,000 | 15 |

*See Glossary

# Kentucky

Kentucky lies in three main regions of the South. These are the Appalachian Highlands, the Interior Plains, and the Coastal Plain.

**The Appalachian Highlands.** The Appalachian Highlands region stretches across the eastern part of Kentucky. Although much of this rugged land is forested, thousands of small farms are located in the broader, more fertile valleys of this region.

**The Interior Plains.** More than two thirds of Kentucky is in the Interior Plains region. Much of the land here is well suited to farming. Some of the best farmland is in the Bluegrass, a basin-shaped area in the northeast corner of this region. In the northwest are important deposits of coal. Near the center of this region, underground streams have formed huge caverns.

**The Coastal Plain.** The western tip of Kentucky lies in the Coastal Plain region. Here there are low hills and swampy lowland. Along the Mississippi River are fertile farmlands.

| Facts About Kentucky | | |
|---|---:|---:|
| | Number or Value | Rank |
| Area (square miles) | 40,395 | 37 |
| Population | 3,396,000 | 23 |
| Capital—Frankfort | | |
| Admission Date: June 1, 1792 | | 15 |
| Colleges and Universities | 36 | 29 |
| Farm Products | $1,355,366,000 | 23 |
|   Cattle and calves | 390,420,000 | 15 |
|   Tobacco | 306,434,000 | 2 |
|   Soybeans | 161,135,000 | 14 |
| Fish | $ 600,000 | 31 |
| Timber Harvested (cubic feet) | 116,764,000 | 24 |
| Minerals | $1,164,762,000 | 9 |
|   Coal | 986,654,000 | 2 |
|   Stone | 70,912,000 | 13 |
|   Petroleum | 34,515,000 | 20 |
| Manufactures* | $5,800,400,000 | 18 |
|   Electrical equipment and supplies | 823,400,000 | 10 |
|   Food and kindred products | 707,100,000 | 16 |
|   Nonelectrical machinery | 685,900,000 | 16 |

*See Glossary

① Appalachian Plateau
② Bluegrass
③ Knobs
④ Western Coalfield
⑤ Pennyroyal

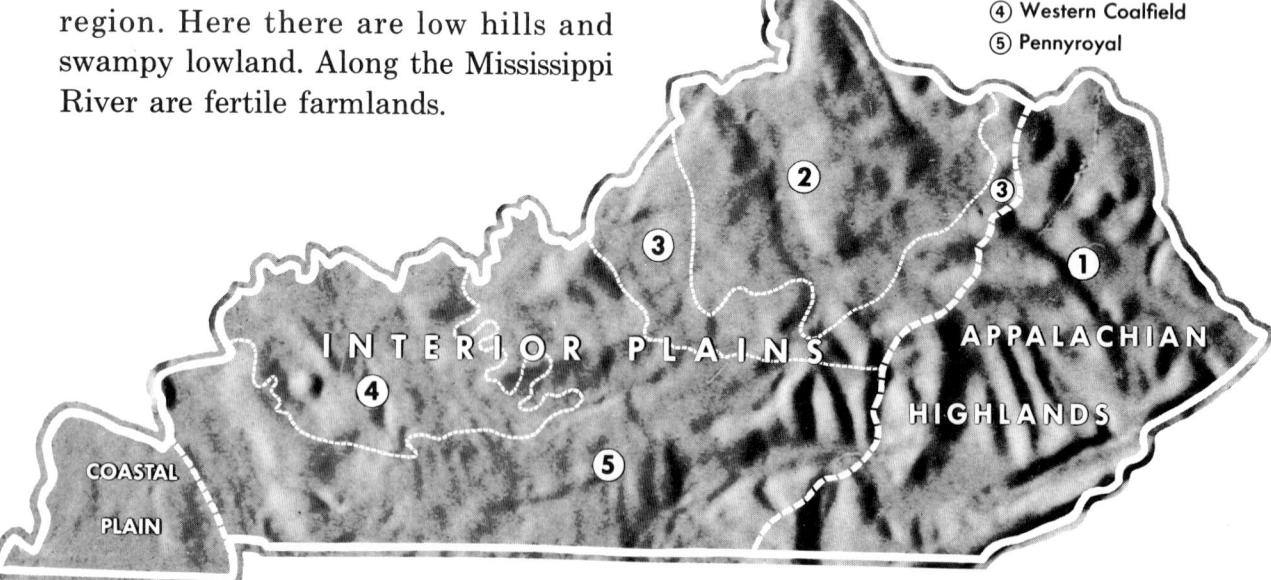

Kentucky lies in three main regions of the South. More than two thirds of the state lies in the Interior Plains. The eastern part of the state is in the Appalachian Highlands. The Coastal Plain extends across the western tip of Kentucky.

# Louisiana

Louisiana lies entirely in the Coastal Plain. As the map shows, however, the state may be divided into three sections.

**The Louisiana Lowland.** Nearly three fifths of Louisiana is covered by the Louisiana Lowland. This low, flat area includes Louisiana's Gulf coast and the fertile floodplains along the Mississippi River. In the past, the river overflowed its banks year after year. Today, huge walls of earth called levees* line the banks of the Mississippi and keep the river from flooding the land.

In southern Louisiana, the floodplains of the Mississippi River merge with low plains along the Gulf coast. Much of this area is crossed by slow-moving streams called bayous, and is dotted with lakes and swamps. Some farmers here grow rice and sugarcane. At the mouth of the Mississippi River is an area called the Mississippi Delta. Over many centuries, the river formed this delta by carrying soil downstream and depositing it in the Gulf.

**The Western Uplands.** The low, wooded hills of the Western Uplands cover about one third of Louisiana. The Red River winds southeastward through this area. Crops such as cotton and corn are raised on the fertile farmlands that border the Red River and other rivers in the Western Uplands.

**The Eastern Uplands.** The map on this page shows where the Eastern Uplands are located. The rolling land of this area is similar to that of the Western Uplands. Pine forests and pastures cover much of the land.

Louisiana lies in the Coastal Plain region. The state may be divided into the Louisiana Lowland, the Western Uplands, and the Eastern Uplands.

| Facts About Louisiana | | |
|---|---:|---:|
| | Number or Value | Rank |
| Area (square miles) | 48,523 | 31 |
| Population | 3,791,000 | 20 |
| Capital—Baton Rouge | | |
| Admission Date: April 30, 1812 | | 18 |
| Colleges and Universities | 23 | 34 |
| Farm Products | $1,181,580,000 | 27 |
|   Rice | 252,828,000 | 3 |
|   Soybeans | 240,344,000 | 9 |
|   Cattle and calves | 229,780,000 | 28 |
| Fish | $ 98,446,000 | 3 |
| Timber Harvested (cubic feet) | 602,353,000 | 7 |
| Minerals | $5,819,610,000 | 2 |
|   Petroleum | 3,327,702,000 | 2 |
|   Natural gas | 1,846,303,000 | 1 |
|   Natural-gas liquids | 420,708,000 | 2 |
| Manufactures* | $4,380,700,000 | 26 |
|   Food and kindred products | 584,300,000 | 23 |
|   Petroleum and coal products | 442,300,000 | 3 |
|   Paper and allied products | 400,200,000 | 14 |

*See Glossary

# Mississippi

Mississippi lies entirely in the Coastal Plain region of the South. As the map on this page shows, however, the state may be divided into four parts.

**The Mississippi River Lowland.** The great Mississippi River forms most of the western boundary of Mississippi. Along the river is a low, flat plain crossed by many slow, muddy streams that empty into the Mississippi. This is an important cotton-growing area. Levees protect the land here from floods.

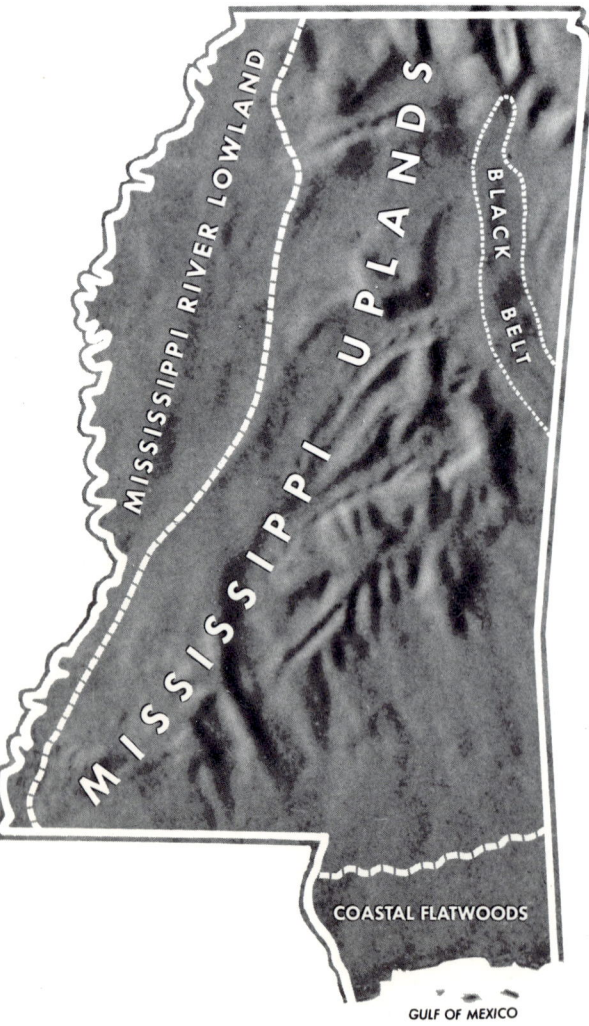

**Mississippi.** This state lies entirely within the Coastal Plain region of the South. However, it may be divided into four sections.

| Facts About Mississippi | | |
|---|---:|---:|
| | **Number or Value** | **Rank** |
| Area (square miles) | 47,716 | 32 |
| Population | 2,346,000 | 29 |
| Capital—Jackson | | |
| Admission Date: December 10, 1817 | | 20 |
| Colleges and Universities | 42 | 26 |
| Farm Products | $1,551,213,000 | 20 |
| Cotton | 386,885,000 | 3 |
| Soybeans | 337,188,000 | 8 |
| Poultry and eggs | 320,357,000 | 7 |
| Fish | $    16,887,000 | 15 |
| Timber Harvested (cubic feet) | 650,891,000 | 6 |
| Minerals | $  281,738,000 | 27 |
| Petroleum | 213,747,000 | 9 |
| Natural gas | 22,846,000 | 13 |
| Sand and gravel | 17,383,000 | 27 |
| Manufactures* | $2,771,600,000 | 29 |
| Lumber and wood products | 309,200,000 | 9 |
| Apparel and other textile products | 285,600,000 | 17 |
| Transportation equipment | 263,500,000 | 22 |

**The Coastal Flatwoods.** The low, sandy area in Mississippi that borders the Gulf of Mexico is called the Coastal Flatwoods.

**The Black Belt.** In northeastern Mississippi is a narrow, curving section of prairie called the Black Belt. It is named for its black, fertile soil. Farming and grazing are important here.

**The Mississippi Uplands.** Nearly three fourths of Mississippi is made up of rolling hills. This section is called the Mississippi Uplands. The highest and most rugged part of this section is a hilly area along the Tennessee River, in the northeastern corner of the state. The southeastern part of the Mississippi Uplands is an important timbering area known as the Piney Woods.

*See Glossary

# North Carolina

| Facts About North Carolina | Number or Value | Rank |
|---|---:|---:|
| Area (square miles) | 52,712 | 28 |
| Population | 5,451,000 | 11 |
| Capital—Raleigh | | |
| Admission Date: November 21, 1789 | | 12 |
| Colleges and Universities | 99 | 8 |
| Farm Products | $ 2,379,764,000 | 10 |
| Tobacco | 719,160,000 | 1 |
| Poultry and eggs | 552,211,000 | 4 |
| Soybeans | 208,863,000 | 10 |
| Fish | $ 16,066,000 | 16 |
| Timber Harvested (cubic feet) | 546,404,000 | 8 |
| Minerals | $ 146,930,000 | 32 |
| Stone | 80,065,000 | 9 |
| Sand and gravel | 19,327,000 | 25 |
| Cement | Not available | |
| Manufactures* | $11,023,100,000 | 10 |
| Textile mill products | 3,036,800,000 | 1 |
| Tobacco | 1,263,700,000 | 1 |
| Chemicals and allied products | 888,800,000 | 12 |

North Carolina lies in two main regions of the South. These are the Coastal Plain and the Appalachian Highlands.

**The Coastal Plain.** In North Carolina, the Coastal Plain is bordered on the east by the Atlantic Ocean. A few miles off the seacoast is a long string of narrow, sandy islands called the Outer Banks. The part of the Coastal Plain that lies nearest to the ocean is low and flat. Here are broad, low prairies, tree-covered swamps, and many lakes. In places where the land is well drained, there are fields of crops. The western part of North Carolina's Coastal Plain is gently rolling. Crops grow well in this fertile area.

**The Appalachian Highlands.** Two sections of the Appalachian Highlands extend through North Carolina. The Piedmont is a broad plateau covered with farms, forests, and manufacturing cities and towns. Dams and power plants on the rivers here provide hydroelectricity for homes and factories. Along the western border of North Carolina are the high, forested mountains of the Blue Ridge. Between the mountains in the Blue Ridge are deep, narrow valleys. Great Smoky Mountains National Park is located along the border between North Carolina and Tennessee.

*See Glossary

**North Carolina,** the widest state east of the Mississippi River, stretches more than five hundred miles from east to west. The Appalachian Highlands region occupies the western three fifths of the state. The rest of North Carolina is in the Coastal Plain region.

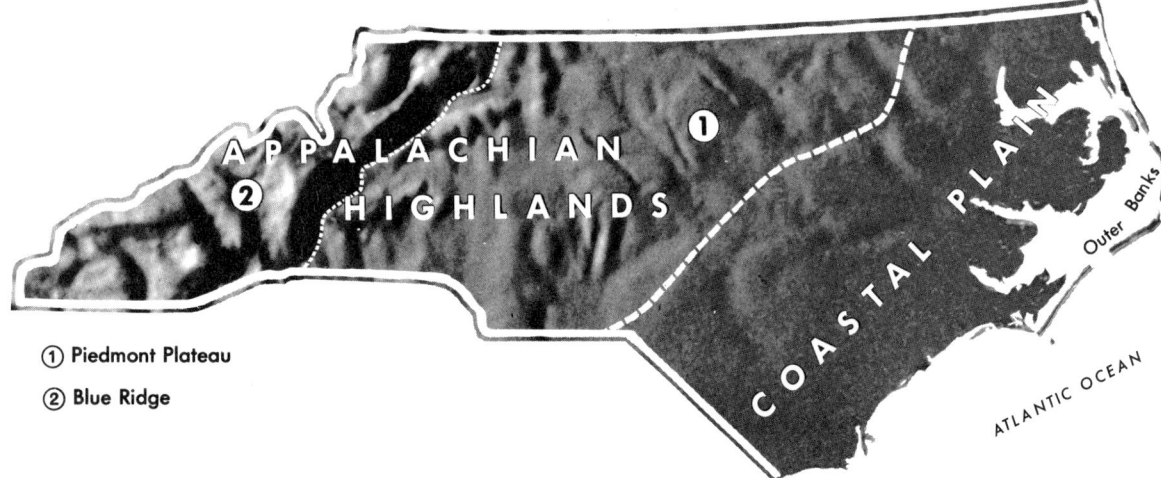

① Piedmont Plateau
② Blue Ridge

# South Carolina

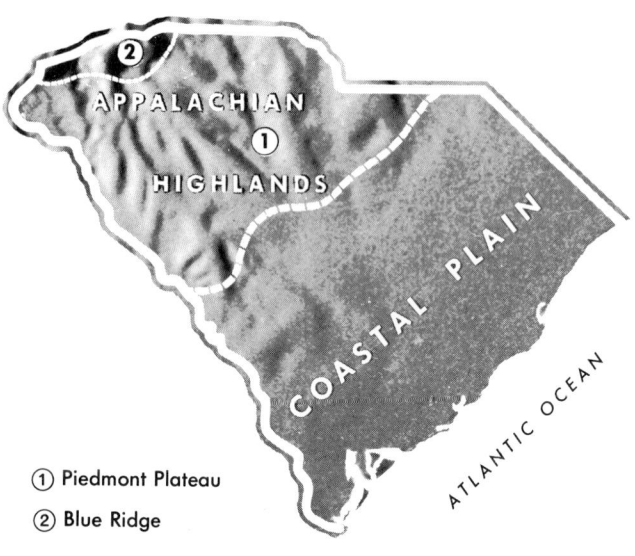

① Piedmont Plateau
② Blue Ridge

**South Carolina.** About two thirds of South Carolina lies in the Coastal Plain. The rest of the state is in the Appalachian Highlands region.

| Facts About South Carolina | Number or Value | Rank |
|---|---:|---:|
| Area (square miles) | 31,055 | 40 |
| Population | 2,818,000 | 26 |
| Capital—Columbia | | |
| Admission Date: May 23, 1788 | | 8 |
| Colleges and Universities | 47 | 21 |
| Farm Products | $ 755,683,000 | 35 |
| Soybeans | 135,985,000 | 15 |
| Tobacco | 115,224,000 | 4 |
| Poultry and eggs | 106,959,000 | 21 |
| Fish | $ 11,258,000 | 18 |
| Timber Harvested (cubic feet) | 405,379,000 | 11 |
| Minerals | $ 88,361,000 | 39 |
| Cement | Not available | |
| Stone | 24,280,000 | 25 |
| Clays | 12,877,000 | 6 |
| Manufactures* | $4,921,000,000 | 22 |
| Textile-mill products | 1,716,900,000 | 2 |
| Chemicals and allied products | 801,000,000 | 14 |
| Nonelectrical machinery | 419,600,000 | 20 |

South Carolina is the smallest state in the South. It lies in the Coastal Plain region and the Appalachian Highlands region.

**The Coastal Plain.** The part of South Carolina that lies in the Coastal Plain is called the Low Country. A broad, smooth beach extends along the northern third of South Carolina's coast. Farther south, the coast is swampy and is broken into many low, flat islands. Cypress and gum trees grow in the dark, quiet waters of swamps in this area. The part of the Coastal Plain that lies farther inland is slightly rolling. Pine forests and farms cover much of this fertile area.

**The Appalachian Highlands.** Two sections of the Appalachian Highlands extend across South Carolina. These are the Piedmont Plateau and the Blue Ridge. The Piedmont Plateau, which lies west of the Coastal Plain, occupies almost one third of the state. Forests and farms cover much of this section of South Carolina. Several large rivers flow across the Piedmont. Dams and power stations have been built on a number of these rivers to provide hydroelectricity. The section of the Piedmont that lies along the Fall Line is an important industrial area and the most densely populated part of South Carolina. (See pages 24-25.)

The Blue Ridge section of the Appalachian Highlands occupies a small area in the northwestern part of South Carolina. In this state, the forested peaks of the Blue Ridge rise only about three thousand feet above sea level.

*See Glossary

# Tennessee

- ① Blue Ridge
- ② Appalachian Ridges and Valleys
- ③ Appalachian Plateau
- ④ Nashville Basin
- ⑤ Highland Rim

**Tennessee lies in three main land regions.** The eastern end of the state is in the Appalachian Highlands, and the western end is in the Coastal Plain. Between these two regions is the Interior Plains.

Tennessee lies in three main regions of the South. These are the Appalachian Highlands, the Interior Plains, and the Coastal Plain regions. The winding Tennessee River drains much of the state. (See map on pages 194-195.)

**The Appalachian Highlands.** Three sections of the Appalachian Highlands extend through Tennessee. The Blue Ridge lies along the eastern border of this state. In this section are the Great Smoky Mountains and several other mountain ranges. West of the Blue Ridge is the Appalachian Ridges and Valleys section. In Tennessee, most of this section is part of the Great Valley. (See page 27.) Still farther west is the Appalachian Plateau. The soil in this rugged, forested area is generally poor. However, large deposits of coal are located here.

**The Interior Plains.** The Interior Plains region of Tennessee is divided into two sections. The Nashville Basin is a lowland shaped somewhat like an oval. The gently rolling land of this area is much like that of Kentucky's Bluegrass. (See pages 30-31.) Surrounding the Nashville Basin is an area of hilly, less fertile land called the Highland Rim.

**The Coastal Plain.** The Coastal Plain region of Tennessee lies between the Mississippi and Tennessee rivers. Many crops are raised in this area.

| Facts About Tennessee | Number or Value | Rank |
|---|---:|---:|
| Area (square miles) | 42,244 | 34 |
| Population | 4,188,000 | 17 |
| Capital—Nashville | | |
| Admission Date: June 1, 1796 | | 16 |
| Colleges and Universities | 62 | 13 |
| Farm Products | $1,164,225,000 | 28 |
| Cattle and calves | 308,339,000 | 19 |
| Soybeans | 206,324,000 | 11 |
| Dairy products | 132,966,000 | 17 |
| Fish | $ 1,200,000 | 26 |
| Timber Harvested (cubic feet) | 161,343,000 | 19 |
| Minerals | $ 275,690,000 | 28 |
| Stone | 71,116,000 | 12 |
| Coal | 66,827,000 | 9 |
| Cement | 50,310,000 | 10 |
| Manufactures* | $7,715,700,000 | 14 |
| Chemicals and allied products | 1,425,000,000 | 8 |
| Food and kindred products | 697,900,000 | 17 |
| Electrical equipment and supplies | 684,100,000 | 14 |

*See Glossary

# Virginia

| Facts About Virginia | | |
|---|---:|---:|
| | Number or Value | Rank |
| Area (square miles) | 40,815 | 36 |
| Population | 4,967,000 | 13 |
| Capital—Richmond | | |
| Admission Date: June 25, 1788 | | 10 |
| Colleges and Universities | 70 | 11 |
| Farm Products | $ 923,400,000 | 33 |
| Cattle and calves | 164,948,000 | 32 |
| Poultry and eggs | 146,754,000 | 16 |
| Dairy products | 127,833,000 | 18 |
| Fish | $ 39,381,000 | 9 |
| Timber Harvested (cubic feet) | 352,786,000 | 13 |
| Minerals | $ 540,595,000 | 18 |
| Coal | 377,679,000 | 5 |
| Stone | 82,719,000 | 8 |
| Sand and gravel | 26,246,000 | 18 |
| Manufactures* | $6,121,800,000 | 17 |
| Chemicals and allied products | 830,600,000 | 13 |
| Food and kindred products | 612,800,000 | 21 |
| Tobacco | 556,700,000 | 2 |

Virginia lies in two main regions of the South. These are the Coastal Plain and the Appalachian Highlands.

**The Coastal Plain.** In Virginia, the Coastal Plain is called the Tidewater. Along the coast of this low, flat region are saltwater marshes, mud flats, and beautiful white sand beaches. These beaches and marshes are interrupted by many bays and river mouths.

**The Appalachian Highlands.** Parts of four sections of the Appalachian Highlands lie in the state of Virginia. The Piedmont of Virginia is a broad plateau. Forests and pastures cover much of this area. Towering above the western edge of the Piedmont is the forested Blue Ridge mountain chain. West of the Blue Ridge is the Appalachian Ridges and Valleys section. The Shenandoah River valley, one of Virginia's most prosperous farming areas, is located here. Near the western end of Virginia is a small section of the Appalachian Plateau, which is rich in coal.

*See Glossary

① Tidewater
② Tidewater (Eastern Shore)
③ Piedmont Plateau
④ Blue Ridge
⑤ Appalachian Ridges and Valleys
⑥ Appalachian Plateau

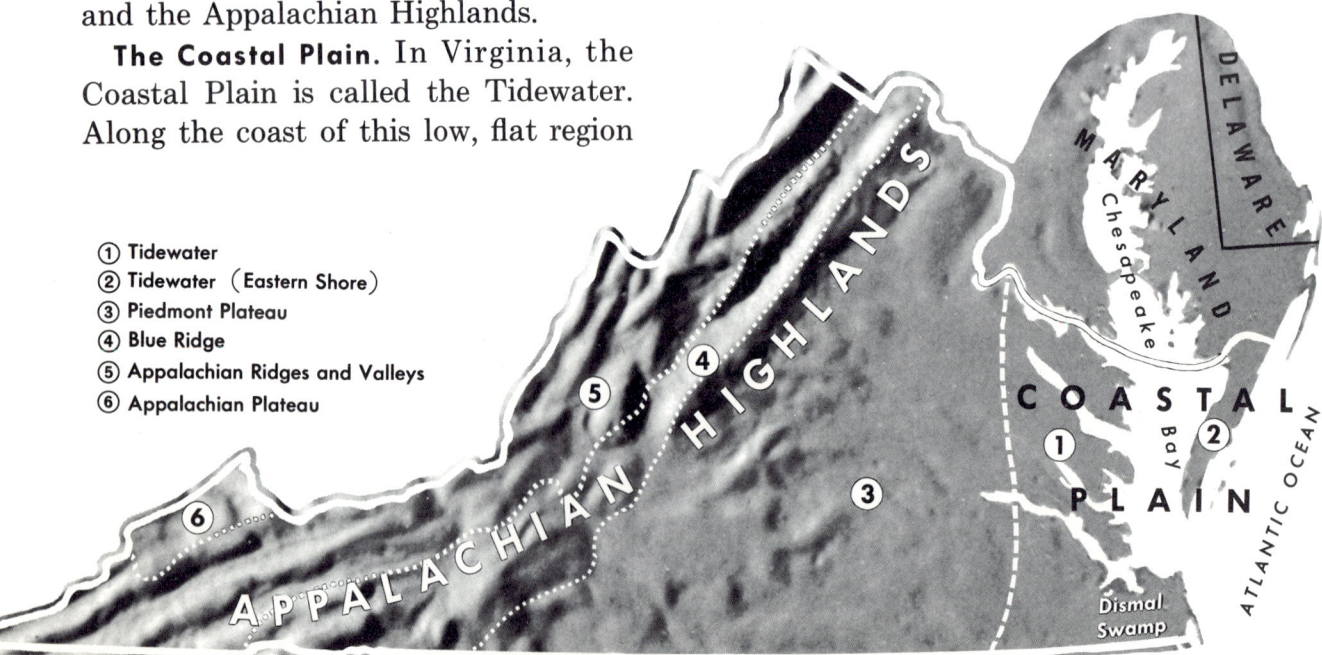

**Virginia** lies in two main regions of the South. The Coastal Plain region of Virginia is divided into two parts by Chesapeake Bay, which is an arm of the Atlantic Ocean. The Appalachian Highlands region covers the remainder of the state.

# Facts About Our States

| State | Capital | Largest City | Area (Square Miles) | Population (1975 Estimates) | Year of Admission |
|---|---|---|---|---|---|
| Alabama | Montgomery | Birmingham | 51,609 | 3,614,000 | 1819 |
| Alaska | Juneau | Anchorage | 586,400 | 352,000 | 1959 |
| Arizona | Phoenix | Phoenix | 113,909 | 2,224,000 | 1912 |
| Arkansas | Little Rock | Little Rock | 53,104 | 2,116,000 | 1836 |
| California | Sacramento | Los Angeles | 158,693 | 21,185,000 | 1850 |
| Colorado | Denver | Denver | 104,247 | 2,534,000 | 1876 |
| Connecticut | Hartford | Hartford | 5,009 | 3,095,000 | 1788 |
| Delaware | Dover | Wilmington | 2,057 | 579,000 | 1787 |
| Florida | Tallahassee | Jacksonville | 58,560 | 8,357,000 | 1845 |
| Georgia | Atlanta | Atlanta | 58,876 | 4,926,000 | 1788 |
| Hawaii | Honolulu | Honolulu | 6,424 | 865,000 | 1959 |
| Idaho | Boise | Boise | 83,557 | 820,000 | 1890 |
| Illinois | Springfield | Chicago | 56,400 | 11,145,000 | 1818 |
| Indiana | Indianapolis | Indianapolis | 36,291 | 5,311,000 | 1816 |
| Iowa | Des Moines | Des Moines | 56,290 | 2,870,000 | 1846 |
| Kansas | Topeka | Wichita | 82,264 | 2,267,000 | 1861 |
| Kentucky | Frankfort | Louisville | 40,395 | 3,396,000 | 1792 |
| Louisiana | Baton Rouge | New Orleans | 48,523 | 3,791,000 | 1812 |
| Maine | Augusta | Portland | 33,215 | 1,059,000 | 1820 |
| Maryland | Annapolis | Baltimore | 10,577 | 4,098,000 | 1788 |
| Massachusetts | Boston | Boston | 8,257 | 5,828,000 | 1788 |
| Michigan | Lansing | Detroit | 58,216 | 9,157,000 | 1837 |
| Minnesota | St. Paul | Minneapolis | 84,068 | 3,926,000 | 1858 |
| Mississippi | Jackson | Jackson | 47,716 | 2,346,000 | 1817 |
| Missouri | Jefferson City | St. Louis | 69,686 | 4,763,000 | 1821 |
| Montana | Helena | Billings | 147,138 | 748,000 | 1889 |
| Nebraska | Lincoln | Omaha | 77,227 | 1,546,000 | 1867 |
| Nevada | Carson City | Las Vegas | 110,540 | 592,000 | 1864 |
| New Hampshire | Concord | Manchester | 9,304 | 818,000 | 1788 |
| New Jersey | Trenton | Newark | 7,836 | 7,316,000 | 1787 |
| New Mexico | Santa Fe | Albuquerque | 121,666 | 1,147,000 | 1912 |
| New York | Albany | New York | 49,576 | 18,120,000 | 1788 |
| North Carolina | Raleigh | Charlotte | 52,712 | 5,451,000 | 1789 |
| North Dakota | Bismarck | Fargo | 70,665 | 635,000 | 1889 |
| Ohio | Columbus | Cleveland | 41,222 | 10,795,000 | 1803 |
| Oklahoma | Oklahoma City | Oklahoma City | 69,919 | 2,712,000 | 1907 |
| Oregon | Salem | Portland | 96,981 | 2,288,000 | 1859 |
| Pennsylvania | Harrisburg | Philadelphia | 45,333 | 11,827,000 | 1787 |
| Rhode Island | Providence | Providence | 1,214 | 927,000 | 1790 |
| South Carolina | Columbia | Columbia | 31,055 | 2,818,000 | 1788 |
| South Dakota | Pierre | Sioux Falls | 77,047 | 683,000 | 1889 |
| Tennessee | Nashville | Memphis | 42,244 | 4,188,000 | 1796 |
| Texas | Austin | Houston | 267,339 | 12,237,000 | 1845 |
| Utah | Salt Lake City | Salt Lake City | 84,916 | 1,206,000 | 1896 |
| Vermont | Montpelier | Burlington | 9,609 | 471,000 | 1791 |
| Virginia | Richmond | Norfolk | 40,815 | 4,967,000 | 1788 |
| Washington | Olympia | Seattle | 68,192 | 3,544,000 | 1889 |
| West Virginia | Charleston | Huntington | 24,181 | 1,803,000 | 1863 |
| Wisconsin | Madison | Milwaukee | 56,154 | 4,607,000 | 1848 |
| Wyoming | Cheyenne | Cheyenne | 97,914 | 374,000 | 1890 |

# Thinking and Solving Problems

**Why the social studies are important to you.** During the next few years, you will make an important choice. You will choose whether or not you will direct your own life. Many people are never aware of making this choice. They drift through life, never really trying to understand what is going on around them or why things turn out the way they do. Without knowing it, these people have chosen not to direct their own lives. As a result, they miss many enriching experiences. Other people make a serious effort to choose a way of life that will bring them satisfaction. If you decide to live by choice instead of by chance, you will be able to live a more satisfying life.

You will need three types of knowledge to live by choice successfully. Living by choice will demand a great deal from you. You will have to keep growing in three different types of learnings — understandings, values and attitudes, and skills. As the chart on the opposite page shows, the type of learnings we call understandings includes the kinds of information you need in order to understand yourself, your country, and your world. The type of learnings we call values and attitudes deals with the way you feel toward yourself and your world. The third type of learnings includes the skills you need to use in gaining understandings and developing constructive values and attitudes. Among these skills are those you need for obtaining and using knowledge, and for working effectively with other people.

The social studies can help you grow in the three types of learnings. Your social studies class is one of the best places in which you can explore the three types of learnings. Here you can obtain much of the information you need for understanding yourself and your world. You can practice many important skills. Through many experiences, you can begin to evaluate what in life is worthwhile to you.

**The problem-solving method will help you achieve success in social studies.** Since the social studies are of such great importance, you want to use the best possible study method. You could just read a textbook and memorize answers for a test. If you did so, however, you would forget much of the information soon after the test was over. Your thinking ability would not improve, and you would not gain new, constructive values and attitudes. You would not have the opportunity to use many important skills, either. We suggest that you use a special way of studying called the problem-solving method. To use this method in learning about the South, you will need to follow these steps.

**1. Do some general background reading** about the South or about one of the states of the South in which you are most interested.

**2. Choose an important, interesting problem** that you would like to solve. Write it down so that you will have clearly in mind what it is you want to find out. (Look at the sample problem on page 258.) If there are small problems that need to be solved in order to solve your big problem, list them, too.

**3. Consider all possible solutions to your problem** and list the ones that seem most likely to be true. These possible solutions are called "educated guesses," or hypotheses. You will try to solve your problem by finding facts to support or disprove your hypotheses.

**4. Test your hypotheses** by doing research. This book provides you with four main sources of information about the South. These are the pictures, the text, the maps, and the Glossary. To locate the information you need, you may use

# Thinking and the Three Types of Learnings

## THINKING

One of the main reasons you are attending school is to develop your ability to think clearly. Thinking includes seven different thought processes. (See definitions below.) If you learn to use your higher thought processes, rather than simply repeat information you have memorized, you will achieve greater success in school and in life. In fact, your ability to fulfill your obligations as a citizen will depend largely on how well you learn to think. Your ability to think clearly will also help you make progress in the three types of learnings included in the social studies. (See chart below.)

### Seven Thought Processes

1. **Remembering** is recalling or recognizing information.
2. **Translation** is changing information from one form into another, such as words into pictures.
3. **Interpretation** is discovering relationships among facts, concepts,* and generalizations.*
4. **Application** is applying the appropriate knowledge and skills to the solution of a new problem.
5. **Analysis** is separating complicated material into its basic parts to see how those parts were put together, how they are related to each other, and how the parts are related to the whole.
6. **Synthesis** is putting ideas together in a form that is not only meaningful but also new and original.
7. **Evaluation** is judging whether something is acceptable or unacceptable, according to definite standards.

## THREE TYPES OF LEARNINGS

| Understandings | Values and Attitudes | Skills |
| --- | --- | --- |
| Concepts | Beliefs | Obtaining knowledge |
| Generalizations | Appreciations | Using knowledge |
| Facts | Ideals | Working with others |

### Understandings

You will truly gain an understanding of important concepts and generalizations when you use your thought processes to organize information in meaningful ways. In turn, the concepts and generalizations you develop will help you learn to think critically about new situations you meet.

### Values and Attitudes

You will develop many constructive values and attitudes as you improve your thinking ability. Success in the higher levels of thinking will bring you faith that you can solve problems and make wise decisions. In turn, positive values and attitudes will help you to develop your thinking ability.

### Skills

You will be more successful in developing the social studies skills when you use your higher thought processes described above. In turn, you will find that the social studies skills will help you do the critical thinking needed for solving the many difficult problems you will face during your lifetime.

*See **Four Words To Understand**, page 258.

the Table of Contents and the Index. The suggestions on pages 259-262 will help you to locate and evaluate other sources of information.

As you do research, make notes of all the information you find that will either support your hypotheses or disprove them. You may discover that information from one source disagrees with information from another. If this should happen, check still further and try to decide which facts are correct.

**5. Summarize what you have learned.** Have you been able to support one or more of your hypotheses with facts? Have you been able to disprove one or more of your hypotheses? What new facts have you learned? Do you need to do further research?

You may want to write a report about the problem. To help other people share the ideas that you have come to understand, you may decide to illustrate your research project with maps, pictures, or your own drawings. You will find helpful suggestions for writing a good report on pages 262-264.

**You can use the problem-solving method throughout your life.** In addition to helping you to achieve success in the social studies, the problem-solving method can help you in another way. By using it, you will learn to deal with problems in a way that will be valuable to you throughout your life. Many successful scientists, business executives, and government leaders use this method to solve problems.

**A sample problem to solve.** As you study the South, you may wish to investigate problems about the South as a whole or about one state in this region. The following sample problem is about the South as a whole.

Farmers in the South grow many crops that cannot be grown successfully in most other parts of our country. **Why is it possible for farmers in the South to grow such crops?** As you make hypotheses to use in solving this problem, consider the following questions.
a. What facts about the climate in the South help to solve this problem?
b. What facts about the land in the South help to solve it?

### Four Words To Understand

1. **A concept** is a big, general idea that includes many smaller, more specific ideas. An example of a concept is the idea of "trade." Many kinds of exchange are included in this idea. Two children who exchange marbles on the playground are carrying on trade. A person who pays money for a loaf of bread is also carrying on trade; so is a factory that buys raw materials from other countries and sells its manufactured products overseas. Only as you come to see the various things that the word "trade" includes do you grow to understand this concept. Another example of a concept is the idea of "climate."

2. **A generalization** is a general rule or principle that expresses a meaningful relationship among two or more concepts. It is formed by drawing a conclusion from a group of facts. For example, "Through trade, all people on the earth can have a better living," is a generalization drawn from facts about trade and the way people live in various parts of the world. It includes four concepts: "trade," "all people," "the earth," and "a better living." These have been put together to give a significant understanding about the world. The many facts you read about, hear about, or experience will make more sense if you think of them as statements that can be combined to form meaningful generalizations. Remember, however, that if a generalization is based on wrong or insufficient facts, or is carelessly thought out, it may be false. Make certain that you understand the concepts in a generalization, and judge carefully whether or not you think it is true.

3. **Values** are the things in life that a person considers right, desirable, or worthwhile. For instance, if you believe that every individual is important, we may say that one of your values is the worth of the individual.

4. **Attitudes** are the outward expression of a person's values. For example, if you truly value the worth of every individual, you will express this value by treating everyone you meet with consideration.

# Learning Social Studies Skills

**What is a skill?** A skill is something that you have learned to do well. To learn some skills, such as swimming, you must train the muscles of your arms and legs. To learn others, such as typing, you must train your fingers. Still other skills require you to train your mind. For example, reading with understanding is a skill that requires much mental training. The skills that you use in the social studies are largely mental skills.

**Why are skills important?** Mastering different skills will help you to have a more satisfying life. You will be healthier and enjoy your leisure time more if you develop skills needed to take part in various sports. By developing artistic skills, you will be able to express your feelings more fully. It is even more important for you to develop skills of the mind. These skills are the tools that you will use in obtaining and using the knowledge you need to live successfully in today's world.

**To develop a skill, you must practice it correctly.** If you ask fine athletes or musicians how they gained their skills, they will say, "Through practice." To develop skills of the mind, you must practice also. Remember, however, that a person cannot become a good ballplayer if he or she keeps throwing the ball incorrectly. The same thing is true of mental skills. To master them, you must practice them correctly.

The following pages contain suggestions about how to perform correctly several important skills needed in the social studies. Study these skills carefully, and use them.

## How To Find Information You Need

Each day of your life you seek information. Sometimes you want to know certain facts just because you are curious. Most of the time, however, you want information for some special purpose. If your hobby is baseball, for example, you may want to know how to figure batting averages. If you collect stamps, you need to know how to identify the countries they come from. As a student in today's world, you need information for many purposes. As an adult, you will need even more knowledge to live successfully in tomorrow's world.

You may wonder how you can possibly learn all the facts you are going to need during your lifetime. The answer is that you can't. Therefore, knowing how to find information when you need it is of vital importance to you. Following are suggestions for locating good sources of information and for using these sources to find the facts that you need.

### Written Sources of Information

1. <u>Books</u>. You may be able to find the information you need in books that you have at home or in your classroom. To see if a textbook or other nonfiction book has the information you need, look at the table of contents and the index.

Sometimes, you will need to go to your school or community library to locate books that contain the information you want. To make the best use of a library, you should learn to use the card catalog. This is a file that contains information about the books in the library. Each nonfiction book has at least three cards, filed in alphabetical order. One is for the title, one is for the author, and one is for the subject of the book. Each card gives the book's special number. This number will help you to find the book, since all the nonfiction books in the library are arranged on the shelves in numerical order. If you cannot find a book you want, the librarian will be glad to help you.

2. <u>Reference volumes</u>. You will find much useful information in special books known as reference volumes. These include dictionaries, encyclopedias, atlases, and other

special books. Some companies publish a book each year with statistics and general information about the events of the preceding year. Such books are usually called yearbooks, annuals, or almanacs.

3. <u>Newspapers and magazines.</u> These are important sources of up-to-date information. Sometimes you will want to look for information in papers or magazines that you do not have at home. You can usually find the ones you want at the library.

The *Readers' Guide to Periodical Literature,* which is available in most libraries, will direct you to magazine articles about the subject you are investigating. This is a series of volumes that list articles by title, author, and subject. In the front of each volume is an explanation of the abbreviations used to indicate the different magazines and their dates.

4. <u>Booklets, pamphlets, and bulletins.</u> Many materials of this type are available from local and state governments, as well as from our federal government. Chambers of commerce, travel bureaus, trade organizations, private companies, and embassies of foreign countries publish materials that contain a wealth of information.

Many booklets and bulletins give accurate information. You should remember, however, that some of them are intended to promote certain products or ideas. Information obtained from such sources should be checked carefully.

### Reading for Information

The following suggestions will help you to save time and effort when you are looking for information in books and other written materials.

1. <u>Use the table of contents and the index.</u> The table of contents appears at the beginning of the book and generally is a list of the chapters in the book. By looking at this list, you can usually tell whether the book has the type of information you need.

The index is a more detailed list of the topics that are discussed in the book. It will help you locate the pages on which specific facts are discussed. In most books, the index is at the back. Encyclopedias often include the index in a separate volume, however.

At the beginning of an index, you will usually find an explanation that makes it easier to use. For example, the explanation at the beginning of the Index for this book tells you that *p* means picture and *m* means map.

The topics, or entries, in the index are arranged in alphabetical order. To locate all the information you need, you may have to look under more than one entry. For example, to find out on what pages in this book there is information about the Civil War, look up the entry for this war, and also see if the Civil War is listed under the entries for history.

2. <u>Skim the written material to see if it contains the information you need.</u> Before you begin reading a chapter or a page, skim it to see if it has the information you need. In this way you will not run the risk of wasting time reading something that is of little or no value to you. When you skim, you look mainly for topic headings, topic sentences, and key words. For example, imagine you are looking for the answer to the question: "What two important basins lie in the Interior Plains region of the South?" You might look for a topic heading that says "Interior Plains." When you find this topic heading, you might look for the key word "basins."

3. <u>Read carefully when you think you have located the information you need.</u> When you think you have found the page that contains the information you are looking for, read it carefully. Does it really tell you what you want to know? If not, you will need to look further.

**Other Ways of Obtaining Information**

1. Direct experience. What you observe or experience for yourself may be a good source of information if you have observed carefully and remembered accurately. Firsthand information can often be obtained by visiting places in your community or nearby, such as museums, factories, or government offices.

2. Radio and television. Use the listings in your local newspaper to find programs about the subjects in which you are interested.

3. Movies, filmstrips, recordings, and slides. Materials on a great variety of subjects are available. They can be obtained from schools, libraries, museums, and private companies.

4. Resource people. Sometimes, you will be able to obtain information by interviewing a person who has special knowledge. On occasion, you may wish to invite someone to speak to your class and answer questions.

## Evaluating Information

During your lifetime, you will constantly need to evaluate what you see, hear, and read. Information is not true or significant simply because it is presented on television or is written in a book, magazine, or newspaper. The following suggestions will help you in evaluating information.

**Learn to tell the difference between primary and secondary sources of information.** A primary source of information is a firsthand record. For example, a photograph taken of an event while it is happening is a primary source. So is the report you write about a field trip you take. Original documents, such as the Constitution of the United States, are primary sources also.

A secondary source is a secondhand report. For example, if you write a report about what someone else told you he or she saw, your report will be a secondary source of information. Another example of a secondary source is a history book.

Advanced scholars like to use primary sources whenever possible. However, these sources are often difficult to obtain. Most students in elementary and high school use secondary sources. You should always be aware that you are using secondhand information when you use a secondary source.

**Find out who said it and when it was said.** The next step in evaluating information is to ask, "Who said it?" Was she a scholar with special training in the subject about which she wrote? Was he a newsman with a reputation for careful reporting of the facts?

Another question you should ask is "When was it said?" Changes take place rapidly in our world, and the information you are using may be out of date. For example, suppose you are looking for information about a country. If you use an encyclopedia that is five years old, much of the information you find will be inaccurate.

**Find out if it is mainly fact or opinion.** The next step in evaluating information is to decide whether it is based on facts or whether it mainly consists of unsupported opinions. You can do this best if you are aware of these three types of statements:

1. Statements of fact that can be checked. For example, "Voters in the United States choose their representatives by secret ballot" is a statement of fact that can be checked by observing how voting is carried on in different parts of our country.

2. Inferences, or conclusions that are based on facts. The statement "The people of the United States live in a democracy" is an inference. This inference is based on the fact that the citizens choose their representatives by secret ballot, and on other facts that can be proved. It is important to remember that inferences can be false or only partly true.

3. Value judgments, or opinions. The statement "It is always wrong for a country

## Seven Propaganda Tricks

People who use propaganda have learned many ways of presenting information to influence you in the direction they wish. Seven propaganda tricks to watch for are listed below.

**Name Calling.** Giving a label that is disliked or feared, such as "un-American," to an organization, a person, or an idea. This trick often persuades people to reject something they know nothing about.

**Glittering Generalities.** Trying to win support by using fine-sounding phrases, such as "the best deal in town" or "the American way." These phrases have no clear meaning when you stop and think about them.

**Transfer.** Connecting a person, product, or idea with something that people already feel strongly about. For example, displaying a picture of a church next to a speaker to give the impression that he or she is honest and trustworthy.

**Testimonial.** Getting well-known persons or organizations to announce in public their support of a person, product, or idea.

**Plain Folks.** Trying to win support by appearing to be an ordinary person who can be trusted. For example, a political candidate may try to win people's confidence by giving the impression that he or she is a good parent who loves children and dogs.

**Card Stacking.** Giving the wrong impression by giving only part of the facts about a person, product, or idea. For example, giving favorable facts, and leaving out unfavorable ones.

**Bandwagon.** Trying to win support by saying that "everybody knows that" or "everyone is doing this."

---

to go to war" is a value judgment. Since a value judgment is an opinion, you need to examine it very critically. On what facts and inferences is it based? For example, what facts and conclusions do you think form the basis of the opinion, "It is always wrong for a country to go to war"? Do you agree or disagree with these conclusions? Reliable writers or reporters are careful to let their readers know which statements are their own opinions. They also try to base their opinions as much as possible on facts that can be proved.

**Find out why it was said.** The next step in evaluating information is to find out the purpose for which it was prepared. Many books and articles are prepared in an honest effort to give you accurate information. For example, scientists writing about new scientific discoveries will usually try to report their findings as accurately as possible, and they will be careful to distinguish between what they have actually observed and the conclusions they have drawn from these facts.

Some information, however, is prepared mainly to persuade people to believe or act a certain way. Information of this kind is called propaganda.

Some propaganda is used to promote causes that are generally considered good. A picture that shows Smokey the Bear and the words "Only *you* can prevent forest fires" is an example of this kind of propaganda.

Propaganda is also used to make people support causes they would not agree with if they knew more about them. This kind of propaganda may consist of information that is true, partly true, or false. Even when it is true, however, the information may be presented in such a way as to mislead you.

Propaganda generally appeals to people's emotions rather than to their reasoning ability. For this reason, you should learn to identify information that is propaganda. Then you can think about it calmly and clearly, and evaluate it intelligently.

## Making Reports

There are many occasions when you need to share information or ideas with others. Sometimes you will need to do this in writing. Other times you will need to do it orally. One of the best ways to develop your writing and speaking skills is by making oral and written reports. The success of your report will depend on how well you have organized your material. It will also depend on your skill in presenting it. Here are some guidelines that will help you in preparing a good report.

**Decide upon a goal.** Have your purpose clearly in mind. Are you mainly interested in communicating information? Do you want to give your own viewpoint on a subject, or are you trying to persuade other people to agree with you?

**Find the information you need.** Be sure to use more than one source. If you are not sure how to locate information about your topic, read the suggestions on pages 259-261.

**Take good notes.** To remember what you have read, you must take notes. Before you begin taking notes, however, you will need to make a list of the questions you want your report to answer. As you do research, write down the facts that answer these questions. You may find some interesting and important facts that do not answer any of your questions. If you feel that they might be useful in your report, write them down, too. Your notes should be brief and in your own words except when you want to use exact quotations. When you use a quotation, be sure to put quotation marks around it.

You will be able to make the best use of your notes if you write them on file cards. Use a separate card for each statement or group of statements that answers one of your questions. To remember where your information came from, write on each card the title, author, and date of the source. When you have finished taking notes, group the cards according to the questions they answer. This will help you arrange your material in logical order.

**Make an outline.** After you have reviewed your notes, make an outline. This is a general plan that shows the order and the relationship of the ideas you want to include in your report. The first step in making an outline is to pick out the main ideas. These will be the main headings in your outline. (See sample outline below.) Next, list under each of these headings the ideas and facts that support or explain it. These related ideas are called subheadings. As you arrange your information, ask yourself the following questions.

a. Is there one main idea I must put first because everything else depends on it?
b. Have I arranged my facts in such a way as to show relationships among them?
c. Are there some ideas that will be clearer if they are discussed after other ideas have been explained?
d. Have I included enough facts so that I can complete my outline with a summary statement or a logical conclusion?

When you have completed your first outline, you may find that some parts of it are skimpy. If so, you may wish to do more research. When you are satisfied that you have enough information, make your final outline. Remember that this outline will serve as the basis of your finished report.

**Example of an outline.** The author of this feature prepared the following outline before writing "Making Reports."

I. Introduction
II. Deciding upon a goal
III. Finding information
IV. Taking notes
    A. List main ideas to be researched
    B. Write on file cards facts that support or explain these ideas
    C. Group cards according to main ideas
V. Making an outline
    A. Purpose of an outline
    B. Guidelines for arranging information
    C. Sample outline of this section
VI. Preparing a written report
VII. Presenting an oral report

**Special guidelines for a written report.** Using your outline as a guide, write your report. The following suggestions will help you to make your report interesting and clear.

Create word pictures that your readers can see in their minds. Before you begin to write, imagine that you are going to make a movie of the subject you plan to write about. What scenes would you like to show on the screen? Next, think of the words that will create these same pictures in your readers' minds.

Group your sentences into good paragraphs. It is usually best to begin a paragraph with a topic sentence that says to the reader, "This is what you will learn about in this paragraph." The other sentences in the paragraph should help to support or explain the topic sentence.

A sample paragraph. Below is a sample paragraph from this book. The topic sentence has been underlined. Notice how clear it is and how well the other sentences support it. Also notice how many pictures the paragraph puts in your mind.

> In the Appalachian Highlands region, climate varies with elevation. The higher you go above sea level, the cooler the air becomes. As you may have learned in your science class, the earth gives off heat that it has received from the sun. At low elevations, much of this heat is absorbed by the moisture and particles of dust in the air. At high elevations, however, the air is much cleaner and drier. Therefore, it cannot absorb as much heat. As a result, the temperature is usually cooler at high elevations than it is at lower elevations. Each three to four hundred feet of altitude makes a difference of one degree in temperature.

Other guidelines. There are two other things to remember in writing a report. First, use a dictionary to find the spelling of words you are doubtful about. Second, make a list of your sources of information to include at the beginning or end of your report. This list is called a bibliography.

**Special guidelines for an oral report.** When you are going to give a report orally, you will also want to organize your information in a logical order by making an outline. Prepare notes to guide you during your talk. These notes should be complete enough to help you remember all the points you want to make. You may even write out certain portions of your report that you prefer to read.

When you present your report, speak directly to your audience. Pronounce your words correctly and distinctly. Remember to speak slowly enough for your listeners to follow what you are saying, and use a tone of voice that will hold their interest. Stand up straight, but try not to be too stiff. Remember, the only way to improve your speaking skills is to practice them.

## Holding a Group Discussion

One of the important ways in which you learn is by exchanging ideas with other people. You do this frequently in informal conversation. You are likely to learn more, however, when you take part in the special kind of group conversation that we call a discussion. A discussion is more orderly than a conversation, and it usually has a definite, serious purpose. This purpose may be the sharing of information or the solving of a problem. In order to reach its goal, the discussion group must arrive at a conclusion or make a decision of some kind.

A discussion is more likely to be successful when those who take part in it observe the following guidelines.

**1. Be prepared.** Think about the topic to be discussed ahead of time. Prepare for the discussion by reading and taking notes. You may also want to make an outline of the ideas you want to share with the group.

**2. Take part.** Contribute to the discussion; express your ideas clearly and concisely. Be sure that the statements you make and the questions you ask deal with the topic being discussed.

**3. Listen and think.** Listen thoughtfully to others. Encourage all of the members of the discussion group to express their ideas. Do not make up your mind about a question or a problem until all of the facts have been given.

**4. Be courteous.** When you speak, address the entire group. Ask and answer questions politely. When you disagree with someone, point out your reasons calmly and in a friendly way.

### Working With Others

In school and throughout life, you will find that there are many projects that can be done better by a group than by one person working alone. Some of these projects would take too long to finish if they were done by a single individual. Others have different parts that can be done best by people with different talents.

Before your group begins a project, you should decide several matters. First, determine exactly what you are trying to accomplish. Second, decide what part of the project each person should do. Third, schedule when the project is to be completed.

The group will do a better job and reach its goals more quickly if each person follows these suggestions:

**1. Do your part.** Remember that the success of your project depends on every member of the group. Be willing to do your share of the work and to accept your share of the responsibility.

**2. Follow the rules.** Help the group decide on sensible rules, and then follow them. When a difference of opinion cannot be settled by discussion, make a decision by majority vote.

**3. Share your ideas.** Be willing to share your ideas and talents with the group. When you submit an idea for discussion, be prepared to see it criticized or even rejected. At the same time, have the courage to stick up for a principle or a belief that is really important to you.

**4. Respect others.** Remember that every person is an individual with different beliefs and talents. Give the other members of the group a chance to be heard, and be ready to appreciate their work and ideas.

**5. Be friendly, thoughtful, helpful, and cheerful.** Try to express your opinions seriously and sincerely without hurting others or losing their respect. Listen politely to the ideas of others.

**6. Learn from your mistakes.** Look for ways in which you can be a better group member the next time you work with others on a project.

### Building Your Vocabulary

When you do research in many different types of reading materials, you are likely to find several words you have never seen before. If you skip over these words, you may not fully understand what you are reading. The following suggestions will help you to discover the meanings of new words and build your vocabulary.

**1. See how the word is used in the sentence.** When you come to a new word, don't stop reading. Read on beyond the new word to see if you can discover any clues to what its meaning might be. Trying to figure out the meaning of a word from the way it is used may not give you the exact definition. However, it will give you a general idea of what the word means.

**2. Sound out the word.** Break the word up into syllables, and try to pronounce it. When you say the word aloud, you may find that you know it after all but have simply never seen it in print.

**3. Look in the dictionary.** When you think you have figured out what a word means and how it is pronounced, check with the dictionary. Have you pronounced it correctly? Did you decide upon the right definition? Remember, most words have several meanings. Do you know which meaning should be used?

**4. Make a list of the new words you learn.** In your own words, write a definition of each word you include in your list. Review this list from time to time.

# Learning Map Skills

**The earth is a sphere.** Our earth is round like a ball. We call any object with this shape a sphere. The earth is, of course, a very large sphere. Its diameter* is about 8,000 miles (12,874 kilometers*). Its circumference is about 25,000 miles (40,233 kilometers). The earth is not quite a perfect sphere, however, for it is slightly flattened at the North and South poles.

**Globes and maps.** The globe in your classroom is also a sphere. It is a model of the earth. The surface of the globe shows the shapes of the earth's landmasses and bodies of water. It also shows their locations. Globes are made with the North Pole at the top, but they are usually tilted to show the way the earth is tilted. Maps are flat drawings that represent part or all of the earth's surface.

**Scale.** Globes and maps give information about distance. When you use them, you need to know what distance on the earth is represented by a given distance on the globe or map. This relationship is called the scale. The scale of a globe or map may be expressed in several different ways.

On most maps, the scale is shown by a small drawing. For example:

Sometimes, the scale is expressed in this way: 1 inch = 400 miles (644 kilometers).

Scale is often shown in another way, especially on globes and large maps. For example: 1:10,000,000. These numbers mean that any given distance on the globe or map represents a distance on the earth that is ten million times as large. When the scale is shown in this way, you may use any kind of measuring unit you wish. If you choose the inch, then one inch on the globe or map equals ten million inches on the earth, or about 158 miles. If, however, you prefer to use measuring units from the metric* system, then one centimeter* on the globe or map would represent ten million centimeters on the earth, or 100 kilometers.

**Locating places on the earth.** Map makers, travelers, and other curious people have always wanted to know just where certain places are located. Over the years, a very accurate way of giving such information has been worked out. This system is used all over the world.

In order to work out a system for locating anything, you need starting points and a measuring unit. The North and South poles and the equator are the starting points for the system we use to locate places on the earth. The measuring unit for our system is called the degree (°).

**Parallels show latitude.** When we want to locate a place on the earth, we first find

*See Glossary

**The Chesapeake Bay area** is a different size on the two maps shown below. This is because one inch on each of these maps represents a different distance on the earth.

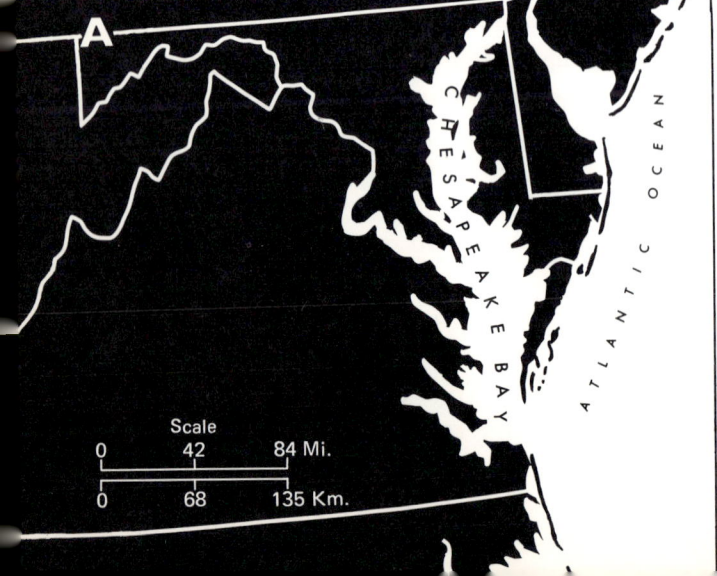
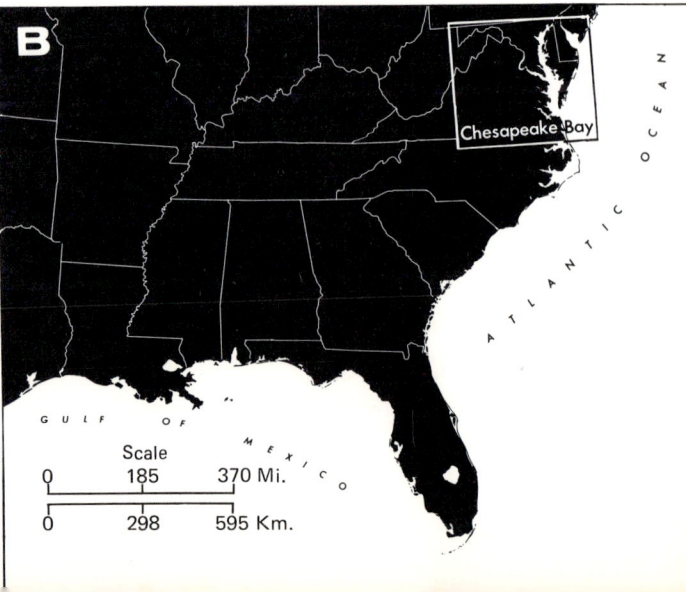

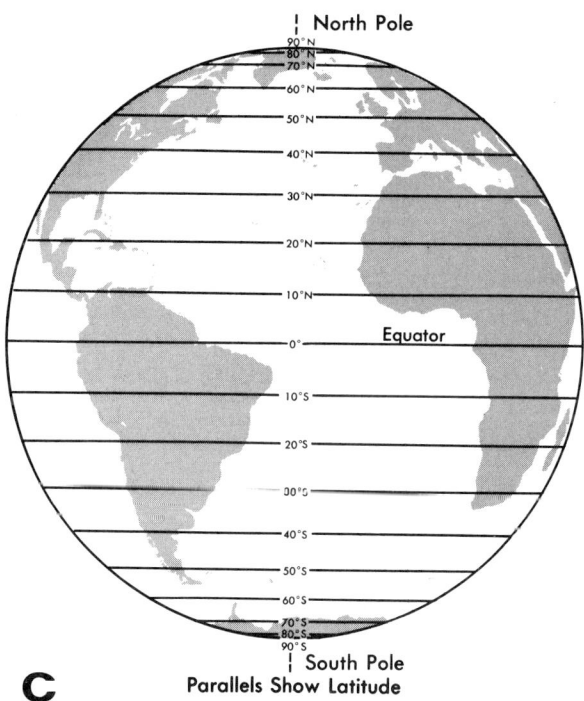

C  Parallels Show Latitude

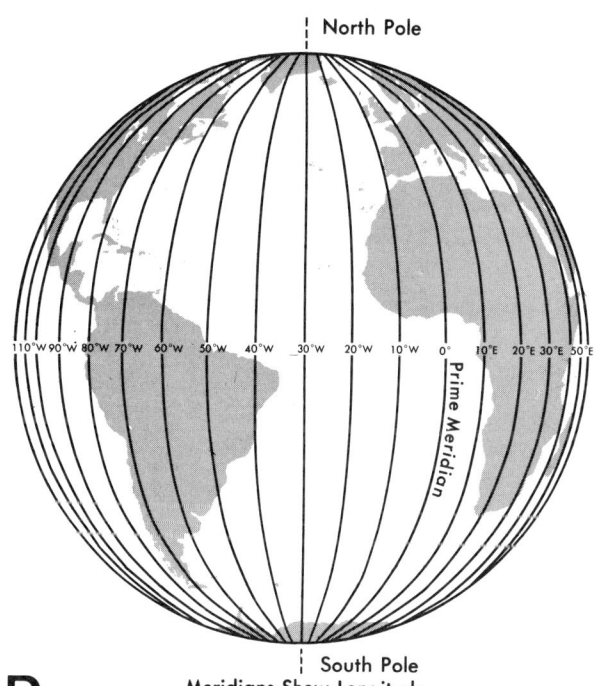

D  Meridians Show Longitude

out how far it is north or south of the equator. This distance measured in degrees is called north or south latitude. The equator represents zero latitude. The North Pole is located at 90 degrees north latitude, and the South Pole is at 90 degrees south latitude.

All points on the earth that have the same latitude are the same distance from the equator. A line connecting such points is called a parallel. This is because it is parallel to the equator. (See illustration C, above.)

**Meridians show longitude.** After we know the latitude of a place, we need to know its location in an east-west direction. This is called its longitude. The lines that show longitude are called meridians. They are drawn so as to connect the North and South poles. (See illustration D, above.) Longitude is measured from the meridian that passes through Greenwich, England. This line of zero longitude is called the prime meridian. Distance east or west of this meridian measured in degrees is called east or west longitude. The meridian of 180 degrees west longitude is the same as the one of 180 degrees east longitude. This is because 180 degrees is exactly halfway around the world from the prime meridian.

**Locating places on a globe.** The location of a certain place might be given to you like this: 30°N 90°W. This means that this place is located 30 degrees north of the equator, and 90 degrees west of the prime meridian. See if you can find this place on the globe in your classroom. It is helpful to remember that parallels and meridians are drawn every ten or fifteen degrees on most globes.

**The round earth on a flat map.** An important fact about a sphere is that you cannot flatten out its surface perfectly. To prove this, you might perform an experiment. Cut an orange in half and scrape away the fruit. You will not be able to press either piece of orange peel flat without crushing it. If you cut one piece in half, however, you can press these smaller pieces nearly flat. Next, cut one of these pieces of peel into three sections, or gores, shaped like those in illustration E, on page 268. You will be able to press these small sections quite flat.

A map like the one shown in illustration E can be made by cutting the surface of a globe into twelve pieces shaped like the smallest sections of your orange peel. Such a map would be fairly accurate. However, an "orange-peel" map is not an easy map to

## A Round Globe on a Flat Surface

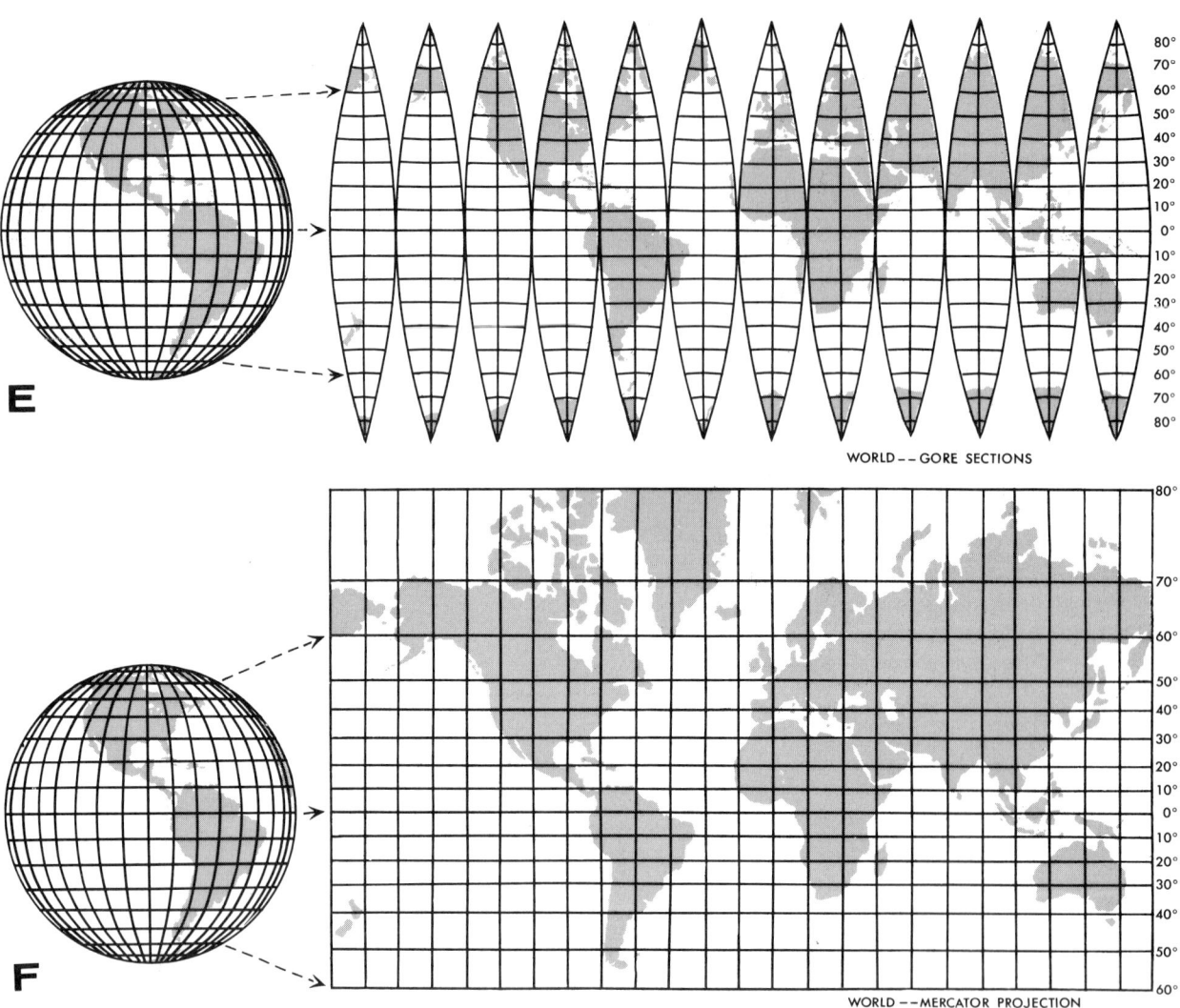

use, because the continents and oceans are split apart.

A flat map can never show the earth's surface as truthfully as a globe can. On globes, shape, size, distance, and direction are all accurate. Although a single flat map of the world cannot be drawn to show all four of these things correctly, flat maps can be made that show some of these things accurately. The various ways of drawing maps of the world to show different things correctly are called map projections.

**The Mercator\* projection.** Illustration F above, shows a world map called a Mercator projection. When you compare this map with a globe, you can see that continents, islands, and oceans have almost the right shape. On this kind of map, however, North America seems larger than Africa, which is not true. On Mercator maps, lands far from the equator appear larger than they are.

Because they show true directions, Mercator maps are especially useful to navigators. For instance, the city of Lisbon, Portugal, lies almost exactly east of Baltimore, Maryland. A Mercator map shows that a ship could reach Lisbon by sailing from Baltimore straight east across the Atlantic Ocean.

**The shortest route.** Strangely enough, the best way to reach Lisbon from Baltimore is not by traveling straight east. There is a shorter route. In order to understand why this is so, you might like to perform the following experiment.

On your classroom globe, locate Lisbon and Baltimore. Both cities lie just south of the 40th parallel. Take a piece of string and connect the two cities. Let the string follow the true east-west direction of the 40th parallel. Now, draw the string tight. Notice that it passes far to the north of the 40th parallel. The path of the tightened string is the shortest route between Baltimore and Lisbon. The shortest route between any two points on the earth is called the great circle route.

**The gnomonic (nō mon′ ik) projection.** Using a globe and a piece of string is not a very handy or accurate way of finding great circle routes. Instead, sailors and fliers use a special kind of map called the gnomonic projection. (See illustration G, below.) On this kind of map, the great circle route between any two places can be found simply by drawing a straight line between them.

**Equal-area projections.** Mercator and gnomonic maps are both very useful, but they do not show true areas. They cannot be used when you want to compare areas in different parts of the world. This is because sections of these maps that are the same size do not always represent the same amounts of the earth's surface.

Maps that do show true areas are called equal-area projections. If one square inch of such a map represents a certain number of square miles on the earth's surface, then every other square inch of the map will represent an equal number of square miles on the earth. In order to draw an equal-area map of the world on a flat surface, the shapes of the landmasses and bodies of water must be distorted. (See illustration H, below.) To avoid this, some equal-area maps are broken, or interrupted. The breaks are arranged to fall at places that are not important. (See illustration I, below.)

**Maps that show part of the earth.** For some purposes, we prefer maps that do not show the entire surface of the earth. A map of a very small area can be drawn more accurately than a map of a large area. It can also include more details.

Illustration J, on page 270, shows a photograph and a map of the same small part of the earth. The drawings on the map that show the shape and location of things on the earth are called symbols. The small drawing that shows directions is called a compass* rose.

**Maps for special purposes.** Maps can show the location of many different kinds of things. For instance, a map can show what minerals are found in certain places, or what crops are grown. A small chart that lists the symbols and their meanings is usually included on a map. This is called the legend, or key. (See map on pages 194-195.)

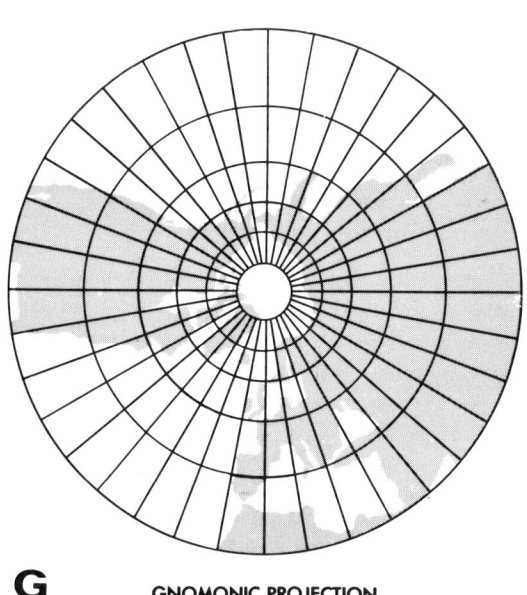

**G**  GNOMONIC PROJECTION

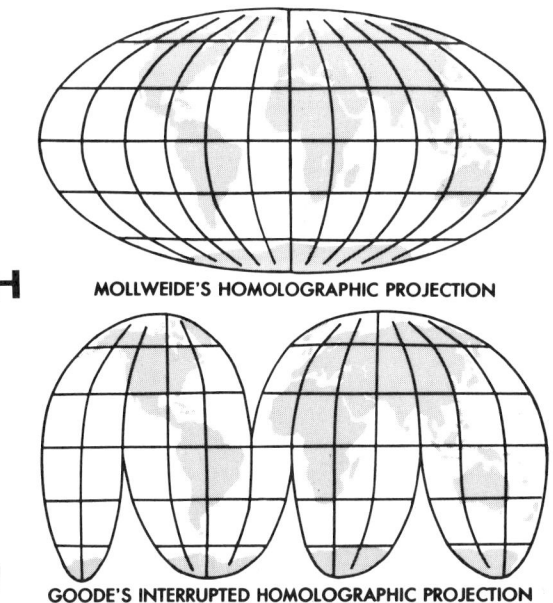

**H**  MOLLWEIDE'S HOMOLOGRAPHIC PROJECTION

**I**  GOODE'S INTERRUPTED HOMOLOGRAPHIC PROJECTION

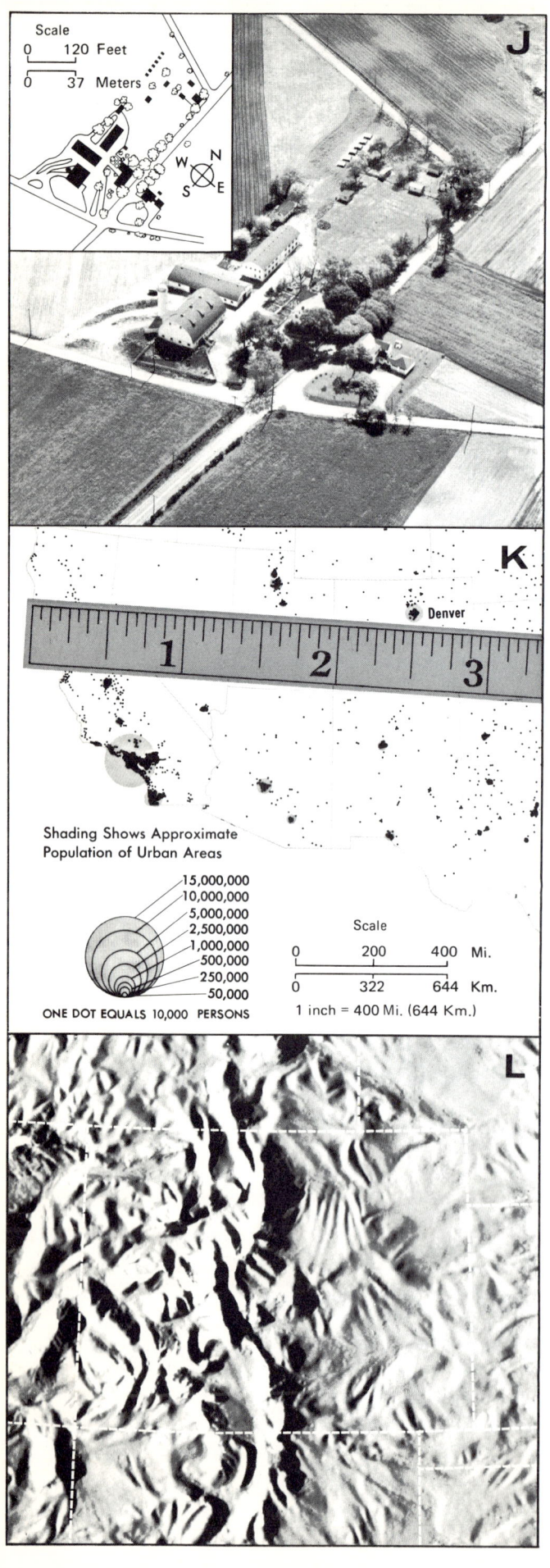

Symbols on some geography maps stand for the amounts of things in different places. For instance, map K, on this page gives information about the number of people in the southwestern part of the United States. The key tells the meaning of the symbols, which in this case are dots and circles.

On different maps, the same symbol may stand for different things and amounts. For example, each dot on map K, stands for 10,000 persons. On other maps, a dot might represent 5,000 sheep or 1,000 bushels of wheat.

There are other ways of giving information about quantity. For example, various designs or patterns may be used on a rainfall map to indicate the areas that receive different amounts of rain each year.

**Some globes and maps show the roughness of the earth's surface.** From a jet plane, you can see that the earth's surface is irregular. You can see mountains and valleys, hills and plains. For some purposes, globes and maps that show these things are needed. They are called relief globes and maps.

Since globes are three-dimensional models of the earth, you may wonder why most globes do not show the roughness of the earth's surface. The reason for this is that the highest mountain on the earth is not very large when it is compared with the earth's diameter. Even a very large globe would be almost perfectly smooth.

In order to make a relief globe or map, you must use a different scale for the height of the land. For example, you might start with a large flat map. One inch on your flat map represents a distance of 100 miles (161 kilometers) on the earth. Now you are going to make a model of a mountain on your map. On the earth, this mountain is two miles (3.2 kilometers) high. If you let one inch represent a height of two miles on the earth, your mountain should rise one inch above the flat surface of your map. Other mountains and hills should be modeled on this same scale.

By photographing relief globes and maps, flat maps can be made that show the earth much as it looks from an airplane. The maps at the top of page 12 of this book are photographs of a relief globe. Map L, on this page, is a photograph of a relief map.

**Topographic maps.** Another kind of map that shows the roughness of the earth's surface is called a topographic, or contour, map. On this kind of map, lines are drawn to show different heights of the earth's surface. These are called contour lines. The illustrations on this page help to explain how topographic maps are made.

Illustration M is a drawing of a hill. Around the bottom of the hill is our first contour line. This line connects all the points at the base of the hill that are exactly twenty feet above sea level. Higher up the hill, another contour line is drawn, connecting all the points that are exactly forty feet above sea level. A line is also drawn at a height of sixty feet. Other lines are drawn every twenty feet until the top of the hill is reached. Since the hill is shaped somewhat like a cone, each contour line is shorter than the one just below it.

Illustration N shows how the contour lines in the drawing of the hill M can be used to make a topographic map. This map gives us a great deal of information about the hill. Since each line is labeled with the height it represents, you can tell how high the different parts of the hill are. It is important to remember that land does not really rise in layers, as you might think when you look at a topographic map. Wherever the contour lines are far apart, you can be sure that the land slopes gently. Where they are close together, the slope is steep. With practice, you can picture the land in your mind as you look at such a map. Topographic maps are especially useful to people who design such things as roads and buildings.

On a topographic map, the spaces between the contour lines may be filled in with different shades of gray. If a different shade of gray were used for each different height of land shown in map N, there would be ten shades. It would be very hard for you to tell these different shades of gray apart. Therefore, on map O, at right, black and four shades of gray were used to show differences in height of forty feet. The key box shows the height of the land represented by the different shades. On some topographic maps, colors are used to represent different heights of land.

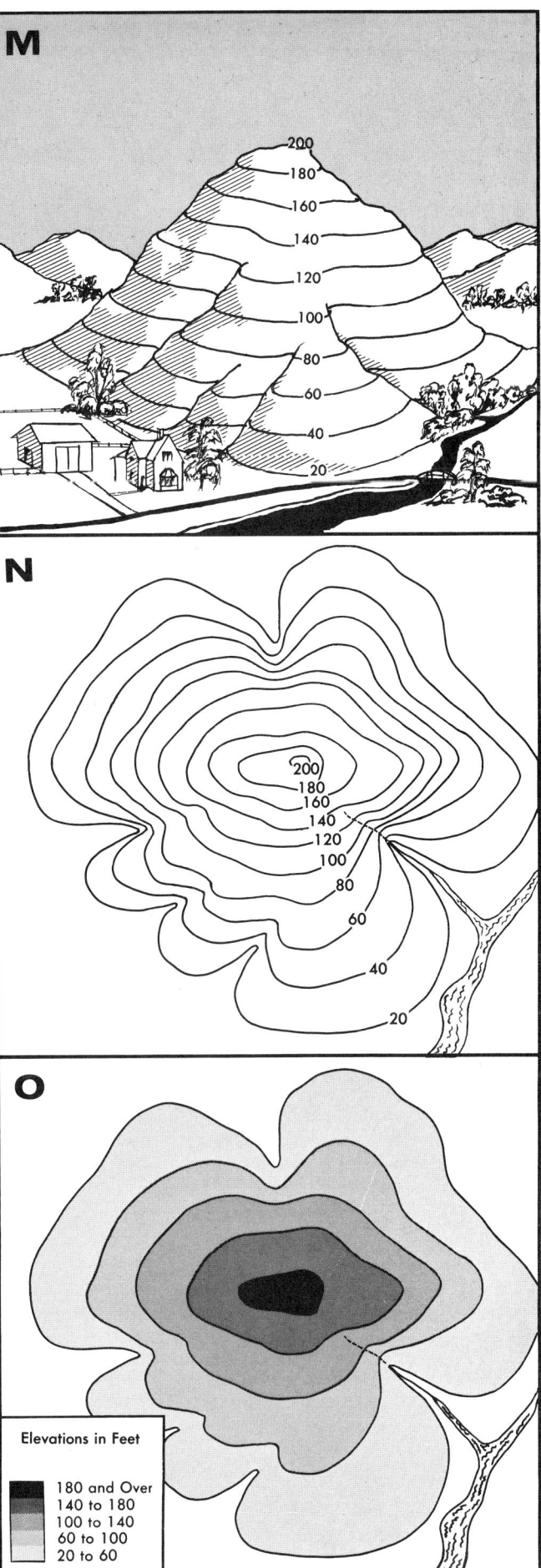

# GLOSSARY

## Complete Pronunciation Key

The pronunciation of each word is shown just after the word, in this way: **alumina** (ə lü′mə nə). The letters and signs used are pronounced as in the words below. The mark ′ is placed after a syllable with a primary or strong accent, as in the example above. The mark ′ after a syllable shows a secondary or lighter accent, as in **Cartier** (kär′ti ā′).

| | | | | | |
|---|---|---|---|---|---|
| a | hat, cap | j | jam, enjoy | u | cup, butter |
| ā | age, face | k | kind, seek | ů | full, put |
| ã | care, air | l | land, coal | ü | rule, move |
| ä | father, far | m | me, am | ū | use, music |
| | | n | no, in | | |
| | | ng | long, bring | | |
| b | bad, rob | | | | |
| ch | child, much | o | hot, rock | v | very, save |
| d | did, red | ō | open, go | w | will, woman |
| | | ô | order, all | y | young, yet |
| e | let, best | oi | oil, voice | z | zero, breeze |
| ē | equal, see | ou | house, out | zh | measure, seizure |
| ėr | term, learn | | | | |
| | | p | paper, cup | | |
| f | fat, if | r | run, try | ə | represents: |
| g | go, bag | s | say, yes | a | in about |
| h | he, how | sh | she, rush | e | in taken |
| | | t | tell, it | i | in pencil |
| i | it, pin | th | thin, both | o | in lemon |
| ī | ice, five | ᴛʜ | then, smooth | u | in circus |

**alluvial** (ə lü′ vi əl). Refers to soil that has been deposited by flowing water.

**alumina** (ə lü′ mə nə). A substance from which aluminum is made. Alumina is usually obtained by processing an ore called bauxite.

**amendment.** A change in, or an addition to, a constitution or a law.

**ammonia** (ə mōn′ yə). A colorless gas composed of nitrogen and hydrogen. It has a sharp smell and is easily dissolved in water. Ammonia is an important industrial chemical. It is used in the manufacture of certain fertilizers and explosives, and also in refrigeration.

**annex.** To make one territory part of another.

**antimony.** A brittle, bluish white metal used by industries in the making of products such as plastics, paint, and batteries.

**Appalachian** (ap′ə lā′chən) **Highlands.** A geographical region of eastern North America. In the United States, these highlands extend from central Alabama and Georgia northeastward to Canada. (See map, page 21.)

**Appalachian** (ap′ ə lā′ chən) **Mountains.** A name often used to refer to mountainous sections of the Appalachian Highlands, such as the Blue Ridge. (Compare maps on pages 15 and 21.)

**Appalachian** (ap′ ə lā′ chən) **Plateau.** The westernmost section of the Appalachian Highlands region. (See map, page 21.) It extends from central Alabama into New York. Most of the Appalachian Plateau in the South is usually known as the Cumberland Plateau.

**Appalachian** (ap′ ə lā′ chən) **Ridges and Valleys.** A section of the Appalachian Highlands region that extends from central Alabama into eastern New York. (See map, page 21.) It includes many long ridges that are separated by narrow valleys. The Great Valley is part of this section.

**atmosphere** (at′ mə sfir). The name given to the layer of air that surrounds the earth.

**atomic energy.** Energy that is stored in atoms. All matter is made up of atoms, which are much too small to be seen except with a special microscope. When atoms are split or combined in certain ways, great amounts of energy are released. This energy can be used for many purposes, including the production of electricity.

**axis of the earth.** An imaginary straight line that passes through the earth, joining the North and South poles. It takes the earth about twenty-four hours to rotate, or turn around, once on its axis.

**bale.** A large bundle of material that is squeezed together and tied with rope, wire, or straps. For example, cotton fiber is squeezed in a machine called a press, wrapped in burlap, and held together by six steel straps. A bale of cotton weighs 500 pounds.

**barite** (bār′ īt). A heavy mineral that may be white, yellow, or colorless. It is used in drilling oil wells and in the manufacture of various paints and chemicals.

**bauxite** (bôk′ sīt). An ore that is the chief source of aluminum. Bauxite may occur as a rocklike or claylike material. It may be red, yellow, or brown in color. Bauxite is processed to obtain alumina, from which aluminum is made.

**bayou** (bī′ ü). A shallow, winding, slow-moving creek or stream. Usually a bayou winds through lowlands or swamps.

**blast furnace.** A cylinder-shaped furnace in which iron is made from iron ore. It is called a blast furnace because a strong blast of air is blown into the bottom of the furnace. The air, which rises through a mixture of iron ore, coke, and limestone, helps the coke to burn at the high temperature needed for producing iron.

**blowgun.** A tube through which a poisoned dart or other object may be blown.

**bluegrass.** Any one of about 200 different grasses with bluish green stems and blue flowers. The best known is Kentucky bluegrass, a useful lawn and pasture grass.

**Blue Ridge.** A section of the Appalachian Highlands region that extends from northern Georgia into Pennsylvania. (See map on page 21.) The Blue Ridge is a chain of forested mountain ranges.

**boll weevil.** A small beetle that lays its eggs in the buds or bolls of cotton plants. The grubs that hatch from the eggs, as well as the adult beetles, cause much damage by eating the buds and bolls.

**burley.** A light-colored tobacco that is used chiefly in cigarettes.

**Cabot** (kab′ ət), **John,** 1450-1498. An Italian sailor who made two voyages to North America for the English.

**carbon.** A common substance found in nature in many different forms. A diamond is pure carbon and so is graphite, the black writing material in your pencil. Anthracite, a high-quality coal, is composed almost entirely of carbon. In combination with other substances, carbon is found in all living things, in many kinds of rock, and in petroleum.

**Cartier** (kär′ ti ā′), **Jacques,** 1491-1557. A French navigator and explorer. He discovered the St. Lawrence River in 1534.

**cash crops.** Crops that farmers raise to be sold, rather than to be used by themselves and their families.

**cellulose acetate** (sel′ yə lōs as′ə tāt). A synthetic material made from cellulose, which is found in trees and other plants. Cellulose acetate is used as a raw material for making synthetic fibers and various plastics. Items often made out of cellulose acetate are photographic film, rayon, and toys. See **synthetic.**

**Celsius** (sel′sē əs). Refers to a scale for measuring temperature. On the Celsius scale, which is part of the metric system, 0° represents the freezing point of water and 100° represents the boiling point. To convert degrees Celsius to degrees on the Fahrenheit scale, multiply by 1.8 and add 32. See **metric system** and **Fahrenheit.**

**centimeter** (sen′ tə mē′ tər). A unit in the metric system for measuring length. It is equal to about .39 inch. See **metric system.**

**circumference** (sər kum′ fər əns). The distance around an object or a geometric figure, especially a circle or a sphere.

**climate.** The average weather conditions of a given place over a period of many years. A description of climate includes such things as wind, sunshine, temperature, the amount of moisture in the air, and the amount of rain, hail, and snow that falls. See **weather**.

**Coastal Plain.** A large region of the United States that borders the Atlantic Ocean and the Gulf of Mexico. (See map, page 21.) The land in this region is level or gently rolling.

**coke.** A fuel made by roasting coal in special airtight ovens. It is one of the three main raw materials used in the production of iron. Coke, together with iron ore and limestone, is loaded into a blast furnace. (See **blast furnace**.) The coke serves as a fuel, burning at a very high temperature, to melt the other materials. The burning coke also provides gases that react with the molten ore to separate the iron from waste materials.

**Colonial Williamsburg.** The restoration of the colonial town of Williamsburg, Virginia. Historic buildings and gardens show what eighteenth-century life was like in this town.

**combine.** A machine that cuts and threshes grain as it moves across a field. See **thresh**.

**Communist.** Refers to an economic system known as communism. (See **economic system**.) Under communism, the government controls industry, farming, trade, education, and most other activities. The term Communist also refers to political parties, governments, and individuals who promote communism.

**compass rose.** A small drawing included on a map to show directions. A compass rose is often used as a decoration. Here are three examples of compass roses:

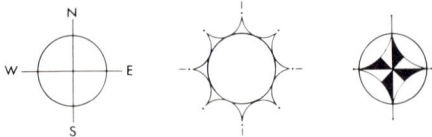

**condense.** To change from a gas to a liquid. For example, when steam is cooled it condenses into water.

**Confederacy** (kən fed′ ər ə si). Common name for the Confederate States of America, a nation made up of the eleven states that withdrew from and fought against the Union in the Civil War. The Confederacy included Texas and all of the states that make up the South except Kentucky.

**Confederate** (kən fed′ ər it). Of or relating to the Confederacy. See **Confederacy**.

**constitution** (kon′ stə tü′ shən). A system of basic principles or rules that provides the basis for a government. When spelled with a capital *C*, this word means the document that outlines the basic principles of the government of the United States, adopted in 1788. The first ten amendments to the Constitution are known as the Bill of Rights.

**conterminous** (kən tėr′ mə nəs) **United States.** The forty-eight states of the United States that are enclosed by an unbroken boundary. The word conterminous means "having the same boundary."

**cotton boll.** The seedpod of the cotton plant. The cotton boll is nearly round and about as large as a golf ball. It contains from thirty to fifty seeds covered with cotton fibers. When the boll is ripe, it splits open and the fibers fluff out.

**cotton gin.** A machine that separates seeds and other materials from cotton fibers. Teeth on a revolving drum hook the cotton fibers and pull them through openings that are too small to allow the seeds and other materials to pass through. The building in which such a machine is operated may also be called a cotton gin.

**coypu** (koi′ pü). A beaverlike animal, native to South America. It was brought to Louisiana in 1930. The coypu is valued for its soft, brownish fur, called nutria.

**crop rotation.** A farming procedure in which various crops are raised on the same land in different years. (See page 167.)

**crude oil.** Petroleum before it has been refined.

**Cuba.** An island country about 90 miles south of Florida. (See map, page 60.)

**Cumberland Gap.** A pass through the Cumberland Plateau, near the point where Virginia, Kentucky, and Tennessee meet. Many pioneers traveled through this pass when they moved westward to settle in Kentucky and Tennessee.

**Cumberland Plateau.** The name usually used for most of the Appalachian Plateau section of the South. See **Appalachian Plateau**.

**cypress.** In the South, this name usually refers to the bald cypress, a kind of tree that grows in swamps and along the banks of streams. The wood of the bald cypress is soft and light, and does not rot easily. There are several other kinds of cypress that are not related to the bald cypress.

**Davis, Jefferson,** 1808-1889. The president of the Confederate States of America. Davis was born in Kentucky but later moved to Mississippi. He served as a United States Army officer, as a member of both houses of Congress, and as secretary of war. In 1861, when Mississippi and several other southern states formed the Confederacy, Davis was chosen to be its president. See **Confederacy.**

**de Bry, Théodore,** 1528-1598. A German engraver. He used drawings and paintings by early explorers and settlers to make engravings portraying life in America in the late 1500's.

**democracy.** A political system in which people govern themselves, or a country with such a system of government. In democratic nations such as the United States, people may form and express their own opinions, choose their leaders, and help decide important issues. In a democracy, government is intended to protect the rights and freedoms of the individual.

**density of population.** The average number of people per square mile, or some other unit of area, in a given place. Density of population may be figured by dividing the total number of people in an area by the area's total number of square miles or other units.

**diameter** (dī am′ ə tər). A straight line that goes through the center of a geometric figure, especially a circle or sphere. The line joins two opposite points on the figure.

**dictatorship.** A government that is run by a single leader or by a small group of leaders who are not responsible to the people.

**Dismal Swamp.** A 750-square-mile area of wild swampland in northeastern North Carolina and southeastern Virginia.

**distill.** To cause a substance to give off vapor by heating it, and then to condense the vapor. The product or products that result may be entirely different from the original substance. Often, however, the product is a purer form of the original substance. For example, pure water can be obtained by distilling seawater.

**dulcimer.** A musical instrument consisting of metal wires stretched across the top of a flat box. The player strikes the wires with small, cork-tipped mallets.

**ecology** (ē kol′ ə jē). Refers to all the various relationships between living things (plants, animals, and human beings) and between living things and their environment. Also, the scientific study of these relationships. See **environment.**

**economic system.** The system followed by the people of a country in deciding what goods and services shall be produced, how they shall be produced, and to whom they shall be distributed.

**environment** (en vī′rən mənt). All of the objects and conditions that surround living creatures and influence their growth and development. The environment of human beings includes such things as air, sunlight, water, rocks, plants, and animals.

**equator** (i kwā′ tər). An imaginary line around the earth, dividing it into a northern half and a southern half.

**equinox** (ē′kwə noks). Either of two times of the year when the sun shines directly on the equator. These occur about March 21 and September 22. At these two times, day and night are of equal length everywhere on earth.

**erosion.** The process by which the rock and soil of the earth's surface are worn away or dissolved by the forces of nature. Erosion includes wearing away by the action of rainfall, running water, ice, wind, and waves. Erosion may benefit human beings, as when soil is formed from rocks, or it may be harmful, as when fertile soil is washed away.

**etcher.** An artist who uses the technique of etching, which is the process of engraving lines in a metal plate with acid. The plate is then used to print copies of the design or picture.

**evaporate** (i vap′ ə rāt). To change from a liquid to a gas or vapor. When water evaporates, it mixes with the air as water vapor.

**Fahrenheit** (far′ən hīt). Refers to a scale for measuring temperature in which the freezing point of water is represented by 32° and the boiling point by 212°. See **Celsius.**

---

PRONUNCIATION KEY: hat, āge, cāre, fär; let, ēqual, tėrm; it, īce; hot, ōpen, ôrder; oil, out; cup, pùt, rüle, ūse; **child;** lo**ng; thin;** ᴛHen; **zh,** measure; ə represents **a** in about, **e** in taken, **i** in pencil, **o** in lemon, **u** in circus. For the complete key, see page 272.

**Fall Line.** The border between the Piedmont Plateau and the Coastal Plain. Many rapids and low waterfalls are formed as rivers flow from the plateau onto the plain.

**federal.** Refers to the national government of the United States, as opposed to a state or local government.

**finfish.** A true fish, as opposed to a shellfish. (See **shellfish**.) Finfish have backbones and breathe through gills.

**flax.** A tall, slender plant with long, narrow leaves and, usually, blue flowers. The fibers of the stem are used to make products such as linen cloth, thread, and rope.

**floodplain.** A plain made up of soil that has been deposited by a flooding river.

**fluorite** (flü′ə rīt). A mineral that occurs in many different colors, usually in the form of transparent crystals. Much of the fluorite mined in the United States is used in the steelmaking process. Fluorite is also used in manufacturing industrial chemicals and ceramic products.

**French Revolution.** The period of violence and disorder in France from 1789 to 1799, during which the people overthrew the king. Although the people gained control of the country, the republic they established did not last. However, even under Napoleon Bonaparte, who ruled France as a dictator from 1799 until 1815, the French people had more equality of opportunity than they had ever known before.

**fuller's earth.** A kind of clay, varying in color from white to brown. It is used mainly to remove impurities from oils and to speed up certain chemical processes.

**Georgian** (jôr′ jən) **style.** In architecture, a style commonly used in Britain and her colonies in the 1700's and early 1800's. A house built in the Georgian style was usually very impressive, with the same number of windows on each side of an elaborate central doorway.

**gorges.** Deep, narrow valleys with steep, rocky walls.

**graphite.** A soft, black form of carbon that has a greasy feel. The "lead" in pencils is really graphite. This material is also used in electrical equipment and lubricants. Graphite occurs in nature as a mineral, but it is also produced from coal and petroleum.

**Great Lakes.** Five huge lakes in the central part of North America. These are Lakes Superior, Michigan, Huron, Erie, and Ontario. (See map, page 29.) The lakes are connected by straits, rivers, and canals.

**Great Valley.** A long chain of river valleys in the eastern part of the United States. The Great Valley forms a large part of the Appalachian Ridges and Valleys section of the Appalachian Highlands.

**growing season.** The period of time when crops can be grown outdoors without danger of being killed by frost.

**gum tree.** Any one of certain kinds of trees that yield a thick gummy substance. In the South, common gum trees are the sweet gum, the sour gum, and the tupelo. The hard, reddish brown wood of the sweet gum is used in making furniture, boxes, and other products.

**Hampton Roads.** A natural channel in southeastern Virginia through which three rivers empty into Chesapeake Bay. The ports of Newport News, Hampton, Portsmouth, and Norfolk are on this channel.

**Havana** (hə van′ ə). The capital and largest city of Cuba. See **Cuba**.

**Henry, Patrick,** 1736-1799. An early American statesman and orator, who urged the colonies to fight for their independence from England.

**hominy** (hom′ ə ni) **grits.** A food made by removing the skins from kernels of corn and then grinding the kernels into a coarse meal. The meal is usually boiled or fried.

**Huguenots** (hū′ gə nots). The name given in the sixteenth and seventeenth centuries to the Protestants in France. The Huguenots were often persecuted by French Roman Catholics.

**hydroelectricity** (hī′ drō i lek ′tris′ə ti). Electricity produced by waterpower. The force of rushing water is used to run machines called generators, which produce electricity.

**inalienable** (in āl′ yə nə bəl) **rights.** Those natural rights that a person cannot give up or transfer to the government. In a democracy, the government respects and protects the inalienable rights of the people. Our Declaration of Independence states that among our inalienable rights are "Life, Liberty, and the pursuit of Happiness."

**indigo** (in′ də gō). A plant from which a deep-blue dye, also called indigo, may be obtained.

**infectious disease.** Any disease that is caused by germs. Measles and scarlet fever are examples of infectious diseases.

**integrate** (in′ tə grāt). The opposite of segregate. See **segregation**.

**Interior Highlands.** A region that includes northwestern Arkansas, part of eastern Oklahoma, most of the southern half of Missouri, and a small area near the southern tip of Illinois. (See map, page 21.) The Interior Highlands region includes the Ozark Plateau and the Ouachita Mountains.

**Interior Plains.** A large region in the central part of North America. (See map, page 21.) Much of the land in this region is level or gently rolling.

**irrigate.** To supply land with water by artificial rather than natural means. Ditches, canals, pipelines, and sprinklers are common means of irrigation.

**Jackson, Andrew,** 1767-1845. The seventh president of the United States. Jackson was born in South Carolina but lived in Tennessee most of his life. He served in both houses of Congress when he was a young man and was a successful general during the War of 1812. He was elected president in 1828 and 1832.

**Jefferson, Thomas,** 1743-1826. The third president of the United States.

**kerosene** (ker′ə sēn). An oily liquid generally obtained from petroleum. Much of the kerosene now being produced is mixed with gasoline and used as fuel for jet-aircraft engines. In many areas where there is no electricity, kerosene is still used as a fuel for lamps and stoves. It is also used in the manufacture of liquids for killing insects.

**kilometer** (kə lom′ ə tər). A unit in the metric system for measuring length. It is equal to about .62 mile. See **metric system**.

**Latin America.** Commonly, all of the lands in the Western Hemisphere south of the United States. Includes Mexico, Central America, the West Indies, and South America.

**Lee, Robert E.,** 1807-1870. The greatest military leader of the Confederacy. Lee, a Virginian, was an officer in the United States Army from the time of his graduation from the United States Military Academy until the Civil War. When Virginia seceded from the Union, Lee resigned from the United States Army and joined the Confederate forces. Early in 1865, near the end of the Civil War, he was appointed general in chief of the Confederate armies.

**Lent.** A period of fasting observed by some churches before Easter.

**levees.** High, wide walls of earth or concrete built along rivers or lakes to prevent flooding. Most levees are at least 15 feet high, 8 feet wide at the top, and 100 feet wide at the base. Hundreds of miles of levees stretch along the southern part of the Mississippi River.

**lime.** A white substance made by burning limestone, bones, or shells in an oven called a kiln. Lime is used in manufacturing fertilizer, glass, and many other products.

**limestone.** A common rock that occurs in various colors, from white to dark gray or brown. Light-colored limestone that can be cut into blocks is valued as building stone. Crushed limestone is widely used in road building and other kinds of construction. Limestone is also used as a raw material in making cement, lime, soda ash, and many other products.

**lint.** The long fibers obtained from the boll of the cotton plant. Lint is used to make cotton textiles.

**literacy test.** A test of a person's ability to read and write used to determine whether a citizen is qualified to vote. Literacy tests were formerly used in some places to prevent certain people from voting even though they could read and write. For example, election boards sometimes denied the right to vote to black citizens who could read and write, just because their answers to certain questions were "unsatisfactory" to the board.

**loam.** A fertile, crumbly soil that is a mixture of clay, sand, and humus. Humus is decayed animal and vegetable matter.

---

PRONUNCIATION KEY: hat, āge, cāre, fär; let, ēqual, tėrm; it, īce; hot, ōpen, ôrder; oil, out; cup, pu̇t, rüle, ūse; child; long; thin; ᴛʜen; zh, measure; ə represents a in about, e in taken, i in pencil, o in lemon, u in circus. For the complete key, see page 272.

**lock.** A section of a canal or river that is used to raise or lower ships from one water level to another. Gates at each end permit ships to enter or leave the lock. When a ship is in the lock, the gates are closed. The water level in the lock is raised or lowered to the level of the part of the canal or river toward which the ship is bound. Then the gates in front of the ship are opened, and the ship passes out of the lock.

**lubricants** (lü′brə kənts). Substances, such as oil and grease, that are used to reduce the amount of heat and wear produced when two solid objects rub together. For example, certain parts of lawnmowers and sewing machines must be coated with oil as a lubricant so they will work easily.

**Madison, James,** 1751-1836. The fourth president of the United States.

**majority** (mə jôr′ə ti) **vote.** The voting procedure in which the larger part of the total votes cast determines a decision or choice. Usually, any number over half is considered a majority.

**manufactures.** The actual value added to goods or to raw materials by factories.

**marble.** A very hard form of limestone that can be highly polished. Marble may be all one color or a mixture of colors.

**Medicare.** A United States government insurance program that helps provide medical and hospital care for certain disabled persons and persons over 65 years of age. Part of the cost of the program is paid for by the insured members and the rest is paid by the federal government.

**menhaden** (men hā′dən). A fish of the herring family. Menhaden are found in abundance along the Atlantic and Gulf coasts of the United States. They are chiefly used to make fertilizer, livestock feed, and oil.

**Mercator** (mer kā′ tər) **projection.** One of many possible arrangements of meridians and parallels on which a map of the world may be drawn. Devised by Gerhardus Mercator, a Flemish geographer who lived from 1512 to 1594. On a Mercator map, all meridians are drawn straight up and down, with north at the top. The parallels are drawn straight across, but increasingly farther apart toward the poles.

**Mesopotamia** (mes′ə pə tā′mi ə). An ancient land in southwestern Asia, between the Tigris and Euphrates rivers. Most of Mesopotamia is part of present-day Iraq. People were living in Mesopotamia more than eight thousand years ago.

**meter.** The basic unit in the metric system for measuring length. It is equal to 39.37 inches. See **metric system.**

**metric system.** A system of measurement used in most countries and by scientists throughout the world. In this system, the meter is the basic unit of length. It is equal to 39.37 inches. In the metric system, 100 centimeters equal one meter, and 1000 meters equal one kilometer.

**metropolitan** (met′ rə pol′ ə tən) **area.** A densely populated area that includes at least one large, central city. In addition to the central city, a metropolitan area usually includes several neighboring towns and settled sections. The people of these outlying areas often work in the central city, or go there for shopping and other business.

**mica.** Any one of a group of minerals that can be split into very thin, often transparent, sheets. Sheets of mica are used chiefly in electrical and electronic devices. When powdered, mica is used in making paints and special papers.

**migration.** The movement of people out of one region or country and into another, with the intention of making it their permanent home.

**Monroe, James,** 1758-1831. The fifth president of the United States.

**Muscle Shoals.** A town in northwestern Alabama, on the Tennessee River.

**national origin.** Generally refers to the country where a person was born, or where his or her parents or grandparents were born.

**natural gas fields.** Areas in which natural gas is produced.

**natural-gas liquids.** Valuable liquids obtained from natural gas. The liquids are separated from the gas before it is piped to homes and factories.

**natural resources.** The things in nature that are useful to people. Natural resources include soil, water, minerals, forests, air, and sunshine.

**newsprint.** An inexpensive, coarse paper made mostly from wood pulp. It is mainly used for newspapers.

**nitrates** (nī′ trāts). Chemicals that contain a certain combination of nitrogen and oxygen. Nitrates are used in fertilizer as a source of the nitrogen needed by plants.

**nitrogen** (nī′ trə jən). A colorless, odorless, tasteless gas that makes up about four fifths of the air in the earth's atmosphere. All plants and animals require foods that contain nitrogen. Most plants obtain the nitrogen they need from the soil in which they grow. Therefore, in order to keep soil fertile, farmers must add plant foods that contain nitrogen.

**Nobel Prize.** One of several prizes given annually for outstanding contributions in the fields of science, literature, and peace. The money for the Nobel prizes was willed by the Swedish inventor Alfred Nobel.

**nonmetallic minerals.** Minerals that are useful for purposes other than the production of metals. Examples of nonmetallic minerals that are important in industry are sulfur, salt, graphite, and limestone.

**Northern Hemisphere** (hem′ ə sfir). The half of the earth that is north of the equator. See **equator**.

**Nova Scotia** (nō′və skō′shə). A province in eastern Canada. It is made up of Cape Breton Island and a peninsula that extends into the Atlantic Ocean. The first European settlers of what is now Nova Scotia were French. These settlers and their descendants became known as Acadians. During and after the French and Indian War, the British forced the Acadians to leave Nova Scotia. Many of them finally settled in the French colony of Louisiana.

**nuclear** (nü′ klē ər). Refers to the production or use of atomic energy. See **atomic energy**.

**oil derrick.** A tower or framework that supports the machinery used for drilling an oil well.

**orbit.** The path followed by the earth as it moves around the sun.

**ore.** Rock or other material that contains enough of some valuable substance, such as a metal, to make it worth mining.

**Orientals** (ô′ri en′təlz). Persons from Asian countries such as China, Japan, and India.

**Ouachita** (wäsh′ə tô) **Mountains.** An area of low, rugged mountains in west central Arkansas and eastern Oklahoma. The Ouachita Mountains are in the Interior Highlands region.

**oxygen** (ok′ sə jən). A colorless, odorless, tasteless gas that makes up about one fifth of the air in the earth's atmosphere. In combination with other substances, oxygen is found in all plants and animals, in water, and in many kinds of rock.

**Ozark Plateau.** A hilly area that extends from central Missouri through northwestern Arkansas and into eastern Oklahoma. It is part of the Interior Highlands region.

**parallel** (par′ ə lel). An imaginary circle drawn east and west around the earth, parallel to the equator.

**parliament** (pär′lə mənt). In some nations, the highest lawmaking body. When capitalized, "Parliament" usually refers to the chief lawmaking body of Great Britain.

**peninsula** (pə nin′ sə lə). An area of land that is almost surrounded by water and is connected to a larger body of land.

**pension.** A fixed amount of money, other than wages, paid regularly to a person or a family. Pensions are sometimes paid by the government or by private business firms to persons who have retired from their jobs.

**petrochemicals** (pet′ rō kem′ ə kəlz). Chemicals obtained from raw materials provided by petroleum or natural gas. Petrochemicals are used in making hundreds of products, such as paint, fertilizer, and synthetic rubber.

**phosphorus** (fos′ fər əs). A nonmetallic substance that is plentiful in rocks, soil, and living cells. In nature, it is always

---

PRONUNCIATION KEY: hat, āge, cãre, fär; let, ēqual, tėrm; it, īce; hot, ōpen, ôrder; **oil, out**; cup, put, rüle, ūse; **child**; **long**; **thin**; ᴛнen; **zh**, measure; ə represents **a** in about, **e** in taken, **i** in pencil, **o** in lemon, **u** in circus. For the complete key, see page 272.

found in combination with other substances. Chemicals containing phosphorus are important ingredients in fertilizer, because plants cannot live without this substance.

**Piedmont** (pēd′ mont) **Plateau.** A section of the Appalachian Highlands that extends from New York into Alabama. (See map, page 21.) Most of the land in the Piedmont is gently rolling or hilly.

**plantation.** A large farm, usually located in regions with a warm climate, where crops such as cotton or tobacco are grown. Generally, the work on a plantation is done by large numbers of laborers who live there. In the South before the Civil War, most of the work on plantations was done by black slaves.

**plateau** (pla tō′). A large, generally level area of high land.

**plutonium** (plü tō′ ni əm). A silvery-white metal, similar to uranium, from which it is formed.

**Proclamation of 1763.** An order by the British King that prohibited the American colonists from settling west of the Appalachian Mountains.

**Puerto Rico** (pwer′tō rē′kō). An island about one thousand miles southeast of Florida. Since 1952, Puerto Rico has been a self-governing commonwealth associated with the United States.

**Pulitzer** (pū′lit sər) **Prize.** Any one of several prizes awarded each year in the United States for achievement in journalism, music, art, and literature. The prizes are named after Joseph Pulitzer (1847-1911), a newspaper editor and publisher. Pulitzer left a fortune to provide money for the prizes.

**pulp.** A soft, damp material usually made from wood or rags. It consists of many tiny threads, or fibers. Pulp is used in making paper and other products.

**pulpwood.** Timber that is used to make pulp. (See **pulp.**) Some common trees cut for pulpwood are pine, hemlock, spruce, and aspen.

**pyrites** (pī rī′ tēz). Various minerals that are combinations of sulfur with metals such as iron, copper, and nickel. Both copper and nickel may be produced by smelting ores that contain pyrites, but it is not practical to obtain iron in this way. A gas formed during the smelting process is used to make sulfuric acid, which is an important industrial chemical. The gas is also used in refrigeration.

**quarry.** An open pit in the earth from which stone is taken.

**ratified.** Given official approval.

**reservation.** An area of land owned by the government and set aside for some special use. Especially, such an area set aside for use by Indians.

**rickets.** A disease of children in which the bones are curved or improperly formed. It is caused by a lack of sunlight or a lack of vitamin D in the diet.

**rosin.** A hard, brittle substance that is prepared, along with turpentine, from the sap of living pine trees or from dead pinewood. Rosin is used in products such as paints, varnishes, and soaps.

**rotation crop.** Any crop, such as clover, alfalfa, or soybeans, that is grown as part of the procedure of crop rotation. See **crop rotation.**

**scholarship** (skol′ər ship). An award of money or other benefits to help a student continue his or her education.

**scrap.** Refers to any pieces of iron or steel that have been discarded, such as worn-out machinery and pieces of steel left over from manufacturing processes.

**Sea Islands.** A chain of flat, marshy islands stretching along the Atlantic coastline of South Carolina, Georgia, and northern Florida.

**secede** (si sēd′). To withdraw from an organization, or to declare oneself no longer part of it.

**segregate.** See **segregation.**

**segregation.** The separation of one group of people from another. In the United States, usually refers to the separation of blacks from white people, either by law or by custom. For example, some of our states formerly had laws that required blacks to attend separate schools, to eat in separate restaurants, and sit in separate sections of buses. Such laws have now been declared unconstitutional. However, segregation still occurs. For example, many all-black and all-white schools remain because they are located in neighborhoods where the people all belong to the same group.

**shellfish.** Any animal, such as a shrimp or an oyster, that lives in water and is covered by a shell or a bony skeleton. Shellfish do not have backbones, gills, or fins. See **finfish**.

**sickle.** A hand tool with a short, curved blade, used for reaping grain.

**siege** (sēj). The surrounding of a fortified place by an army that is attempting to capture it. A siege may last for months or even years.

**slag.** The waste material that is produced when ore is smelted to obtain metal. See **smelt**.

**smelt.** To separate the metal from the other materials in ore by melting the ore in a special furnace.

**solstice** (sol′stis). Either of two times of the year when the direct rays of the sun are farthest from the equator. This occurs about June 21, when the sun shines directly on the Tropic of Cancer, and about December 22, when the sun shines directly on the Tropic of Capricorn. See **Tropic of Cancer** and **Tropic of Capricorn**.

**sound.** A passage of water that separates an island from the mainland, or that connects two larger bodies of water. A sound may also be an arm or inlet of the ocean.

**Southern Hemisphere** (hem′ə sfir). The half of the earth that is south of the equator. See **equator**.

**standard of living.** The average level of conditions in a community or a country, or the level of conditions that people consider necessary for a happy, satisfying life. Among the factors considered in determining standard of living are the general living and working conditions of the people, and the amount and kind of things they possess. In countries with a high standard of living, many different goods and services are generally considered to be necessities. In countries with a low standard of living, many of these same items are luxuries enjoyed by only a few people.

**strait.** A narrow passage of water that connects two larger bodies of water.

**sulfur.** A pale-yellow substance found in large quantities in nature, either pure or combined with other substances. It is used to make fertilizer, paper, medicine, and many chemicals.

**sulfuric** (sul fyūr′ ik) **acid.** A heavy, colorless, oily liquid that is widely used in manufacturing. Sulfuric acid is a strong acid that eats away many materials. It is used in refining petroleum and in making fertilizer, chemicals, steel, explosives, and plastics.

**Supreme Court.** The highest court in the United States.

**synthetic** (sin thet′ ik). Refers to certain artificial substances, such as plastics and nylon, developed to replace similar natural materials.

**tanning.** The process in which animal hides or skins are treated with chemicals to make leather.

**tenant farmers.** Farmers who work land owned by someone else and pay rent to the owner, either in money or in shares of what they produce.

**terminus.** The end of a transportation route.

**three-dimensional** (də men′ shə nəl). Having length, width, and height.

**thresh.** To separate the grain from the husks and stems of the plant.

**tidal waves.** Unusually high ocean waves, caused by earthquakes or hurricanes. Tidal waves rush against a shore and cause great damage as they wash inland.

**titanium** (tī tā′ni əm) **ores.** Ores from which the metal titanium is obtained. Titanium, which is both strong and light in weight, is used in the construction of aircraft. It is also used in certain kinds of steel.

**topographic** (təp′ə graf′ ik). Refers to the physical features of an area, such as lakes, rivers, and hills. A topographic map shows the elevation of these features and their location in relation to each other.

---

PRONUNCIATION KEY: hat, āge, cāre, fär; let, ēqual, tėrm; it, īce; hot, ōpen, ôrder; oil, out; cup, pùt, rüle, ūse; child; long; thin; ŧHen; zh, measure; ə represents a in about, e in taken, i in pencil, o in lemon, u in circus. For the complete key, see page 272.

**topsoil.** The top layer of soil on the earth's surface. It is seldom much more than one foot deep. Normally, topsoil is more fertile than the soil beneath it, because it contains a larger amount of decayed plant material.

**tributary** (trib′yə ter i). A stream or river that flows into a larger stream or a lake.

**Tropic of Cancer.** An imaginary line around the earth, about 1,600 miles north of the equator. (See top chart, page 42.)

**Tropic of Capricorn.** An imaginary line around the earth, about 1,600 miles south of the equator. (See top chart, page 42.)

**tropics.** The part of the earth that lies between the Tropic of Cancer and the Tropic of Capricorn. (See top chart, page 42.) The weather in the tropics is generally hot all year round.

**truck farm.** A farm on which vegetables are raised to be sold. One meaning of the word "truck" is to trade things. Formerly, vegetables often were traded for other products.

**tung nuts.** Seeds obtained from the fruit of the tung tree. A poisonous, pale-yellow oil produced from tung nuts is used in paints, varnishes, and similar products.

**turpentine.** An oily liquid prepared from the sap of living pine trees or from dead pinewood. It is often used for thinning paints and varnishes.

**TVA.** Abbreviation for Tennessee Valley Authority. (See pages 192-195.)

**unconstitutional** (un′ kon stə tü′ shə nəl). Contrary to a constitution. Especially, contrary to the Constitution of the United States.

**Union.** The United States. When used in referring to the Civil War period, means the states that did not secede.

**uranium** (yu rā′ni əm). An extremely heavy, silvery-white metal. It is important as the source of certain materials used to produce atomic energy. See **atomic energy**.

**vegetation.** Any plant life, such as trees, grass, shrubs, and flowers.

**watershed.** The land drained by a river or a system of rivers.

**weather.** The condition of the atmosphere at a given time and place. A description of weather includes such things as wind, sunshine, temperature, and moisture. The average weather conditions of a particular place over a long period of time make up its climate. See **climate**.

**West Virginia.** The state of West Virginia was once the western part of the state of Virginia. At the beginning of the Civil War, Virginia seceded from the Union. However, most of the people in the state's western counties supported the Union. These counties declared their independence from Virginia and set up a new government. In June, 1863, the state of West Virginia was admitted to the Union.

**World War I, 1914-1919.** The first war in history which involved nearly every part of the world. The Central Powers—Germany, Austria, Turkey, and Bulgaria—were defeated by the Allies. These included Great Britain, France, Russia, Japan, and the United States.

**World War II, 1939-1945.** The second war in history which involved nearly every part of the world. The Allied Powers, which included the United States, Great Britain, the Soviet Union, France, and many other countries, defeated the Axis Powers. These included mainly Germany, Italy, and Japan. The Soviet Union, the United States, and Japan did not enter World War II until 1941.

**yarn.** A thread or a strand of twisted threads used in weaving cloth. Knitted materials are also made from yarn.

# INDEX

Explanation of abbreviations used in this Index:

*p* — picture    *m* — map

**agriculture,** *see* **farming**
**Alabama,** 37, 39, 41, 46, 181, 182-183, 185, 188, 193, 198, 204, 206, 207, 244; *p* 192-193, 200-201, 208-209; *m* 114, 183, 244; *graph* 188
   facts about, 244
**Alaska,** 13; *m* 13, 14
**alumina** (ə lü′ mə nə), 183, 206-207, 272
**aluminum,** 183, 206, 207; *p* 206-207
**Appalachian** (ap′ ə lā′ chən) **Highlands,** 22-28, 44-46; *p* 22-23, 25-28, 45-47; *m* 21, 22
   of Alabama, 244; *m* 244
   climate, 44-46; *p* 45-47
   forests in, 26, 28, 46, 186
   of Georgia, 44, 247; *p* 25; *m* 247
   of Kentucky, 248; *m* 248
   minerals in, 181, 182
   of North Carolina, 251; *p* 46-47; *m* 251
   of South Carolina, 252; *m* 252
   of Tennessee, 253; *m* 253
   of Virginia, 44, 254; *p* 45; *m* 254
**Appalachian Plateau,** 22, 28, 244, 253, 254; *p* 28; *m* 21
**Appalachian Ridges and Valleys,** 22, 27-28, 244, 247, 253, 254; *m* 21
**architecture,** *see* **arts**
**Arkansas,** 32, 33, 245; *p* 18-19, 32, 50-51; *m* 114, 245; *graph* 188
   facts about, 245
**Arkansas Valley,** 33, 245; *m* 245
**Armstrong, Louis,** 157; *p* 157
**arts,** 152-159; *p* 152-159
   architecture, 152-154; *p* 94-95, 152-153
   crafts, 158-159; *p* 159
   literature, 155-157; *p* 156
   music, 157-158; *p* 157, 158
   painting and sculpture, 154-155; *p* 154-155
**astronauts,** 11, 218
**Atkins, Chet,** *p* 158
**Atlanta, Georgia,** 106, 107-108; *p* 92-93, 107; *m* 114
**atmosphere,** 12-13

**atomic energy,** 273. *See also* **industry**
**automation,** 129, 132; *p* 128-129

**basic needs,** 99-102, 125-126; *p* 38-39, 100-101, 124-127
**Baton Rouge** (bat′ ən rüzh′), **Louisiana,** *m* 29, 114
**bauxite** (bôk′sīt), *see* **minerals**
**bayous** (bī′üz), 249, 273
**Biloxi, Mississippi,** 62; *p* 104-105; *m* 114
**Bingham, George Caleb,** 154; *p* 154-155
**Birmingham, Alabama,** 88, 105, 206; *m* 114, 183
**Black Belt,** 244, 250; *m* 244, 250
**Black Mountains,** 26
**blacks,** *see* **people**
**Bluegrass,** 31, 170, 248; *p* 30-31; *m* 248
**Blue Ridge,** 22, 26, 45, 46, 251, 252, 253, 254; *p* 2-3, 26, 46-47; *m* 21
**boll weevil,** 166, 273
**Boone, Daniel,** 66; *p* 154-155
**Boston Mountains,** 32
**British Parliament,** 70, 216

**Cabot** (kab′ət), **John,** 63, 273
**Cartier** (kär′ti ā′), **Jacques,** 61, 273
**cattle,** *see* **farm products, livestock**
**Charleston, South Carolina,** 89, 96; *m* 29, 114
**Charlotte** (shär′lət), **North Carolina,** 105; *m* 114
**Chattanooga, Tennessee,** 27; *m* 29, 114
**chemical products,** 183, 185
**chemicals,** *see* **industry**
**Cherokee Indians,** 73, 98
**Chesapeake** (ches′ ə pēk) **Bay,** *m* 29, 254
**cities,** 99-117, 132; *p* 20, 107-113, 116-117; *m* 114. *See also* names of cities
**citizenship,** 118-148
**city government,** 102-103
**civil rights,** 143
**Civil Rights Act of 1964,** 143
**Civil War,** 78-83; *p* 79-81; *m* 78, 82

**clay,** *see* **minerals**
**Clay, Henry,** *p* 76-77
**climate,** 34-51; *p* 34-41, 45-47, 50-51; *m* 41, 44, 48, 49; *charts* 42, 43, 48, 49
   Appalachian Highlands, 44-46; *p* 45-47
   Coastal Plain, 37-41, 44; *p* 36-41
   hurricanes, 41, 49; *p* 40-41; *m* 49; *chart* 49
   Interior Highlands, 51; *p* 50-51
   Interior Plains, 46, 51
   rainfall, 37, 39, 41, 46, 48; *m* 41
   seasons of the year, 42-43; *charts* 42, 43
   summer, 34, 36, 37-39, 44-45, 46; *p* 36-37; *charts* 42, 43
   temperatures, 34, 37, 39, 43, 44, 51; *m* 44
   thunderstorms, 39, 48; *m* 48; *chart* 48
   winter, 34, 36, 37, 41, 44, 45, 51; *p* 45; *charts* 42, 43
**clothing,** *see* **industry**
**coal,** *see* **minerals**
**Coastal Flatwoods,** 250; *m* 250
**Coastal Plain,** 19-20, 37-41, 44; *p* 20, 38-41; *m* 19, 21
   of Alabama, 37, 39, 41, 244; *m* 244
   of Arkansas, 245; *m* 245
   climate, 37-41, 44; *p* 38-41
   of Florida, 41, 44, 246; *p* 20; *m* 246
   forests in, 186
   of Georgia, 247; *m* 247
   of Kentucky, 248; *m* 248
   of Louisiana, 249; *p* 38-39; *m* 249
   of Mississippi, 250; *m* 250
   of North Carolina, 251; *m* 251
   of South Carolina, 252; *m* 252
   of Tennessee, 253; *m* 253
   of Virginia, 254; *m* 254
**coke,** 180, 182, 274
**colonists,** *see* **history,** colonial
**Columbus, Christopher,** 57-58; *p* 57
**communication,** *see* **great ideas, language**
**Confederacy** (kən fed′ər ə si), 78, 82, 83, 274; *m* 78, 82

---

PRONUNCIATION KEY: hat, āge, cāre, fär; let, ēqual, tėrm; it, īce; hot, ōpen, ôrder; oil, out; cup, put, rüle, ūse; child; long; thin; ᴛʜen; zh, measure; ə represents a in about, e in taken, i in pencil, o in lemon, u in circus. For the complete key, see page 272.

**Confederate states,** *see* **Confederacy**
**conservation** (kon'sər vā'shən), 166-167, 193; *p* 166-167
**Constitution,** 213, 216, 274
**constitutional** (kon' stə tü'shən əl) **amendments,** 83-84, 85, 122, 213, 216
**continents,** 13; *chart* 12
**contour** (kon'tür) **farming,** 167; *p* 166-167
**cooperation,** *see* **great ideas**
**corn,** *see* **farm products**
**cotton,** *see* **farm products**
**cotton boll,** 162, 165, 274
**cotton gin,** 165, 274
**crafts,** *see* **arts**
**crime,** 144-148; *p* 144-147; *graph* 145
**crop rotation,** 167, 274
**crops,** *see* **farm products**
**Cubans,** *see* **people**
**Cumberland Gap,** 66, 274
**Cumberland Plateau,** 274. *See also* **Appalachian Plateau**

**dams,** 191-195; *p* 26-27, 192-194; *m* 194-195
**de Bry, Théodore,** 228, 275; *p* 228-229
**democracy,**
  growth of, 215-216; *p* 214-217
  principles of, 118-125; *p* 118-121, 123
  problems for, 125-148
**depressed areas,** 128-129
**de Soto, Hernando,** 59-60; *p* 58-59; *m* 60
**discrimination and prejudice,** 138-143
**division of labor,** *see* **great ideas**
**Duveneck, Frank,** 155

**Eastern Uplands,** 249; *m* 249
**ecology,** 275; *p* 181
**education,** *see* **great ideas**
**elections,** 122, 143, 151, 213, 216; *p* 84, 123, 216-217
**electric power,** 193, 195. *See also* **hydroelectricity** *and* **natural resources,** waterpower
**Emancipation Proclamation,** 83
**Everglades,** 75, 174; *m* 246
**exchange,** *see* **great ideas**
**explorers,** *see* **history**

**Fall Line,** 24-25, 198, 247, 252; *p* 24-25; *m* 29
**farm equipment,** 165, 168; *p* 18-19, 171-175, 232
**farming,** 16-17, 162-175, 226, 230; *p* 18-19, 160-169, 171-175, 232; *m* 170
  in the Appalachian Highlands, 22, 24, 26, 27, 28
  on the Coastal Plain, 20, 162, 172, 174; *p* 18-19
  in the Interior Highlands, 32, 33
  in the Interior Plains, 31
  tenant, 86-87, 89; *p* 86
  *See also* **grazing**
**farming methods,** 16-17, 22, 166-168
**farm products,**
  corn, 20, 28, 31, 46, 174
  cotton, 17, 22, 33, 46, 113, 162, 165, 166, 167, 168, 170-172; *p* 164-165, 171; *m* 170
  fruit, 32, 33, 173; *p* 34-35, 124-125
  indigo, 162, 165
  livestock, 31, 46, 168-170; *p* 160-161, 168-169
  oats, 174
  peanuts, 17, 20, 174; *p* 174
  poultry and eggs, 168-169
  rice, 20, 113, 162, 174; *p* 18-19
  soybeans, 17, 167, 172-173
  sugarcane, 20, 113, 174; *p* 175
  tobacco, 17, 20, 22, 28, 31, 46, 162, 165, 166, 167
  vegetables, 20, 173-174; *p* 172-173
  wheat, 174
**Faulkner, William,** 155; *p* 156
**Fifteenth Amendment,** 85, 122
**fish,** *see* **natural resources**
**flood control,** 193, 194-195; *m* 194-195. *See also* **levees**
**floodplains,** 249, 276
**Florida,** 34, 44, 59, 61, 73, 94, 108-110, 113-115, 173, 185, 189, 191, 246; *p* 16-17, 20, 34-35, 108-109, 120-121, 124-125, 172-173, 184-185, 190, 201, 204, 219; *m* 114, 246; *graphs* 188, 189
  facts about, 246
**Florida Keys,** 246; *m* 246
**Florida Lowlands,** 246; *m* 246
**Florida panhandle,** 246
**Florida Uplands,** 246; *m* 246
**food processing,** *see* **industry**
**forest products,** 186-188, 204, 205; *p* 186-187, 227. *See also* **industry,** wood products
**forests,** *see* **natural resources**
**Fort Knox,** 115
**Fort Sumter, South Carolina,** 78; *p* 79
**Fourteenth Amendment,** 83-84, 85, 122
**freedom,** *see* **great ideas**
**French and Indian War,** *see* **history**
**French Quarter,** 113
**fruit,** *see* **farm products**
**fuller's earth,** *see* **minerals**
**furniture,** 205; *p* 205

**galaxy,** 9; *p* 9
**Georgia,** 44, 64, 107-108, 173, 174, 185, 188, 247; *p* 6-7, 25, 88-89, 92-93, 107, 134-135; *m* 114, 247; *graph* 188
  facts about, 247
**global view,** 8-17; *p* 8-9, 16-17; *m* 13-16; *charts* 10-12
**Grant, Ulysses S.,** 83
**grazing,** 31; *p* 30-31
**great ideas,** 210-241; *p* 210-225, 227-232, 234-241
  cooperation, 106, 218-219; *p* 146-147, 218, 219
  division of labor, 105-106, 236-237; *p* 198-199, 236, 237
  education, 102, 103, 134-135, 137, 224-225; *p* 103, 132-135, 224, 225
  exchange, 106, 238-239; *p* 164-165, 238-239
  freedom, 106, 212-213; *p* 58-59, 96-97, 142-143, 212-213
  language, 103, 156, 220-223; *p* 156, 220-223
  loyalty, 106, 240-241; *p* 79, 240, 241
  rules and government, 102-103, 143, 214-217; *p* 140-141, 214-217
  using natural resources, 105, 226-229; *p* 18-19, 168-169, 176-177, 227-229
  using tools, 105, 230-235; *p* 54-55, 136, 137, 206-207, 230-232, 234-235
**Great Smoky Mountains,** 26
**Great Smoky Mountains National Park,** 251
**Great Valley,** 27, 253, 276; *p* 26-27
**growing season,** 36-37, 41, 44-45, 46; *m* 170

**Handy, W. C.,** 157
**Harris, Joel Chandler,** 155
**health,** 137-138; *p* 136, 137
**Henry, Patrick,** 276; *p* 68-69
**history,** 52-89; *p* 52-55, 57-59, 62-63, 66-69, 71-77, 79-81, 84, 86-89; *m* 60, 63, 65, 70, 72, 78, 82
  Civil War period, 77-83; *p* 79-81; *m* 78, 82
  colonial, 61-67, 162, 165, 216, 228; *p* 66-67, 218, 229
  explorers, 57-63; *p* 57-59, 62-63; *m* 60, 63
  French and Indian War, 64-65; *p* 66-67; *m* 65
  Indians, 54-56, 60, 73, 75, 228; *p* 54-55, 228-231
  Reconstruction, 83-85; *p* 84
  Revolutionary War, 68-70, 240; *p* 240

the South since Reconstruction, 85-89; *p* 86-89
  territorial claims, 57-67; *p* 62-63; *m* 65
  territorial expansion, 70-75; *p* 71; *m* 70, 72
**Huguenots,** 61, 276
**hurricanes,** *see* **climate**
**hydroelectricity** (hī′drō i lek′-tris′ə ti), 25, 27, 176, 198, 251, 252, 276. *See also* **natural resources,** waterpower

**inalienable rights,** 216, 276
**Indians,** *see* **history** *and* **people**
**industrial areas,** *m* 208
**Industrial Revolution,** 232-233; *m* 233
**industry,** 196-209, 233; *p* 196-209, 234-235, 237
  appliance, 208
  atomic energy, 195, 208
  chemical, 193, 202-203; *p* 192-193
  clothing, 198, 200
  development of, 196, 198
  electrical equipment, 208; *p* 234-235
  electronics, 208
  food processing, 201; *p* 104-105, 200-201
  iron and steel, 183, 198, 206
  metal, 206-207; *p* 206-207
  oil refining, 202; *p* 202-203
  pulp and paper, 204; *p* 88-89, 196-197
  since Reconstruction, 87-89; *p* 86-89
  resources for, 198
  services, 237
  space, 218; *p* 208-209, 219
  textile, 198-200; *p* 25, 86-87, 198-199
  tobacco products, 201
  tourist, 110, 113, 114
  transportation equipment, 208
  wood products, 17, 204-205; *p* 204, 205
**inflation,** 130-131; *p* 131
**Interior Highlands,** 32-33, 50; *p* 32, 50-51; *m* 21
  of Arkansas, 245; *p* 50-51; *m* 245
  climate, 51; *p* 50-51
**Interior Plains,** 31, 46, 51; *p* 30-31; *m* 21
  of Alabama, 31, 244; *m* 244
  climate, 46, 51
  of Kentucky, 31, 51, 248; *p* 30-31; *m* 248

  of Tennessee, 31, 51, 253; *m* 253
**Intracoastal Waterway,** *m* 29
**inventions,** 165, 222, 230, 232, 233; *p* 232
**iron ore,** *see* **minerals**

**Jackson, Andrew,** 115, 277
**Jacksonville, Florida,** 61; *p* 20; *m* 114
**Jamestown, Virginia,** 63-64, 218; *p* 52-53, 215, 218; *m* 114
**Jefferson, Thomas,** 152, 155, 217; *p* 152-153
**Johnson, Andrew,** 83

**Kentucky,** 31, 51, 78, 115, 165, 172, 181, 201, 248; *p* 30-31, 181, 235; *m* 114, 248; *graph* 188
  facts about, 248
**Kentucky Derby,** 115
**Knoxville, Tennessee,** 27; *m* 114

**Lake Okeechobee** (ō′ki chō′bi), 246; *m* 246
**Lake Pontchartrain** (pon′ chər-trān), 110; *p* 36-37; *m* 249
**land,** 18-33; *p* 6-7, 18-20, 22-23, 25-28, 30-32; *m* 21. *See also* **Appalachian Highlands, Coastal Plain, Interior Highlands,** *and* **Interior Plains**
**language,** *see* **great ideas**
**La Salle, René Robert Cavelier, Sieur de,** 61-62; *p* 62-63; *m* 63
**Lee, Robert E.,** 83, 277; *p* 80-81
**legumes** (leg′ ūms), 172
**levees,** 111, 249, 250, 277
**Lincoln, Abraham,** 78, 83
**literacy tests,** 85, 143, 151, 277
**literature,** *see* **arts**
**livestock,** *see* **farm products**
**locks,** 195, 278
**Louisiana,** 61, 62, 96, 110-113, 170, 174, 176, 179, 185, 189, 201, 202, 206, 207, 239, 249; *p* 36-39, 71, 110-113, 164-167, 178, 202-203, 238-239; *m* 114, 249; *graphs* 188, 189
  facts about, 249
**Louisiana Lowland,** 249; *m* 249
**Louisiana Purchase,** 72; *m* 72
**Louisville** (lü′ i vil), Kentucky, 106, 115; *m* 114
**loyalty,** *see* **great ideas**
**lumbering,** 33, 186, 188, 205; *p* 186-187, 204, 227

**Madison, James,** 155, 278
**manufacturing,** *see* **industry**
**map skills,** 266-271
**Mardi Gras** (mär′di grä′), 113; *p* 112-113
**Mars,** 11; *chart* 10-11
**Memphis** (mem′ fis), **Tennessee,** 106, 115-116, 201; *p* 116-117; *m* 114
**Miami, Florida,** 106, 108-110; *p* 108-109; *m* 114
**Miami Beach, Florida,** 108; *m* 114
**Milky Way,** 9; *p* 9
**minerals,** 176-186, 226, 228, 229; *p* 176-178, 181, 182, 184-185; *m* 179, 180, 183
  bauxite, 183, 206-207, 273
  clay, 185-186
  coal, 180-182, 183; *p* 181; *m* 180, 183
  fuller's earth, 186, 276
  granite, 185
  iron ore, 182-183; *p* 182; *m* 179, 183
  kaolin, 185
  limestone, 183, 185, 277; *m* 179, 183
  marble, 185, 278
  natural gas, 176, 179; *m* 179
  oil, 176-179; *p* 176-178; *m* 179
  phosphate rock, 185; *p* 184-185
  pyrites, 183, 280
  salt, 185
  sulfur, 185, 281
  zinc, 183
**Mississippi,** 169, 172, 173, 176, 250; *p* 104-105, 171, 196-197; *m* 114, 250; *graph* 188
  facts about, 250
**Mississippi River,** 202, 245, 249, 250; *p* 110-111; *m* 29
  discovery of, 60; *p* 62-63; *m* 60
  exploration of, 61-62; *m* 63
**Montgomery, Alabama,** 37, 39, 41; *m* 114
**Monticello** (mon′tə sel′ō), 152; *p* 152-153
**moon,** 10, 11
**Mount Mitchell,** 26
**Mount Vernon,** *p* 74-75
**Muscle Shoals, Alabama,** 202, 278; *m* 114

**Nashville, Tennessee,** 158; *m* 114
**Nashville Basin,** 31, 253; *m* 253
**Native Americans,** *see* **people, Indians**
**natural gas,** *see* **minerals**
**natural resources,** 176-195, 226-229, 278; *p* 176-178, 181,

---

PRONUNCIATION KEY: hat, āge, cāre, fär; let, ēqual, tėrm; it, īce; hot, ōpen, ôrder; oil, out; cup, pùt, rüle, ūse; **ch**ild; lo**ng**; **th**in; ᴛʜen; zh, measure; ə represents **a** in about, **e** in taken, **i** in pencil, **o** in lemon, **u** in circus. For the complete key, see page 272.

182, 184-190, 192-194, 227-229; *m* 179, 180, 183, 188, 194-195
   fish, 188-190; *p* 188-190; *graph* 189
   forests, 186-188; *p* 186-187, 227; *m* 188
   sponges, 191; *p* 190
   waterpower, 191, 195; *p* 192-194
   *See also* **minerals** *and* **great ideas**
New Orleans (ôr′li ənz), Louisiana, 89, 106, 110-113, 157, 239; *p* 71, 110-113, 238-239; *m* 114
Newport News, Virginia, 208; *m* 114
Nobel Prize, 155, 279
North America, 13; *chart* 12
North Carolina, 63, 98, 106, 162, 165, 169, 170, 172, 174, 188, 200, 201, 203, 205, 251; *p* 2-3, 46-47, 198-199, 205, 234-235; *m* 114, 251; *graphs* 188, 209
   facts about, 251
Northern Hemisphere, 42, 43, 279; *charts* 42, 43

Oak Ridge, Tennessee, 195; *m* 114
oceans, 13; *chart* 12
Oglethorpe, James, 64
Ohio River, 115; *m* 29
Okefenokee (ō′kə fə nō′kē) Swamp, 247; *m* 247
Ouachita (wäsh′ə tô) Mountains, 33, 245, 279; *m* 245
Ozark Plateau, 32, 245, 279; *p* 32; *m* 245

Paducah, Kentucky, 195; *m* 114
painting, *see* **arts**
peanuts, *see* **farm products**
people, 90-106; *p* 90-91, 96-98, 100-101, 103-105
   ancestry, 95-99
   basic needs, 99-102, 125-126; *p* 38-39, 100-101, 124-127, 148-149
   blacks, 64, 75, 83-85, 97, 140, 143, 151
   Cubans, 97-98; *p* 98
   early, 226, 228, 230-232; *p* 230-231
   famous southerners, 152, 154-155, 157; *p* 68-69, 76-77, 80-81, 138-139, 156-158

   Indians, 54-56, 60, 73, 75, 98, 228, 230; *p* 54-55, 72-73, 228-231
   rights and freedoms, 120, 122, 140, 143, 145, 216; *p* 96-97, 123, 138-139, 142-143, 216-217
   *See also* **citizenship** *and* **social problems**
petrochemicals (pet′rō kem′ə-kəlz), 179, 202, 279
petroleum, *see* **minerals**, oil
petroleum products, 179, 202
Piedmont (pēd′mont) Plateau, 22, 24, 44, 198, 280; *m* 21
planets, 10, 11; *chart* 10-11
plantations, 75, 77, 86, 162, 280; *p* 74-75
Ponce de León (pänsə dā lē ōn′), Juan, 58-59
population, 94-95, 99; *m* 95. *See also* names of states
ports, 110, 111, 113, 114, 115, 182, 239; *p* 110-111, 116-117, 238-239; *m* 29
power, 232, 233. *See also* **hydroelectricity**
prejudice, *see* **social problems**
Pulitzer (pū′lit sər) Prize, 155, 157, 280

rainfall, *see* **climate**
Raleigh (rô′li), North Carolina, 106; *m* 114
Raleigh, Sir Walter, 63
raw materials, 176, 196, 198, 200, 202, 203
Reconstruction, *see* **history**
Reconstruction Acts, 84, 85
Red River, 249; *m* 29
Revolutionary War, *see* **history**
rice, *see* **farm products**
Richmond, Virginia, 96; *m* 114
rivers, 20, 24, 27, 194-195; *p* 20, 110-111; *m* 29, 194-195
rotation crops, 167, 172, 280
rules and government, *see* **great ideas**

St. Augustine (ô′gəs tēn), Florida, 61; *m* 114
St. Petersburg, Florida, 106, 113, 114-115; *m* 114
Sea Islands, Georgia, 247; *m* 247
seasons, *see* **climate**
segregation, 85, 280-281. *See also* **discrimination** *and* **prejudice**
Seminole Indians, 73, 75, 98; *p* 72-73

settlements, *see* **territorial claims**
sharecroppers, *see* **tenant farming**
shellfish, 190, 281; *p* 188-189
Shenandoah (shen′ ən dō′ ə) River, 27; *m* 29
shipyards, 208
slavery, 64, 77-78, 83, 98; *m* 78
Smith, Captain John, 218
social problems, 126-151
   definition, 126
   discrimination, 140, 143, 151
   handicaps and illness, 137-138; *p* 136, 137
   lack of education, 133-135, 137; *p* 132-135
   lack of jobs, 128-129, 132; *p* 128-129
   prejudice, 138-140, 151; *p* 138-139
   progress in the South, 149-151; *p* 148-151
soil erosion, 166
solar system, 10-11; *chart* 10-11
South Carolina, 61, 78, 162, 173, 185, 208, 252; *p* 79; *m* 114, 252; *graph* 188, 189
   facts about, 252
soybeans, *see* **farm products**
space, 11, 218; *p* 16-17, 208-209, 219
sponges, *see* **natural resources**
standard of living, 17, 281
states' rights, 77, 78
steel, *see* **industry**, iron and steel
sulfuric (sul fyūr′ik) acid, 183, 185, 203, 281
sun, 10, 42-43; *charts* 10-11, 42, 43
synthetic (sin thet′ ik) fibers, 200, 203
synthetics, 179, 202, 281

Tampa, Florida, 106, 113-114; *m* 114
Tampa Bay, 113, 114
Tarpon Springs, Florida, 191; *p* 190; *m* 114
temperature, *see* **climate**
tenant farming, 86-87, 89; *p* 86
Tennessee, 31, 46, 115-116, 181, 183, 203, 207, 208, 253; *p* 116-117, 207; *m* 114, 253
   facts about, 253
Tennessee River, 27, 191, 193, 194, 195; *p* 192-194; *m* 29, 194-195
Tennessee Valley Authority, 191, 193-195; *m* 194-195

---

**PRONUNCIATION KEY:** hat, āge, cãre, fär; let, ēqual, tėrm; it, īce; hot, ōpen, ôrder; oil, out; cup, pùt, rüle, ūse; **ch**ild; lo**ng**; **th**in; ᴛнen; **zh**, measure; ə represents **a** in about, **e** in taken, **i** in pencil, **o** in lemon, **u** in circus. For the complete key, see page 272.

territorial claims,
  British, 62-64, 65; *m* 65
  French, 61-62, 64-65; *p* 62-63; *m* 65
  Russian, *m* 65
  Spanish, 58-61, 65; *p* 58-59; *m* 65
textiles, *see* industry
Thirteenth Amendment, 83, 122
thunderstorms, *see* climate
Tidewater, 254; *m* 254
timber, 186, 188, 204; *p* 186-187, 227; *graph* 188
tobacco, *see* **farm products** *and* **industry**
transportation equipment, *see* **industry**

unemployment, 128-129, 132

Union, the, 78, 83, 84-85; *m* 78, 82
United States,
  Congress, *p* 140-141
  conterminous, 13, 16; *m* 13, 16
  facts about states, 255
  history, 68-85; *p* 68-69, 71-77, 79-81, 84; *m* 70, 72, 78, 82
  location, 13; *m* 13
using natural resources, *see* **great ideas**
using tools, *see* **great ideas**

Valley Forge, 240; *p* 240
vegetables, *see* **farm products**
Virginia, 44, 63, 83, 162, 181, 189, 201, 208, 218, 254; *p* 45, 52-53, 68-69, 74-75, 162-163, 210-211, 215, 218, 220-221, 229, 232; *m* 114, 254; *graphs* 188, 189
  facts about, 254
Voting Rights Act of 1965, 143

Washington, George, 240; *p* 66-67, 74-75, 240
waterpower, *see* **natural resources**
waterways, *m* 29
Whitney, Eli, 165
Wilderness Road, 66
Williams, Tennessee, 157
Williamsburg, Virginia, 274; *p* 210-211, 220-221, 229
Wolfe, Thomas, 155
world industrial development, 233; *m* 233

## Maps, Charts, and Special Features

**PART 1  Land and Climate**
The Solar System . . . . . . . . . . . . . . 10-11
Continents and Oceans . . . . . . . . . . . . 12
The United States . . . . . . . . . . . . . . . . 13
The United States . . . . . . . . . . . . . 14-15
The Regions of the Conterminous United States. . . . . . . . . . . . . . . . . 16
Coastal Plain . . . . . . . . . . . . . . . . . . . . 19
Land Regions . . . . . . . . . . . . . . . . . . . 21
Appalachian Highlands . . . . . . . . . . . . 22
The Fall Line. . . . . . . . . . . . . . . . . 24-25
Exploring Waterways. . . . . . . . . . . . . . 29
Interior Plains . . . . . . . . . . . . . . . . . . . 31
Interior Highlands . . . . . . . . . . . . . . . . 32
Average Annual Rainfall . . . . . . . . . . . 41
The Seasons of the Year . . . . . . . . 42-43
Average January and July Temperatures . . . . . . . . . . . . . . . . . . . . . . . 44
Thunderstorms . . . . . . . . . . . . . . . . . . 48
Hurricanes. . . . . . . . . . . . . . . . . . . . . . 49

**PART 2  History**
Explorations of De Soto . . . . . . . . . . . 60
Explorations of La Salle . . . . . . . . . . . 63
Before and After the French and Indian War. . . . . . . . . . . . . . . . . . . 65
How the United States Began . . . . . . . 70
How Our Country Grew . . . . . . . . . . . 72
Our Country Divided. . . . . . . . . . . . . . 78
Exploring the Civil War With Maps . . . . 82

**PART 3  People**
United States Population Distribution. . .95
Cities of the South . . . . . . . . . . . . . . .114
Serious Crimes in the United States. . . .145

**PART 4  Earning a Living**
Exploring the Growing Season . . . . . . .170
Cotton Harvested . . . . . . . . . . . . . . . .170
Mineral Resources: Iron Ore, Limestone, Natural Gas, and Oil . . . . . . .179
Coalfields of the United States . . . . . .180
Iron and Steel . . . . . . . . . . . . . . . . . .183
Timber Harvested and Forest Lands . . .188
Leading Fishing States of the South . . .189
Main Industrial Areas . . . . . . . . . . . . .208

**PART 5  Great Ideas That Built Our Nation**
World Industrial Development. . . . . . .233

**PART 6  States of the South**
Alabama . . . . . . . . . . . . . . . . . . . . . .244
Arkansas . . . . . . . . . . . . . . . . . . . . . .245
Florida . . . . . . . . . . . . . . . . . . . . . . .246
Georgia . . . . . . . . . . . . . . . . . . . . . . .247
Kentucky . . . . . . . . . . . . . . . . . . . . . .248
Louisiana. . . . . . . . . . . . . . . . . . . . . .249
Mississippi . . . . . . . . . . . . . . . . . . . . .250
North Carolina . . . . . . . . . . . . . . . . . .251
South Carolina . . . . . . . . . . . . . . . . . .252
Tennessee . . . . . . . . . . . . . . . . . . . . .253
Virginia. . . . . . . . . . . . . . . . . . . . . . .254

# ACKNOWLEDGMENTS

Grateful acknowledgment is made to the following for permission to use the illustrations found in this book:

A. Devaney, Inc.: Pages 25, 92-93, and 120-121; pages 152-153 by David W. Corson
Alabama Department Offices: Pages 150-151
Alpha Photo Associates, Inc.: Pages 124-125 and 204
American Telephone and Telegraph Company: Pages 222-223
Arkansas Department of Parks and Tourism: Page 32
Atlanta Chamber of Commerce: Page 107
Black Star: Page 123 by Leo Chaplin; pages 132-133 by Peter Hastings; pages 140-141 by Dennis Brack; pages 142-143 by Doug Wilson
Camerique: Pages 202-203
Chicago Historical Society: Page 71
Colfield's Studio: Page 156
Colonial Williamsburg: Pages 210-211 and 229
David Redfern Photography: Page 157
DeWys, Inc.: Pages 137 and 201
Edward L. DuPuy: Page 159
Freelance Photographers Guild, Inc.: Pages 200-201, 213, 237 (lower), and 242-243; pages 2-3 by A. C. Shelton; page 26 by D. Pietrzyk; pages 30-31 by Lehrt; pages 100-101 by A. Felix
General Electric Company: Page 235
Georgia State University: Pages 134-135
Globe Photos: Pages 108-109 by Eamon Kennedy
Grant Heilman: Pages 18-19, 50-51, and 174; pages 38-39 by Alan Pitcairn
H. Armstrong Roberts: Pages 20, 22-23, 52-53, 74-75, 96-97, 118-119, 126-127, 131, 146-147, and 162-163
Harold M. Lambert Studios, Inc.: Pages 40-41, 90-91, 216-217, and 220-221
Harper's Weekly: Page 84
Harrison Forman: Page 45
International Harvester Company: Page 232
Johnson Publishing Co.: Pages 138-139
Joseph Steinmetz: Page 190
J. R. Eyerman: Pages 8-9
Ken Heyman: Pages 148-149 and 171
Kentucky Tourist and Travel Division: Page 28
Knox College Library: Pages 238-239
Library of Congress: Pages 94-95; page 57 repainted by Nichols
Louisiana Tourist Commission: Pages 36-37
Magnum Photos: Page 236 by Erich Lessing
Memphis Chamber of Commerce: Pages 116-117
Minute Maid Company: Pages 34-35
Mississippi Agricultural and Industrial Board: Pages 196-197
Mobil Oil Corporation: Pages 176-177
Musée Des Beaux-Arts De Paux: Pages 164-165
NASA: Pages 16-17, 208-209, and 219
National Coal Association: Page 181
National Film Board: Page 225

New York Historical Society—New York, New York: Pages 76-77
Patrick Henry Memorial Foundation: Pages 68-69
Photo Researchers, Inc.: Pages 128-129; pages 112-113 by Glaubach
Photoworld: Page 86 (upper)
Rapho Guillumette Pictures: Pages 168-169 and 221 by Bruce Roberts; page 237 (upper) by Donald Getsug
RCA Records: Page 158
Reynolds Metals Company: Pages 206-207
Richard Marsh: Page 98
St. Louis Art Museum: Pages 154-155 painted by Bronson
Shostal Associates, Inc.: Pages 4-5, 6-7, 88-89, 104-105, 186-187, 198-199, 227, and 234-235
Smithsonian Institution: Page 212 painted by L. G. Ferris
Soviet Information Bureau—Moscow, USSR: Page 217
Staatliche Museum—Berlin, Germany: Page 224
State of Florida Development Commission: Florida News Bureau: Pages 172-173 and 184-185; pages 72-73 by Ozzie Sweet; pages 188-189 by Frederic Lewis
Tennessee Department of Education: Page 207
Tennessee Valley Authority: Pages 26-27, 46-47, 160-161, 192-193, and 194
Texaco: Page 178 by John Keller
The Bettmann Archive: Pages 86-87 and 240
The Fideler Company: Pages 58-59, 62-63, 215, and 230-231; pages 54-55 by Janet Johnson; pages 214-215 by Robert Bauer
Thomas Williams: Page 218
Travel and Promotion Division: Department of Construction and Development—Raleigh, North Carolina: Page 205
United States Department of Agriculture: Page 175
United States Department of Agriculture: Soil Conservation Service: Pages 166-167
United States Department of Commerce: Weather Bureau: Page 48 by Klein
United States Department of Health, Education, and Welfare: Page 136 by Robert Pumphrey
U. S. News and World Report: Pages 144-145
Van Cleve Photography: Pages 110-111 by Burton McNeely
Virginia Commonwealth University: Page 103
Virginia Historical Society: Pages 80-81
Virginia Museum of Fine Arts: Pages 66-67
Vivienne della Grotta: Page 241
William L. Clements Library: Pages 228-229
Woodward Iron Company: Page 182

Grateful acknowledgment is made to Scott, Foresman and Company for the pronunciation system used in this book, which is taken from the Thorndike-Barnhart Dictionary Series. Grateful acknowledgment is made to the following for permission to use cartographic data in this book: Creative Arts: Pages 42 and 43; Nystrom Raised Relief Map Company, Chicago 60618: Pages 21, 244-254, and 270; Panoramic Studios: Page 12; Rand McNally & Company: Pages 14 and 15, 54, and 236; United States Department of Agriculture: Forest Service: Page 188; United States Department of Commerce: Bureau of the Census: Page 95.